Female Combatants After Armed Struggle

This book stems from a simple 'feminist curiosity' that can be succinctly summed up into a single question: what happens to combatant women after the war? Based on in-depth interviews with 40 research participants, mostly former combatants within the Irish Republican Army (IRA), this book offers a critical exploration of republican women and conflict transition in the North of Ireland.

Drawing on the feminist theory of a continuum of violence, this book finds that the dichotomous separation of war and peace within conventional approaches represents a gendered fiction. Despite undertaking wartime roles that were empowering, agentic, and subversive, this book finds that the 'post-conflict moment' as experienced by female combatants represents not peace and security, but a continuity of gender discrimination, violence, injustice, and insecurity. The experiences and perspectives contained in this book challenge the discursive deployment of terms such as post-conflict, peace, and security, and moreover, shed light on the many forms of post-war activism undertaken by combatant women in pursuit of peace, equality, and security.

The book represents an important intervention in the field of gender, political violence, and peace, and more specifically, female combatants and conflict transition. It is analytically significant in its exploration of the ways in which gender operates within non-state military movements emerging from conflict and will be of interest to students and scholars alike.

Niall Gilmartin is a lecturer in the Department of Sociology, University of Dublin, Trinity College, Ireland.

Routledge Studies in Gender and Global Politics
Series Editor: Laura J. Shepherd
UNSW Australia

This series aims to publish books that work with, and through, feminist insights on global politics, and illuminate the ways in which gender functions not just as a marker of identity but also as a constitutive logic in global political practices. The series welcomes scholarship on any aspect of global political practices, broadly conceived, that pays attention to the ways in which gender is central to, (re)produced in, and is productive of, such practices.

There is growing recognition both within the academy and in global political institutions that gender matters in and to the practices of global politics. From the governance of peace and security, to the provision of funds for development initiatives, via transnational advocacy networks linked through strategic engagement with new forms of media, these processes have a gendered dimension that is made visible through empirically grounded and theoretically sophisticated feminist work.

Human Capital in Gender and Development
Sydney Calkin

Women, Global Protest Movements and Political Agency
Rethinking the Legacy of 1968
Edited by Sarah Colvin and Katharina Karcher

Gender, Emancipation, and Political Violence
Rethinking the Legacy of 1968
Edited by Sarah Colvin and Katharina Karcher

Gendering Peace
UN Peacebuilding in Timor-Leste
Sarah Smith

Female Combatants After Armed Struggle
Lost in Transition?
Niall Gilmartin

Female Combatants After Armed Struggle
Lost in Transition?

Niall Gilmartin

LONDON AND NEW YORK

First published 2019
by Routledge
2 Park Square, Milton Park, Abingdon, Oxon OX14 4RN

and by Routledge
52 Vanderbilt Avenue, New York, NY 10017

Routledge is an imprint of the Taylor & Francis Group, an informa business

© 2019 Niall Gilmartin

The right of Niall Gilmartin to be identified as author of this work has been asserted by him in accordance with sections 77 and 78 of the Copyright, Designs and Patents Act 1988.

All rights reserved. No part of this book may be reprinted or reproduced or utilised in any form or by any electronic, mechanical, or other means, now known or hereafter invented, including photocopying and recording, or in any information storage or retrieval system, without permission in writing from the publishers.

Trademark notice: Product or corporate names may be trademarks or registered trademarks, and are used only for identification and explanation without intent to infringe.

British Library Cataloguing-in-Publication Data
A catalogue record for this book is available from the British Library

Library of Congress Cataloging-in-Publication Data
A catalog record has been requested for this book

ISBN: 978-0-415-78637-9 (hbk)
ISBN: 978-1-31522-769-6 (ebk)

Typeset in Times New Roman
by Wearset Ltd. Boldon, Tyne and Wear

Printed and bound in Great Britain by
TJ International Ltd, Padstow, Cornwall

For Ann-Marie, Beth, Anna, and Clara.

Contents

	Foreword	viii
	Acknowledgements	x
1	Introduction	1
2	Who fought the war? The gendered constructions of soldiering roles in post-war commemorative processes	40
3	Gendering the post-conflict narrative	73
4	From the front lines of war to the sidelines of peace? Republican women and the Irish peace process	113
5	Beyond regression: change and continuity in women's post-war activism	151
6	Conclusion	177
	Index	189

Foreword

We're all trying to figure it out. We read between the lines of seemingly bland documents. We avidly digest each other's newest reports and studies, often in their still-in-progress drafts. We exchange observations, usually with a healthy dose of irreverence. We grab time during official debates to trade hunches and tactics in the corridors of hotels and agencies. We cobble together travel funds so that we can meet together in Geneva or Sarajevo or New York to hold day-long conferences about it.

The specific 'it' is the exclusion of women – especially combatant women and civil society activist women (both) – from wartime peace negotiations. The larger 'it' is the marginalisation of diverse, knowledgeable local women from the deals that will structure rebuilding a war-torn society after the formal peace agreement is signed by the men with guns.

I've been reading Niall Gilmartin's engaging book with these intense conversations at the front of my mind. *Female Combatants After Armed Conflict* makes an important contribution to this on-going transnational urgent conversation. As you read the pages that follow, think of what they mean for women in Yemen today, for women in Ukraine, South Sudan, and, of course, Syria today. Think what Gilmartin's findings mean for women strategising and organising in post-war Bosnia, Guatemala, and Sri Lanka today. Niall Gilmartin and the women whose voices you will be carefully listening to in these chapters are hoisting a bright neon yellow feminist flag of warning over every supposedly effective and blatantly ineffective peace political process and post-war political process that does not include women and that does not take seriously women's experiences, women's needs, and women's ideas.

Female Combatants After Armed Struggle is based on Niall Gilmartin's extensive and sensitive in-depth interviews with women who were directly involved with the nationalist armed groups during the three long decades of Northern Ireland's armed conflict, a conflict that allegedly ended with the signing of the Good Friday Agreement in 1998.

Many of these women, not surprisingly, did not want to talk to him. It may have been more than ten years since they put down their arms. By the time Gilmartin introduced himself to them, these women were leading quite different lives than those they led when they were combatants during 'the Troubles'.

Those changes, however, did not mean these women's wars were over. Those changes in the surface of their lives did not mean they easily could trust a stranger with their personal wartime experiences and their candid thoughts about the workings of sexism in post-war life.

Thus, among the several notable aspects of this book is its tracing the building, the slow, step by uneasy step building trust. It is the foundation on which this book rests. Anyone planning to interview women in any war zone or in any country haltingly recovering from armed violence would do well to read Niall Gilmartin's book – slowly.

Cynthia Enloe
Clark University, USA

Acknowledgements

Undertaking, researching, and writing a book such as this is an incredibly enjoyable and rewarding experience, but as many will attest, can also be a lonely and solitary endeavour. While at many stages this book was no exception, it could not, however, have come to fruition without the love, support, and encouragement of a number of people. I owe a huge debt to the interviewees involved and I wish to express my heartfelt gratitude to the republican women who participated in this research. Thank you for generously sharing your stories, your homes, and your time. I wish to sincerely thank Eibhlín Glenholmes, Tony Miller, Stephanie Lord, and Seán Ó. Murchadha for their help and support throughout this project. I wish to express sincere thanks to all the staff at *Tar Anall* Belfast, *Tar Abhaile* Derry, and the Sinn Féin offices in Dublin, Belfast, and Stormont.

Although born on the southern side of the Irish border in the 1970s, most school holidays throughout the 1980s and 1990s were spent with family in west Belfast. While I maintain nothing but fond and happy memories of this period, it was lucidly clear that this was a 'place apart'. Unquestionably, the situation that existed there in that part of the city provoked in me a life-time of interest in the conflict there and for all intents and purposes represents the kernel of this book. I would like to acknowledge all the Gilmartin family of Mooreland Crescent, Belfast, for love and support throughout the decades, and especially for those who are sadly no longer with us. A very special thank you to my mum and dad who have constantly encouraged me in all my endeavours in life and to my sisters, Rowena, Joanne, and Michelle, and wider Gilmartin and Behan family circle. Special thanks to my long-standing friends who have always provided good times when they're needed most.

I wish to express sincere thanks to my colleagues Fidelma Ashe, Maire Braniff, Mary Corcoran, Laurence Cox, Pauline Cullen, David Landy, Richard Layte, Michelle Maher, Mary Murphy, John O'Brennan, Claire Pierson, and Peter Shirlow for friendship, encouragement, and support throughout. A special mention and thank you to Colin Coulter for support and friendship over the course of many years, not only to me but my family. A huge thank you to Cynthia Enloe for her work, time, humour, and support during previous drafts and for her generous foreword to this book. Thank you to Laura Sjoberg for advice in the early parts of this process. The publication of this book owes a huge debt to the dedication and professionalism of Laura Shepherd; thank you for your constant advice and support. Thank you also to the editorial staff at Routledge, Nicola Parkin, Lucy Frederick, Lydia de Cruz, and Sophie Iddamalgoda.

I wish to extend sincere gratitude to Honor Fagan for her friendship, and invaluable thoughts and contributions throughout this entire process as well as her painstaking diligence on previous manuscript drafts. While familial connections to Belfast undoubtedly ignited my interest in the North of Ireland, the feminist activism, research, and teaching of Theresa O'Keefe was the primary source of inspiration for this research and ultimately this book. Thank you for showing me that feminism is for everybody.

Finally, to my wife, Ann-Marie, and daughters, Beth, Anna, and Clara – undoubtedly it was you guys who bore the brunt of this project and witnessed first-hand the good times and, unfortunately, the bad. Thank you for your love, patience, and encouragement throughout this entire process.

1 Introduction

> War also destroys the patriarchal structures of society that confine and degrade women. In the very breakdown of morals, traditions, customs, and community, war also opens up new beginnings
>
> Meredith Turshen (1998: 20)

Introduction

Given the pain, loss, and suffering that invariably accompanies the eruption of armed conflict, Meredith Turshen's contention may be considered perplexing and perhaps unfathomable. Feminist investigations into the perspectives of combatant women over the last three decades however, reveal demonstrable evidence of wartime power, agency, politicisation, and mobilisation (Åhäll and Shepherd 2012; Alison 2009; Henshaw 2017; MacKenzie 2012; Shekhawat 2015; Sjoberg 2010, 2014). Such perspectives indicate that the realm of war can be a site for some women to subvert and resist patriarchal formations. During the transition from war to peace however, the rhetoric of equality and rights tends to mask the reconstruction of patriarchal power. Though the social and political flux generated by war and conflict transition creates numerous possibilities and perils for women (and men), conventional processes of conflict resolution however, are as gendered as wars, and typically adhere to and reproduce gendered stereotypes (De Alwis *et al.* 2013: 171, 192). When women do appear in post-war peace processes, invariably they are positioned and valued for their 'peace-making qualities' and informal contributions, with little attention given to the breadth and scope of women's wartime roles, including that of armed fighter. Moreover, women's apparent propensity for peacefulness as so expressed in both dominant nationalist discourse and conventional narratives consistently fails to transfer into the political capital required for entry into the 'hard talk' of formal negotiations. Given their perceived 'unconventional' role as combatants and the centrality of their wartime contributions, one might therefore expect to find female combatants taking their rightful place at the negotiating table alongside their male comrades as part of conflict transition processes. Despite the centrality and importance of their wartime contributions, the small but burgeoning body of work documenting the post-war experiences of female fighters reveals consistent patterns of loss, regression, and marginalisation.

This book stems from a simple 'feminist curiosity' (Enloe 2004) that can be succinctly summed up in a single question: what happens to combatant women after the war? Based on in-depth interviews with 40 research participants, mostly former combatants within the Irish Republican Army (hereafter the IRA), this book offers a critical exploration of republican women and conflict transition in the North of Ireland.[1] The purpose of the book is twofold; first, it explores the hidden story of women's eclectic and vital roles within a non-state nationalist movement in transition. And second, it seeks to uncover the ways in which gender, which being the multiple workings of masculinity and femininity, shapes combatant women's conflict transition experiences. The overarching aim, therefore, is to provide an alternative vision of conflict transition, one that differs significantly from both the male-dominated mainstream perspective and many existing feminist approaches. While acknowledging and building upon current feminist critiques of conflict transition as a thoroughly gendered enterprise, the key point of departure is a critical analysis of post-war scenarios from the unique perspective of female combatants.

Though conflict transition is often cited as a period of opportunity to construct a new post-war society, gender equality, and women's struggle for emancipation are rarely afforded priority. Those who challenge the gendered and often patriarchal understandings that underpin conventional approaches to resolving armed conflicts are typically advised to focus their energies more on the 'bigger picture' – that being elite-led negotiations, structures of governance, functioning economies, and law, order, and stability. While established approaches to war and peace are zealous in their efforts to render invisible the multiple workings of masculinity and femininity within conflict transition, the diligent endeavours of feminist scholars bring to light the centrality of gender and gender power to post-war processes (Alison 2009; Anderlini 2007: Cockburn 1998; Cohn 2013; Confortini 2006; El-Bushra 2007; Meintjes *et al.* 2001; Moser and Clark 2001). Furthermore, conventional visions of peace and security are constituted by subjective ideological standpoints that address certain forms of violence and conflict that draws ideological sustenance and legitimation by masquerading as objective, universal, self-evident, and unproblematic. Feminist interrogations of peace and security demonstrate the clear links between many forms of violence, highlighting the continuity between various forms of violence enacted before, during, and after wars, and thus eroding the foundations of conventional thinking regarding peace and security. In doing so, feminist analyses of violence using a continuum framework challenge the discursive deployment of terms such as post-conflict, peace, and security, and moreover, makes visible many forms of violence and insecurities concealed by a limited and partial form of peace that address certain forms of violence while normalising others. Drawing on the feminist theory of a continuum of violence, this book finds that the dichotomous separation of war and peace represents a manufactured falsehood, and ultimately a gendered one. Despite undertaking wartime roles that were empowering, agentic, and subversive, this book argues that the post-conflict moment as experienced by female combatants represents not peace and security, but a continuity of gender discrimination, violence, and insecurity. While a limited but burgeoning crop of existing research on female combatants and post-conflict invariably reveal clear patterns of regression in the post-war period (Shekhawat 2015), simplified suggestions that combatant women return to pre-war domestic life conceals their agency and overlooks the nuanced complexities involved within a cohort of women who do not fit the gendered archetype. Therefore, this book further argues that it is the presence of post-war violence that ensures a continuity of combatant women's struggle, from wartime mobilisation to post-war activism. In other words, there is no return to pre-conflict roles precisely because violence, domination, and insecurity exist long after the ending of armed actions.

Hence, while this book is, of course, concerned with exposing the deleterious gendered effects of both nationalism and conflict transition on combatant women, it is equally concerned with examining the ways in which they position themselves and their political activism after the war. Exploring the post-war lives of combatant women allows for a greater excavation of gender, war, and conflict transition, generating important questions for feminist interrogations of war and peace. How are women's wartimes roles marginalised, silenced, and ignored? What ways do combatant women resist such regression? Combatant women are often portrayed as 'empowered agents', yet we know little about the threats and insecurities they face during and after war. What does peace and security look like to combatant women? What role, if any, do they play in formal peace negotiations? What happens to the political spaces opened by combatant women during armed conflict? What happens to their political struggles after the war? Do combatant women carry over their wartime empowerment into conflict transition? Examining the ways in which combatant women organise for peace and equality yields a far stronger feminist analysis of patriarchy and women's eclectic forms of resistance in post-war scenarios.

Theorising the 'post-conflict' moment

The models and prescriptions for peace invariably depend upon the overarching explanations of the violence that preceded it. War and armed conflict are conventionally presented as arbitrary events; a crisis or emergency involving physical, direct acts of violence, typically book-ended with a start and end date. The principal concern of those charged with devising a new 'post-conflict' landscape are issues such as state security, sovereignty, law and order, democratic governance, and functioning capitalist economies. The establishment and delivery of such approaches requires a political, cultural, and discursive framework that legitimises this 'negative peace', that being the absence of military violence, and recasting it as universally beneficial for all. The power of those who propagate the ending of armed actions as signifying 'post-conflict' resides in their capacity to normalise all other forms of violence that do not sit within the narrow confines of physical violence. Traditional approaches to war, peace, and security, as embodied by the dominant schools of realism and liberalism, seek to analytically differentiate armed conflict from everyday violence through cultural and discursive representation of war as something exceptional and a source of insecurity for all. Traditional International Relations (IR) assiduously nurture a highly limited understanding of violence as something conducted by state and non-state actors in the pursuit of political objectives, and therefore embedding violence in conventional, state-centric terms. The enabling conditions to make distinct certain forms of violence are centrally constituted through the politics of discourse and presentation. The construction of meaning with regards to war not only solidifies its privileged status as an exceptional and therefore paramount existential source of insecurity; in doing so, it diminishes the meaning associated with other forms of violence as less important. The use of binary categorisation and resulting hierarchy of violence is legitimised and expressed through a series of politically expedient dichotomies such as public/private; collective/individual; extraordinary/everyday, which serve to deflect critical questions regarding the structural and cultural conditions in which these forms of violence are trivialised and de-politicised within processes of conflict transition.

Feminist scholars, among others, have long taken issue with the apparent orthodoxy that pervades these conventional tropes and practices. While prevailing forms of peacebuilding are delineated as universally beneficial for all, evidence from the so-called post-conflict period around the world demonstrates a continuity of violence for women, with many also facing new forms of violence. A vast body of work documenting the many instances of violence against women in the aftermath (and, of course, during) war challenges the prevailing discourse of 'post-conflict' or a 'return to normal' (Pillay 2001). Female insecurity and exposure to various acts of violence during the so-called 'peace time' indicates the androcentric bias within mainstream conflict resolution processes, particularly levels of sexual violence, which remain high in the aftermath of wartime violence (Handrahan 2004; M'Cormack-Hale 2012: 8). 'Post-conflict' is therefore reconceptualised by feminists as a period of continued violence and insecurity for women (McLeod 2011: 599), where they remain socially, politically, and economically marginalised, and exposed to various forms of physical violence, which paradoxically appears to increase in the aftermath of war (Cockburn 2013; Karam 2001; Kelly 2000; Krog 2001). There is now a vast body of feminist work (broadly grouped as Feminist Security Studies) challenging the androcentric discourse and meanings of peace and security. The existing state of knowledge provides incredibly useful concepts and categories, offering valuable insights into how women re-conceptualise peace. Given that feminists take a broad approach in defining conflict and violence as all forms of exploitation, marginalisation, and oppression (Reardon 1993: 71), it is unsurprising that feminist visions of peace also conceptualise peace in more profound ways. A common distinctive characteristic of feminist visions of peace is the consensus that peace is not merely the absence of 'conventional violence' but is a broader tackling of all forms of violence and discrimination (Anderlini 2007; Bouta *et al.*

2005; Karam 2001; Kelly 2000; Pankhurst 2008; Porter 2007; Reardon 1993). Of importance to feminists is the work of Johan Galtung (1969) and John-Paul Lederach (1997), which distinguished between a 'negative' and a 'positive' peace. While the former adheres strictly to conventional ideas around ending armed conflict, the latter encompasses structures and cultures of violence which pervade the so-called post-war peace. Structural violence exists when people suffer or die because of economic or social structures, not because of direct, physical violence (Galtung 1969). In many respects, the emphasis on social justice provides a theoretical link between women's pursuit of peace and their struggle for emancipation, arguing that a genuine peace 'is the antithesis of exploitation, marginalisation, and oppression. Ending discrimination against women and achieving peace are mutually interdependent, virtually inseparable goals' (Reardon 1993: 71).

The violence of armed conflict cannot be separated from other expressions of violence. In every militarised society, war zone and refugee camp, violence against women and men transcends the simple diplomatic dichotomy of war and peace. The continuum of violence resists any division between public and private domains (Giles and Hyndman 2004). While the continuum of violence highlights various forms of violence affecting women and men, a gendered continuum of violence demonstrates how gender links violence at different points on a scale reaching from the personal to the international; from the domestic home to the manoeuvres of tank columns (Cockburn 2004: 43). While many non-feminist critical approaches to peace and security exist, Catia Confortini (2006, 2010) argues that feminism brings its own distinctive understandings and challenges to the status quo. First, feminist theorising of violence and peace expand definitions of peace that suggest continuity between different forms of violence; second, they highlight the diverse roles women, and other marginalised groups, play in violent conflicts and in peace processes; third, they complicate our understanding of peace and violence while foregrounding gender as a social and symbolic construct involving relations of power, and fourth, propose transformative ways of conceptualising peace, war, and post-conflict transitions. Furthermore, gender relations penetrate and shape the political, economic, and cultural forms of violence, and so therefore, any attempt to tackle violence of whatever sort or source must be attentive to gender relations and their power imbalances. Using a threefold continuum of political, economic, and social violence, the gendered continuum of violence argues that a genuine peace can only be achieved when all three types of violence are viewed and treated as interrelated. All three forms of violence are connected in their use of violence to gain or maintain power. Caroline Moser (2001) contends that since gender is embedded in relations of power/powerlessness, each of the three categories of violence is therefore gendered.

Evidence clearly indicates that women are disproportionately victims of structural violence, which, of course, is directly linked to gender inequalities such as gender pay gap or gender role segregation, which only exacerbates women's exposure to structural violence (Tickner 2014: 31). In many respects the linking of peace and social justice not only responds to the prevailing narrow trend within traditional, male-dominated approaches, it also highlights the 'invisible violence' daily experienced by many women (Caprioli 2004). By centralising social justice, the struggle for peace is conceptualised by feminists as a struggle for humane and equitable social conditions, particularly in areas of poverty, exploitation, education, housing, and ecological well-being (Anderlini 2007; Reardon 1993).

The strategic and discursive practice of conventional peace-making operates through a denial of its subjective ideological construction, relies upon a pretence of universality, which consequently mollifies those who question its output. Therefore, the gendered continuum of violence framework is vital in explaining why the reduction of one type of violence does not automatically lead to reductions in other forms of violence. To be sure, it is self-evident that the ending of war or significant decrease in direct, physical armed actions is undoubtedly beneficial to women and men. The neat dichotomy of 'war and peace', however, distorts the lived violent reality for many women before, during and after armed conflict. Such realities propel us to question the androcentric logic and assumptions inherent within the practices and discourse of 'post-conflict'. Moreover, feminist research reveals persistent patterns of increases in gender-based violence in the aftermath of ending armed actions. The contribution of this theoretical approach is that it challenges the orthodoxy of conventional approaches, which seek to package and present the ending of armed actions as the axiomatic signifiers of peace. Furthermore, the failure by conventional forms of conflict transition to take gender seriously as an analytical category of war and peacebuilding leaves normative gender and heterosexual practices firmly in place and free from the rigours of conflict transformation. The inability or unwillingness to engage with gender advances a model of peace that ironically creates the conditions that both enables and masks multiple forms of gender violence and insecurity in a so-called post-conflict society.

An awareness of structural and cultural violence therefore challenges the traditional notion of peace and alerts us to the ways that states and/or groups can exercise power and domination over others without recourse to weapons (Cockburn 2001: 17). Once the exceptionalism that is so often associated with war is illuminated and challenged, the gender continuum of violence provides a greater understanding of why many combatant and nationalist women, such as republican women in the North of Ireland, do not return to pre-war roles, despite the insistence of their male leaders. Quite simply, violence, and conflict are not ended by armistice or military ceasefires. Given their wartime experiences of challenging oppression and injustice, it surely follows that the existence of postwar violence, insecurity, and injustice ensures that many combatant women continue their political struggles in pursuit of a genuine peace, thus demonstrating the long-term benefits for women's participation in non-state military movements. The analysis contained in the following chapters of this book clearly demonstrate that levels of politicisation and mobilisation among combatant women are successfully transferred over into the post-war period.

Women, gender, and conflict transition: contextualising the study

In the course of the last three decades, feminist research and theorising of gender, war, and conflict transition has produced a voluminous and diverse body of work that has not only challenged the masculine bias within conventional approaches but has also ignited much debate within feminist scholarship (for example, see Cohn 2013; El-Bushra 2007; Enloe 2014; Giles and Hyndman 2004; Lorentzen and Turpin 1998; Meintjes *et al.* 2001; Moser and Clark 2001; Pankhurst 2003; Porter 2007). Notwithstanding the debate and diversity among feminist scholars, most are united in their belief that women and gender are largely excluded from dominant, conventional understandings of armed conflict, peace, and conflict transition. While this book is critically attentive to nationality, social class, and ethnicity, gender is the primary category of analysis throughout. Gender is, 'more broadly, a way of categorising, ordering, and symbolising power, of hierarchically structuring relationships among different categories of people, and different human activities symbolically associated with masculinity or femininity' (Cohn 2013: 3). While gender can be used or incorporated by many non-feminist approaches, the key point of departure is that feminists take a critical approach to the use of gender, devoting their energies to exposing the processes – social; structural; cultural; discursive – which constitute and reproduce gender. As a relational concept, femininity and masculinity depend upon each other for the way each is defined, but moreover, that relationship is one based on power and power differentials. Feminists, therefore, are centrally concerned with power and its use to construct and regulate gender roles and identities across different regions and cultures. Despite the vast diversity, feminists are generally united in seeking to better understand women's subordination to prescribe strategies to change it (Tickner 2014).

According to Laura Sjoberg (2014), feminist scholarship in the context of war, conflict, and peace has two common interests; first, it aims to understand where both women and gender are in war and conflict, and second, seeks to draw attention to (and often redress) gender subordination in scholarship studies of war and peace. A feminist gender analysis sees the differentiation and relative positioning of women and men as an important ordering principle that pervades all systems of power and is sometimes its very embodiment. Gender does not have primacy in this respect. Economic class and ethnic differentiation can also be important relational hierarchies, structuring a regime and shaping its mode of ruling. But these other differentiations are always also gendered, and in turn help construct what is a man and a woman in any given circumstance (Cockburn 2004: 28). This book follows Cockburn's contention that gender power shapes the dynamic of every site of human interaction, no more so than in the realm of war and peace. As a social construct, gender varies in its shape, configuration, and assertion, but, nevertheless, the universality of masculine dominance and feminine subordination remains a constant feature of most, if not every society. I use Carol Cohn's (2013) argument that gender as a structural power relation not only shapes individual identities, it also shapes and is shaped by the institutional and symbolic universe we inhabit and material processes such as globalisation and militarisation. It is well established that key ingredients of war and peace – nationalism; the state; militaries – are imbued with gender in that they are constructed and function in ways that draw upon specific notions of masculinity and femininity.

With the post-structural and intersectional turn within feminist theory, the concept of patriarchy has perhaps fallen out of fashion. While gender as a category of analysis can yield new insights, or be utilised to explore women's marginalised or silences voices, the concept of patriarchy provides the tools for examining gender power relations. I follow Cynthia Enloe's contention that to talk only of gender is to miss out on the power relationship between both constructs. Patriarchy allows us to examine femininities and masculinities as relational concepts in terms of power. I draw on the work of Cynthia Enloe (2004; 2014) and define patriarchy as the structural and ideological system that perpetuates the privileging of masculinity while subordinating most women and femininity itself. While patriarchy allows us to theorise the ways in which relationships are structured and constituted, gender is also a set of values, discourses, symbols, and meanings that permeate and shape the ways we think about the world, including issues such as war, peace, and security. The vast body of feminist work on war, peace, and conflict transition is demonstrative of the ways that militaries, states, formal peace processes, rely upon particular ideas about gender. That gender is never fixed or immutable means that the relationship between gender and wider structures is a dynamic process of managing, producing, and, as needed, altering ideas about appropriate and valued masculinities and femininities (Cohn 2013: 19). Laura Sjoberg contends that seeing gender analysis as a key part of thinking about war, and conflict is an important step to make visible gender hierarchy, gender-based expectations, gender's intersections with race, class, ethnicity, and religion, and what happens to women and men in wars and conflicts. Therefore, it is only possible to fully understand gender in the context of war and conflict, and that it is only possible to fully understand war and conflict considering their gendered aspects (2014: 4–5). A feminist gender approach therefore rejects the notion that gender is fixed or innate, and instead interrogate gender not as a category of analysis but as a relationship imbued with power. The ontological position of this book holds that while patriarchy is a structural and cultural feature across all societies, its character and form is culturally constituted, and therefore it differs across time and space. The books use of a pluralised standpoint, explained in detail later in this chapter, is premised upon the heterogeneity among women and men, and femininities and masculinities, and a rejection of universalisms and generalisations.

Given the plurality of masculinities and femininities, feminist theorising of women's relationship to war and peace has expanded considerably over the last 20 years with a distinct departure from previous approaches, which emphasised women's role as peace-makers and victims towards a broader spectrum of vision which considers women's multiple wartime roles (Lorentzen and Turpin 1998;

Moser and Clark 2001; Meintjes *et al.* 2001; Jacobs *et al.* 2000). Moreover, recent feminist scholarly interventions regarding female combatants pointedly challenged essentialist tropes regarding 'men's violence' and 'women's peacefulness' (Alison 2004, 2009; Henshaw 2017; MacKenzie 2012; Sharoni 2001; O'Keefe 2003, 2013; Shekhawat 2015; Sjoberg 2010, 2014). Whereas the scope of feminist analyses of war and peace has significantly broadened in recent times, the balance of attention, some would suggest, understandably continues to fall to those who situate themselves as opponents of violence, peace-makers, or anti-militarists (for example, see Anderlini 2007: 2; Baines 2005; Cockburn 2007, 2013; De Alwis *et al.* 2013; DeLargy 2013; Giles 2013; Porter 1998, 2000, 2003). By necessity, feminist interrogations of conflict transition must consist of multiple narratives emanating from differing viewpoints and perspectives regarding the gendered nature and outcomes of war.

While the notion of 'womenandpeace'[2] (El-Bushra 2007) offers an enticing niche standpoint for women within war and conflict resolution, it nevertheless comes at the expense of marginalising those who fall outside the gendered archetype. The foregrounding of women's opposition to violence and war within mainstream and some feminist approaches are criticised by some for presenting an over-simplified and generalised narrative depicting women as either victims or the proverbial peace-builder (El-Bushra 2003, 2007; Pankhurst 2003), while neglecting those women who occupy other roles, including that of armed fighter. According to Seema Shekhawat, among many others, while women as victims of war or their role as 'peaceniks' has gained maximum attention, the fixation with these two-fold experiences of women does not do justice to the multiple experiences of women during conflict and post-conflict situations (2015: 3). These approaches and narratives become deeply problematic when they gain a hegemonic grip within feminist (and mainstream) explorations of conflict transition, constitute women as a homogenous group, and treat relations among women as non-hierarchical (Jansson and Eduards 2016: 8). The persistent conflation of women with peace and the imposition of gendered dichotomies has little to do with the reality of women's lives during armed conflict nor is it an amalgamation designed to empower the role of women. Associating women solely with peace is a mechanism designed to de-politicise women's actions and marginalise their experiences and needs.

Furthermore, using the notion of women as victims, either of various forms of violence or as a group excluded from meaningful participation, however, 'undermines their desire to be taken seriously as political players' (El-Bushra 2007: 140). Women's apparent propensity for peacefulness as so expressed in both dominant nationalist discourse and conventional narratives, consistently fails to transfer into the political capital required for entry into the 'hard talk' of formal negotiations. For the most part, women's participation in peace processes has been largely restricted to the 'feminised', less valued, informal level, typically cross-community grassroots engagement (Cockburn 1998, 2013; De Alwis *et al.* 2013; Karam 2001; Murtagh 2008; Porter 2003). While such activism is important and powerful, it nevertheless sits quite comfortably in the stereotypical behaviour associated with mainstream trope of women's innate peacefulness. Gendered segregation between formal and informal peace-building augments the prevailing assumption that somehow women, more than men, possess abilities for reaching across the divide in times of conflict, accentuating the myth of women being 'outside' of conflict. Furthermore, women's role as peace activist is easily discounted and disregarded as non-political; there is no greater illustration of this dismissal in the fact that despite their apparent innate talent for 'peace-making' and the widely lauded United Nations SCR 1325,[3] women continue to be universally absent and excluded from formal processes of peace negotiations the world over (Bouta *et al.* 2005; De Alwis *et al.* 2013; Jacobson 2013; Kaufman and Williams 2010; M'Cormack-Hale 2012; Mazurana and Cole 2013; Ni Aolain *et al.* 2011; Romanova and Sewell 2011; Shekhawat 2015). Regardless of the valuable feminist insights documenting women's multiple and vital wartime contributions, some have suggested that much of feminist scholarship on gender, war, and peace has been largely inclined to focus on either the victimisation of women or women's informal attempts at peace (Shekhawat 2015: 2–4). Due to both their perceived 'unconventional' roles as fighters, and the centrality of their labour to military movements, female combatants provide alternative visions of conflict transition, precisely because they do fit the gendered archetypes. Giving voice to those who are marginalised remains a cornerstone of feminist scholarship, and, in keeping with that tenet, this book examines the largely unexplored post-war voices and experiences of republican combatant women, and by doing so, sheds light on the ways in which gendered constructions operate within a transitioning non-state military movement.

Female combatants: the outsiders' outsider?

Despite the ill-informed and long-standing conflation of women with peace within mainstream narratives, there is now a relatively sizable amount of feminist research documenting women's role as armed activists during armed conflict, presenting insightful theoretical contributions to the field of women, armed conflict, peace, and security (Åhäll and Shepherd 2012; Alison 2009; Coulter 2009; Henshaw 2017; Lorentzen and Turpin 1998; Moser and Clark 2001; Meintjes *et al.* 2001; Jacobs *et al.* 2000; MacKenzie 2012; O'Keefe 2003, 2013; Parashar 2014; Sharoni 2001; Shekhawat 2015; Sjoberg 2010, 2014; Sjoberg and Gentry 2007). Over the course of the last 20 years, these significant studies challenged the dichotomies of male/violence and female/peace, demonstrated women's politicisation and mobilisation, examined women's motivations and experiences, and defied the notion that women and political violence are somehow mutually exclusive. The ending of armed actions, however, appears to function as a natural cut-off point for many explorations of combatant women, leaving their post-war experiences relatively under-researched. Of course, I am not suggesting that there are no feminist explorations of female combatants and conflict transition. On the contrary, a burgeoning body of work on combatant women has documented issues such as post-war levels of empowerment

(MacKenzie 2012), exclusion from formal peace processes (McEvoy 2009) gender discrimination (Shekhawat and Pathak 2015), and processes of reconciliation (Boutron 2015). The overriding focus for many however, has been women's experiences and exclusions of Demilitarisation, Demobilisation, and Reintegration (DDR) programs. DDR programs are now widely recognised as an integral element of peace processes. At a basic level, they constitute a process whereby combatants voluntarily turn in arms at designated centres and begin a process of demilitarisation and reintegration. The key debates within women and DDR centre first on the ways in which women are victimised and excluded by androcentric norms and second, on the various strategies to remedy such predicaments (Anderlini 2007; Bouta *et al.* 2005; MacKenzie 2012; Mazurana and Cole 2013; Ni Aolain *et al.* 2011).

While such explorations offer incredibly rich and important insights into the gendered and often patriarchal assumptions underpinning such programs, they also tend to implicitly (and unintentionally) re-establish a link between women and victimhood. Megan MacKenzie takes issue with some of the recent developments regarding DDR, citing the reports of women 'being left behind' by gendered DDR programs as 'oversimplified' (2012: 86). Much of the current debate focuses on women's right to be included to yield the same benefits and services as their male counterparts (Anderlini 2007). Again, the dominant demand appears to be the inclusion of women within existing, top-down processes to benefit as equally as men do. A significant limitation is that the focus appears to be on policy formation, program design, all of which emanate from a top-down position which invariably neglects women's voices and agency from below. The key to women's empowerment is that their voices and experiences must be heard, something largely overlooked within many attempts to explore the post-war experiences of female fighters including DDR programs (MacKenzie 2012). Hence, even in the case of female combatants, where women may emerge from armed conflict with consolidated gains of political consciousness and mobilisation, the overwhelming focus is on their victimisation and exclusion from formal DDR processes, effectively reinvigorating the dubious linkages between women and victimhood. While DDR is an important *part* of the story concerning female combatants and conflict transition, focusing solely on their 'demobilisation' as armed fighters neglects the ways in which combatant women use consolidated gains from wartime experiences to organise politically in conflict transition. Moreover, such approaches also rely on top-down structures to illuminate women's wartime roles at the expense of examining how women themselves conceptualise their wartime roles and sacrifices. The existing gaps in research ensures that the ways in which female combatants organise their post-war political struggles for peace and equality within non-state, nationalist movements remain largely under-studied.

Nationalist movements continue to represent a key challenge for feminist theorists. There remains a vexed contradiction at the heart of the debate regarding gender and nationalism. On the one hand, masculine constructions of the nation have consistently relied upon specific symbolic and practical roles for women that are largely appraised as supplementary, despite the centrality of women's biological reproductive role. On the other hand, it is axiomatic that women's eclectic roles and contributions are essential to the establishment and sustainment of most nationalist military movements. Despite their rhetorical promises, revolutionary nationalist movements do not have a good record with regards to women's emancipation; promises to improve the status of women and end their subordination have gone largely unfulfilled (Luciak 1999; McClintock 1993; Seidman 1993). A key departure now for feminist scholars examining nationalist women in conflict transition is to move beyond the ways in which male-led movements' position women, and focus more on the ways in which nationalist women themselves organise their political struggle in their pursuit of peace (O'Keefe 2013). While field research on female combatants and nationalist women from Palestine (Abdulhadi 1998; Farr 2011; Holt 2003; Richter-Devroe 2012), South Africa (Axelsson 2015; Seidman 1993), and Latin America (Chinchilla 1990; Luciak 1999; Molyneux 1985) uncovers a consistent pattern of regression in the political fortunes for women within transitioning nationalist movements, they do, however, also reveal the ways in which nationalist women resist such moves. While the reneging on wartime promises regarding gender equality by male-led nationalist movements is an important part of the story, the notion of mobilised women returning to pre-conflict, domestic roles does not reflect the post-war realities for combatant women around the globe.

Female Farabundo Martí National Liberation Front (FMLN) members in post-war El Salvador re-energised their semi-autonomous activism during conflict transition period to ensure women's demands were visible (Luciak 1999: 48). The post-war period in Nicaragua witnessed significant advancements for women there due to the formation of AMNLAE, a mass-based women's popular organisation that ran in parallel to other Sandinista organisations. To consolidate these successes, Chinchilla advocates for vigorous grassroots pressure as well as international solidarity and links to other feminist groups (1990: 393). A common trend across case-studies of female combatants and nationalist women in Latin America is their visions of women's rights as something far more than participation in formal politics. Issues of health care, education, childcare, gender-based violence, struggle against sexism, the burden of unpaid domestic labour are all consistently cited as barriers to women's emancipation (Chinchilla 1990). There remains a perpetual failure of formal democratisation to deliver any meaningful change for women's immediate needs or their interests in ending women's subordination (Reif 1986; Waylen 1994)

In South Africa, the main anti-apartheid movement, the African National Congress (hereafter the ANC) women organised in semi-autonomous groups to pursue women's rights alongside the anti-apartheid struggle agenda, broadening the political agenda of the ANC. Many of these demands resided in the immediacy (or what Molyneux refers to as practical gender concerns) of the State's failure to provide basic resources. The feminist demands that emerge within the ANC in the early 1990s and throughout the transition emanated not from the few at a leadership level but from the grassroots popular base from which the ANC draws its support (Seidman 1993: 315). The pressure to question male control in the transition comes from women who have organised independently or semi-autonomously, and who clearly insist that their gender-specific needs be addressed alongside the national question (Axelsson 2015; Britton 2002; Seidman 1993: 315).

Field research from Palestine also reveals a distinct trend of regression as institutional politics re-emerges. The gendered political structures of the Palestinian Authority (PA) presented restrictions and limitations for Palestinian women. The numerous case studies from Palestine, particularly in the aftermath of the 1993 Oslo Accord, illustrate the ways in which nationalist women continue their political activism, framing it in a way that challenges many gendered assumptions. While operating to resist on-going Israeli aggression, Palestinian women also face the constraints of conservative gender ideologies within their own movement (Farr 2011: 545). Palestinian women channel their energies into all aspects of women's lives including health, education, legal literacy, income generation, advocacy of rights, among others. Such activism has increased women's role in public life and to some extent has challenged patriarchal control, helping Palestinians understand the interconnections between public, militarised violence and violence in the home (Farr 2011: 545). Most practically, 'they argue that the gap between where ordinary people find themselves and where politicians focus is so significant that nothing decided at the top will have meaning when attempts are made to apply it on the ground' (Farr 2011: 546). Considering this, women's autonomous organising in the face of post-war patriarchal barriers offers women the best site and opportunities for continuing their political struggle (Holt 2003; Richter-Devroe 2012). Palestinian female resistance activism can potentially affect social and political change; the underlying gender identity of the 'courageous female protestor' also challenges the reductionist gender binaries of male/protector and female/protected that undergird traditional conceptualisations of political activity (Richter-Devroe 2012: 182). The case of Palestinian women demonstrates that different groups of women live different experiences and wage their struggle for emancipation according to their location and needs (Abdulhadi 1998: 669).

Sophie Richter-Devroe (2012) contends that female popular resistance by nationalist women's autonomous groups in Palestine forces us to rethink what 'doing politics' means for women; it challenges established norms associated with women's politics. First, women's grassroots activism within the normally male-dominated public sphere challenges the patriarchal notion that women are valued for their reproductive capacity; their bodies can also be weapons of resistance. Second, their grassroots organising challenges the notion that women's politics is best channelled through formal institutions. It is a radical alternative to the male-dominated social and political cultures in Palestine. In other words, gender equality tackled solely through legislative or formal guarantees changes little in the daily lives of women where they experience 'other forms' of violence, including from religious traditions, domestic violence. (Farr 2011; Holt 2003).

In the North of Ireland, Sandra McEvoy (2009) finds that loyalist female combatants were marginalised not only by their political opponents but also by their male comrades who deliberately restricted their participation in the subsequent peace process, thus creating a 'structural barrier' to further political participation. The absence of combatant women at the bargaining table, according to McEvoy, ensures that peace agreements are unrepresentative and therefore risk being untenable. Studies of republican women in conflict transition thus far reveal a gender differentiation within their communities around the issue of prisoner releases whereby communities treated them rather differently, as female ex-prisoners (Alison 2009). Likewise, Sara McDowell (2008) asserts that republican commemoration since the advent of peace has continued to 'project a hyper-masculine interpretation of the past (and present)' (2008: 336), while Fidelma Ashe (2009) illuminates how gender justice and gender equity have been sidelined, reinforcing men's positions as leaders in the community and 'reaffirm[ing] male hegemony in communities in the conflict transformation period', thereby resulting in processes which 'privilege male interpretations of the past' (2009: 310). Recent research also suggests a back-peddling by the republican leadership with regards to the position of women in the aftermath of the GFA (O'Keefe 2013). This certainly raises pertinent questions regarding women's political activism within the republican movement as it radically shifts away from 'revolutionary' standpoints towards a more mainstream position. Given the dearth of attention to republican women and their post-war experiences, this book represents an important intervention in the field of women and conflict transition both globally and in the North of Ireland.

The abundance of case-studies demonstrating the myriad of ways in which women are mobilised and politicised by nationalism, particularly anti-imperial/ occupation forms of national collective action are often tempered by unequivocal patterns of post-war marginalisation. It is well-established that women are rarely central to nationalist state-building, and moreover, women's emancipation has yet to be fulfilled through nationalism, despite the promising wartime rhetoric. Women's suffering and victimisation through ethno-national wars is, of course, not in doubt. That nationalism is gendered and often oppressive to women is equally a valid standpoint. These narratives, however, become problematic when they assume homogeneity of women's experiences. While Western-based feminist critics of nationalism consistently point to the temporal nature of their activism, others suggest that women's roles and contributions to national independence struggles can have long-term, positive outcomes. While their male comrades, and others, may see women's mobilisation as nationalist actors as an abeyance, the evidence from combatant women indicates a more nuanced and ambiguous transition, replete with instances of continued agency and activism on the one hand, and regression and marginalisation on the other. This book argues that high levels of wartime politicisation, mobilisation, and activism by nationalist women is carried forward into the post-war, thus demonstrating the discernible benefits yielded by women's wartime participation in non-state nationalist movements.

Despite the mounting and compelling evidence contradicting the dubious links between femininity and peacefulness, the women and peace hypothesis remains a strong conceptual framework that enables political actors to mobilise for change. It is, however, both an empowering and restricting framework (Aharoni 2016: 1). The propensity for those who work within such a framework is undoubtedly validated by the discernible levels of agency accrued by such approaches. It does also, however, augment reductive conventional approaches that continue to propagate the dualism of warring male and peaceful female, and as a direct consequence, often precludes those who fail to fit within the stereotyped straitjacket. Furthermore, an examination of female combatants *after* the war identifies the discernible benefits in expanding the emphasis beyond their involvements in war to a point where combatant woman are also recognised and valued for their capacity as peace-builders. Within the realm of women, peace, and conflict transition, I suggest that female combatants embody the proverbial 'other'. If gender and women are both generally positioned as 'outsiders' to mainstream accounts of war and peace, then combatant women are undoubtedly the outsiders' outsider. As stated, while the wartime experiences of combatant women are finally receiving the academic and policy attention warranted, the ending of armed actions represents a paucity in research and understandings on their post-war experiences. Without following the journey of combatant women in its entirety, from the battlefields through to the negotiating tables and beyond, the feminist post-war picture yielded is distorted and unfinished. While this book is attentive to their experiences of war and violence, it is primarily concerned with issues, mechanisms, and possibilities open to combatant women in the aftermath of armed actions. In doing so, it advances their often-omitted understandings of conflict transition and, moreover, reconstitutes combatant women as a relatively untapped feminist resource for conflict resolution.

Why republican women? The purpose and significance of the study

This is a qualitative research project based on 40 semi-structured interviews with republican women that occurred in 2012 and 2013, mainly in the North of Ireland.[4] Ideological splits (most of which are often marred by bitter divisions culminating in violent feuds) are a trademark characteristic of Irish Republicanism, so my use of such a generalised term like 'republican women' requires precise clarification. Research participants all self-identified as members or activists within the Provisional IRA and Sinn Féin,[5] generally referred to as the Republican Movement. While there have been many republican groupings throughout the recent armed conflict, the group known as the Provisional IRA (PIRA), became the main militant republican protagonist in terms of its size, capabilities, and support. While Sinn Féin initially played a subordinate role alongside armed struggle, electoral successes by the republican movement in 1981 resulted in a change of strategy, leading to a much stronger emphasis and focus on electoral politics in co-existence with armed actions. To explore the

16 *Introduction*

transition experiences of republican women, it is vital that an overview of their wartime experiences and insights contextualise the research findings. In doing so, it provides a comprehensive insight into the motivations, roles, and experiences of republican women during the years of armed conflict, right up to the 1994 ceasefires.

The armed conflict, euphemistically dubbed the 'Troubles', which engulfed the North of Ireland from 1969 until its peace accord of 1998, claimed over 3600 lives and injured over 22,000 people. While the roots and trajectory of the conflict are historically complex, broadly speaking, the state of Northern Ireland represents a contested territory between two competing ethno-national blocs.[6] Typically, the Protestant population identify themselves as unionist, loyalist and/or pro-British, while Catholics self-identify as Irish, nationalist or republican. Often erroneously labelled as a 'religious war', religion's role in the conflict functioned more as a marker of ethno-national allegiance, and therefore the violence that engulfed the region cannot be reduced or explained by differing confessional status or theological beliefs (Coulter 1999). Following a guerrilla war for independence waged by Irish republicans between 1919 and 1921, a peace settlement in 1921 partitioned Ireland into two separate states. Twenty-six counties would eventually go on to be the Republic of Ireland, which overwhelmingly comprised those who identified with an Irish nationalist and republican identity. The six-county state of Northern Ireland remained part of the United Kingdom of Great Britain and was purposefully designed to ensure a protestant, pro-British majority. This new state, however, also contained a significant minority population of Catholics who overwhelmingly identified as Irish.

Catholic alienation was apparent in many obvious organs of the state; the state police force, the Royal Ulster Constabulary[7] (RUC) was perceived as a partial and armed wing of unionism, augmented by the exclusively Protestant B Specials, largely viewed by Catholics as a paramilitary force. Various forms of discrimination against Catholics in housing, voting, and employment are now widely accepted as endemic.[8] Uninterrupted one-party unionist rule, coupled with repressive state powers for policing, meant that the Northern Ireland state failed to function as a normal, liberal democratic state. Inspired by civil rights marches in the United States, public marches and demands for civil and equal rights for Catholics in the late 1960s were met with brutal state violence and repression. Ethno-religious tensions were exacerbated in the wake of the civil rights protests. The inter-communal violence that erupted in 1969 witnessed widespread violence and the forced displacement of thousands in cities like Belfast, culminating with the deployment of the British Army in August of that year. While initially welcomed as 'saviours' by some Catholics, the subsequent actions of state forces in the following months, including curfews, internment, as well the killing of hundreds of Catholic civilians alienated many Catholic nationalists and emboldened the re-emerging IRA, setting Northern Ireland on a course of armed violence for the next 30 years. The primary protagonists in the conflict were Irish republican non-state militaries (with the Provisional IRA being the most significant), various pro-British Loyalist non-state militaries (Ulster

Defence Association/Ulster Freedom Fighters;[9] Ulster Volunteer Force[10]), and state forces such as the British Army and the RUC.

Women actions on the front lines of Irish national struggles are not a phenomenon unique to 'the Troubles' in the North. Historically, there were relatively high levels of women's activism in the cause of militant Irish republicanism during the revolutionary period of 1916 to 1921, ranging from armed combatant to weapons transportation (Coulter 1993; Ward 1983).[11] The rebirth of armed republicanism in 1969 (particularly in the form of the Provisionals), however, resides more with the immediacy of protecting families and communities as opposed to any semblance of latent nationalist ideology or theologian republicanism. The invasion of state violence into the working-class streets and homes of nationalists is frequently cited as the main motivating factor in mobilising women (and men) as active republican combatants. State repression such as the Falls curfew, internment, and events such as Bloody Sunday augmented the collective trauma and sense of impending attack, directing women towards militant republicanism as the 'only option'. The magnitude of these events, and others, would see the IRA go from what it termed as a defensive stance towards taking the war to the British (Taylor 1998).

For all its rhetoric regarding its revolutionary and socialist credentials, the Provisional republican movement operated along a strict gender division of roles. Breaking with 'tradition', republican women in the early 1970s were not sated with the prospect of playing the auxiliary role in this evolving conflict and so, demanded a full and equal role in the IRA.[12] While, initially, women's contributions were restricted solely to the auxiliary roles of *Cumann na mBan*[13] (Alison 2009: 187), their demands for full entry into all aspects of militant republicanism meant that women became a vital part of the IRA (Ward 2004: 191). Some suggest the decision by the republican leadership to allow women to join the IRA as full members stemmed not from ideological considerations but more pragmatic concerns regarding the loss of male volunteers through internment and the spiralling levels of violence in the early 1970s (Power 2010). Within the IRA, 'initially women were assigned roles *because* of their gender, not in spite of it' (O'Keefe 2013: 66). The state's initial analysis and approach to the conflict assumed and accepted the gendered myth of women's innocence (Mukta 2000), thus ensuring that women's republican activities such as communications, weapons smuggling, or reconnaissance escaped largely unnoticed by state forces. Using gender stereotypes as a means of subversion meant that baby prams and underwear were often used as a means of transporting weapons and other resources (Alison 2009; O'Keefe 2013). While bombings (particularly car bombs) and gun attacks were the trademark characteristics of the IRA's campaign, other actions including armed robberies (banks, trains, post offices), community 'policing' (beatings, knee capping, tar and feathering[14]), internal security,[15] and high-profile kidnapping were also widely used. Women's progression from auxiliary to front-line fighter saw them trained as proficient bomb-makers. Even as early as 1972, the first IRA bombing team in England involved women and was allegedly led by the Price sisters, Dolours and Marion, who each received lengthy prison sentences for their role in the bombings.

Women convicted for bombing and shooting offences as well as the instances in which some died on 'active service' is indicative of women's permeations throughout the ranks of the IRA. This is not to suggest, however, that widespread sexism and even patriarchal views did not exist within the ranks of the IRA. Despite the active participation of women at all levels, the area of leadership presents a glaring absence of women. As a secret (and illegal) organisation, it is impossible to accurately determine the extent of women's participation at a leadership level, but some suggest that women's leadership roles were located firmly at a cell or brigade level, never reaching the upper echelons. As in 'any hierarchical organisation (e.g. political parties), male prejudice and gendered norms dictated what leadership looked like, at the expense of women' (O'Keefe 2013: 78). Other reasons cited are women's lack of 'seeking power' through positions while others refer to the gendered division of labour as primary explanations for the alleged dearth of women at the higher levels of leadership. Despite an overhaul in its gender regime at a rank and file level, women faced formidable structural barriers when the dearth of women at a leadership level are examined (Keenan-Thomson 2010: 235).

Women's bodies became sites of struggle and resistance, no more so than in the prison struggle of the late 1970s and early 1980s. While the attention of British state forces initially focused on men, in March 1972, Liz McKee was the first woman interned. From 1972 onwards, republican women would find themselves arrested, detained, interrogated, tortured, and imprisoned. Women's bodies were often used by state forces as key 'battlegrounds', attempting to interrogate or extract information from female suspects using sexual slurs, strip-searches, overtones, and actual threats of rape (O'Keefe 2013: 35). Menstruating women in detention were also denied sanitary towels and personal hygiene. As their bodies were used as weapons against them, republican women became critically aware of the gendered ways in which they, unlike their male comrades, were experiencing the conflict. Through the state's widespread use of gendered violence against women's bodies, many women came to feminism through republicanism (Power 2010: 154).

Following the removal of special category status by the British Government in 1976,[16] 32 women sentenced after March 1976 embarked on a campaign of non-cooperation with the prison regime, refusing to comply with compulsory work, withdrawal from prison education programs, and nonconformity with prison discipline (Corcoran 2006: 120). In February 1980, after a particularly violent assault on female prisoners during a prolonged search of their cells in Armagh jail, women were then subject to total confinement to their cells and denied access to toilet and shower facilities. When toilet facilities were reopened to the women several days later, the women refused to 'slop out', as a weapon of protest against their treatment. As the women joined their male comrades on the No-Wash protest, they also had one further resource, menstrual blood. By smearing this alongside their bodily waste on the cell walls, prison authorities only entered cells when they needed to, albeit covered in full-body suits and masks in order protect themselves from the surroundings of the No-Wash protest. Strip searching was routinely used by the state against both men and women, viewed by republicans as attempts to demoralise and sap the political energy from republicans. Although the 1981 hunger strike[17] signalled an end to the 'mirror searches' against the men, ironically, between 1982 to 1986 strip searching of women increased with precise regularity.[18] Refusing to consent to such practices, women were physically restrained by several prison warders (usually male warders) and clothing forcibly removed. Sexual slurs, beatings, and mass cell searches, alongside strip searches were regular parts of the prison regime for women throughout the 1980s and into the 1990s.

Both the prison struggle of 1976–1981 and the continued use of strip searching raised gender consciousness among many republican women, particularly those inside the jail. Ironically, it was the 'freedom' of jail that also provided many female prisoners with the space and opportunity to engage in political education, discussion, and debate. Feminist literature and informal education classes provided the foundations for the development of republican feminist consciousness. Links with other feminist groups forced republican women to confront the patriarchy not only of the state but also within the republican movement; the linkages made between national and gender identities led to a realisation that they were 'dually oppressed' (O'Keefe 2013: 127). By the 1980s republican feminism, particularly in the establishment of the Sinn Féin Women's Department, emerged as a robust political force within the republican movement, 'aggressively campaigning' on issues of prisoner rights, reproductive rights and a lack of equality based on sexual orientation and class (O'Keefe 2013: 133). By now, 'women's liberation was an integral part of the overall struggle against oppression' (Gillespie 1994: 17), indicating the synthesis between women's emancipation and national self-determination. Like many other non-state liberation movements around the world, republican women carved out political spaces within the republican movement to develop a broad social and political agenda that reached far beyond the national question, including gender equality, Lesbian Gay Bisexual Transgender (LGBT) rights, ethnic and racial minorities and reaching out to other struggles in places such as Palestine and South Africa (Maillot 2005). The remainder of this book seeks to uncover the transition of republican women within a movement previously dedicated to armed political violence to a largely mainstream institutional political party. Given this seismic departure, it is important to uncover the ways in which the shift away from armed struggle shaped women's levels of political mobility and activism.

Feminist research methodologies and methods

If feminism is a political project that attempts to 'speak for women' (Hekman 1999: 24), it presents the problem of who exactly is qualified to 'speak' on behalf of women? In recognising the diversity of roles and experiences of women, I apply a feminist standpoint approach that contends that knowledge is situated and perspectival and, that 'there are multiple standpoints from which knowledge is produced' (Hekman 1999: 30). Moreover, many feminist IR scholars also cite standpoint as the ideal method of challenging masculine domination while remaining attuned to the differences between women (Tickner 2014). Formative standpoint theorists such as Nancy Hartstock (1983) and Dorothy Smith (1987) argue for two important yet ultimately contradictory positions; first, that all knowledge is situated (and therefore socially constructed in multiple ways) and second, that there is epistemic privilege among the oppressed allowing a true vision of social relations. Linking directly to Marxist theories regarding how knowledge is constructed through material human activity, standpoint theory maintains that the dominant groups vision of reality is 'partial and perverse', an 'ignorance' derived from their stake in maintaining the prevailing social order and status quo. It argues instead that the oppressed possess the 'truth' regarding the reality of social relations. Early feminist standpoint suffered from the contradiction of being a 'situated knowledge' while also claiming a core, universal truth by one's gender, thus the perennial battle between the universal and the particular. In other words, if standpoint is 'situated knowledge', then all perspectives and narratives emanate from subjective positions which are profoundly shaped by specific contexts of intersecting identities. So, while Hartstock claims that 'women's lives make available a particular and privileged vantage point on male supremacy' (1983: 284), I refute the notion that all women share similar experiences of male supremacy due to women's differential social and political positioning.

The focus in recent times towards differences between women has led to a reformulation of standpoint to a more pertinent pluralised '*standpoints'* or what Tickner terms 'modified standpoints' (1997: 622). In other words, it is self-evident that if women possess multiple experiences they will therefore produce multiple standpoints, presenting the obvious question; which standpoint is the truer vision of society? Hekman (1999) posits that if the vast and multiple differences between women are accepted, there is, in fact, a danger of abandoning the very idea of feminism itself as a political movement. Yet such a predicament, I suggest, can be reconciled. We must examine not the ways in which gender 'competes' with other intersecting structures of power but recognise the fluid ways in which patriarchy intertwines with other structural forces to produce differentially positioned women. Such a position abandons the highly simplistic dualism of dominant/oppressed narratives and instead views both categories as profoundly plural and heterogeneous. Sandra Harding, possibly more than any other theorist, attempted to move standpoint theory away from the essentialist pitfalls and argued that standpoint provides feminists with the necessary solution to the perpetual battle between essentialist and relativist positions. Harding insists that there are multiple standpoints given the vast differences among women but also challenges the post-modern relativism by insisting that women's lives provide an objective location for research. Harding argues for a 'strong objectivity' that acknowledges the contextual positioning of all knowledge, yet argues that certain 'social situations tend to generate the most objective claims'

(Harding 1991: 142). Harding is severely critiqued by some for assuming that the experience or existence of oppression alone guarantees a more objective account (Hekman 1999: 45). Moreover, I would argue that a fundamental building block of feminist theory and methodology is the rejection (or at the very least a deep suspicion) of claims regarding objectivity and truth, and so Harding's demands for a 'strong objectivity' appear to revert towards a more positivist stance. In this, I would tend to agree with the position of Hekman that feminist standpoint is theoretically and epistemologically sounder when it acts as a powerful counter-discourse to the prevailing hegemonic order as opposed to claiming it as privileged and stronger in objectivity (1999: 45). While the existence of multiple standpoints stood accused of undermining the very premise upon which standpoint is based, the fact remains that overwhelmingly women and femininities remain subordinate to men and masculinities. Feminist standpoint does not abandon the category of gender or the idea of theorising from women's lives and therefore remains a credible and useful method (particularly for men engaging in feminist research) for generating feminist epistemology. It retains gender as a primary category of exploration while also recognising the vast differences between women who are differentially situated.

The research process

This feminist study of republican women in conflict transition utilised 40 semi-structured, in-depth interviews to examine their unique perspectives and their current political activity.[19] Qualitative research, particularly non-hierarchical interviewing, is often cited as a primary feminist methodology as it 'gives voice' to women's experiences (Oakley 1981; Stanley and Wise 1993). In addition, secondary materials including political literature, party policy documents, and various websites were also valuable sources throughout the research. Using interviewee narratives and placing emphasis on personal experiences within transitioning societies illuminates the ways in which female combatants negotiate their post-war roles. To explore and elucidate women's lives, DeVault cites the use of personal testimony, particularly through ethnographies and qualitative interviews 'as extremely effective ways in making women visible' (1999: 30). Silverman asserts that interviews 'provide access to the meanings people attribute to their experience and their social worlds' (2004: 126), thus generating theories and knowledge from women's standpoint. To undertake a thorough exploration of republican women's transitioning away from armed conflict, I chose in-depth interviews as the strongest method for two main reasons. First, semi-structured interviews give voice and meaning to the personal narrative and second, by applying the non-hierarchical model advocated by Oakley (1981), it allowed the amelioration of power dynamics within the interview process. From a feminist perspective, interviewing is a powerful research tool in exploring women's experiences as it allows the participant to tell their stories (Denzin and Lincoln 1998: 74), while also enabling the participation of the interviewee as a collaborator within the research. According to Holstein and Gubrium, interviews are interactive and therefore constructional. The 'active interview' allows knowledge to be assembled whereby participants become constructors of knowledge (2001: 142) resulting in a process of 'meaning production' (DeVault 1999; Reinharz 1992; Smith 1987).

Of the 40 participants, 31 identified themselves as members of the IRA, six were solely members of Sinn Féin, while three identified their role as 'republican activist'.[20] In terms of age, participants ranged from 31 years old up to the late seventies. Most interviewees, however, were aged in their fifties and sixties. Given that the epicentres of conflict occurred mainly in urban working-class communities, it is unsurprising that most participants hailed from either Belfast or Derry. In all, 20 interviews occurred in Belfast, eight in Derry, four in Dublin and the remaining eight occurred in various town and villages along the border. Fieldwork began on 26 May 2012 and concluded on 25 November 2013.

Given the clandestine nature of the republican movement and the on-going court cases dealing with the Boston College tapes, which I will deal with in detail a little further on, the task of accessing republican women was helped enormously by my familial connection to west Belfast. My father is from the Andersonstown area of west Belfast and my grandfather was a well-known publican who owned two bars on the Falls road in west Belfast.[21] My familial connection to west Belfast reduced my 'stranger' status greatly and was essential in establishing trust and rapport between the participants, gatekeepers, and me. Furthermore, my familiarity with their northern vernacular as well as knowledge of place names, people, and events were invaluable during the interview process. Using a 'snowball' technique, participants were located using three separate gatekeepers. The first gatekeeper worked within the *Coiste* organisation, established in the late 1990s to help republican ex-prisoners and their families, who provided access to 16 participants; ten in Belfast and eight in Derry. I first met this gatekeeper in 2009 when undertaking some research for an undergraduate dissertation but we established a relationship and stayed in touch with sporadic emails and correspondence related to republican women. A second gatekeeper who also participated in the research is a Sinn Féin member in Belfast, and introduced me to three participants while finally, a family friend, again in Belfast, introduced me to a further two participants. As part of the reflective process upon the conclusion of each interview, several participants then recommended other women to interview and passed on my contact details accordingly, leading to more participants.

The IRA is (and was) an illegal organisation and its members, even today, are still incredibly difficult to access for interview. I would also add here that there was a double-difficulty when attempting to locate female combatants for the simple reason that their role is still considered by some as being 'non-conventional'. Women's numbers within the ranks of the IRA were also much lower than men's, and this certainly adds to the difficulty of locating female research participants. In addition, it is also important to qualify that although 40 interviewees is a relatively high number, it is undoubtedly a small percentage of the actual number of women involved in the republican movement. Nevertheless, as a researcher, I was more than satisfied that I managed to locate and interview 40 participants, which form the bulk of analysis for this book. The process, however, was not without its difficulties.

The Provisional IRA is now officially disbanded, although contentious enquiries by the new police force, Police Service of Northern Ireland[22] (PSNI) into past actions remain on-going. Many research participants in this project deliberately eschewed talking of instances that could be legally harmful to them. This is particularly important given the on-going debacle regarding the Boston College tapes. The Boston College Oral History Archive on 'the Troubles' initiated a research project in 2001 to collect recorded testimonies of former paramilitary members, both loyalist and republican. Interviewees were guaranteed that their recordings would only be released after their deaths. This extraordinary scenario, where former paramilitaries spoke on tape recording of their role and the role of others in various illegal armed actions, sparked a series of subpoenas issued to Boston College by the US Department of Justice on behalf of the United Kingdom in May and August of 2011, requesting the tapes and transcripts for use in criminal investigations. In 2013 a court in the United States ordered that the tapes be handed over to PSNI investigating officers, some of which have led to the arrest and charging of one veteran republican, Ivor Bell in April 2014. In May 2014, Sinn Féin president Gerry Adams was arrested by the PSNI for questioning about the killing, an arrest allegedly stemming directly from the Boston College tapes.[23] There is currently an on-going court battle by the PSNI to secure the entire archive of 46 interviews. I can recall that only three of the 40 participants did not mention the words 'Boston College' to me, particularly prior to commencing the recorded interview and it undoubtedly cast a shadow over this research. I know from speaking to other scholars in the field of combatants that it looms large over their research also.

The initial 15 interviews occurred in two ex-prisoner centres in Belfast and Derry respectively, where gatekeepers arranged a schedule of interviews to be conducted in a designated room within the centre. After these initial 15 interviews, snowballing meant that interviews moved beyond the initial three gatekeepers, but it was clear that many subsequent interviewees were only taking part because it had been 'OK'd' by others. In many of these cases, an initial meeting or correspondence (phone calls or email) was initiated by me. It was only then at the time of interview that I discovered that many of these participants had checked with other participants as to my background and credentials before deciding to participate. Of the remaining 25 interviews, 24 occurred in family homes with one at a place of work. Overwhelmingly, there were marked differences between these interviews and those earlier ones at ex-prisoner centres and Sinn Féin offices. While the initial 15 had the feeling of a 'formal interview' around them (which can be restrictive to both researcher and interviewees), the interviews in the family home felt more like conversations and this is clear when it came to the analysis of the transcripts. It was during the preparation for the tea where informal chat 'broke some of the ice' and built up a rapport well before the commencement of interviews. That, coupled with the safety and comfort of familiar surroundings in the home produced a setting whereby I feel research participants felt far more relaxed, resulting in a far more fluid exchange between us. This is probably most apparent in the length of interviews. On most occasions, I would spend two to three hours at the home, leaving with a recording of at least over an hour, 90 minutes in most cases. After interviews, time was spent reflecting on the interview and on certain issues that were raised during the process, as well as general chat about political developments or personal stories about our own families.

Prior to the rise of feminist methodologies, little attention had been paid to the role of researchers in perpetuating the power dynamics within the research process with traditional 'textbook' methods on research portraying the researcher as an expert yet also a 'disinterested observer' while participants are viewed as 'units of analysis' and 'variables' (Lynch 2000: 78; Oakley 1981). The privileging of the 'expert' perspective enshrines inequality within the research process whereby the detached view of the expert is imposed as the interpreted 'truth' upon a participant's personal experience (Daly 2000). Smith asserts that it is vital that the researched are not objectified (1987: 111); ethical research preserves and encourages their presence as subjects and active agents within the process (ibid.: 151). Similarly, Lather (1991) advocates interactive approaches to research produce a dialectical process whereby participants move away from mere objects of research and become active subjects empowered to their conditions, experiences and perspectives.

Challenging this, Letherby (2003) insists it is impossible to attain a research process that is equal, emancipatory, and fully participatory. The researcher has control over the research process, responsible for transcribing and analysing, will write the research data, and is ultimately the person who delivers the final research findings. Stanley and Wise (1993), acknowledging that inequalities are impossible to eradicate, have argued for a process of 'equalisation' within research, one that mitigates inequalities between the researcher and the researched achieved through process transformation and empowerment. Given my own background and male subjectivities, I concurred that eradicating all inequalities completely was impossible. I did, however, utilise various strategies to at least attempt to 'equalise' the process, including the returning of interview transcripts and sending out the research questions prior to the interview, among others which will discussed in detail below. Whereas feminist methodologies are committed to literally 'giving voice to women's experiences', this is not always a guaranteed outcome of implementing feminist principles and can be problematic. During my research, it was quite clear that choices around topics for discussion during interviews as well as themes for analysis afterwards were choices that I alone made. While the semi-structured interview allowed space for participants to freely discuss any issue they deemed relevant to their experience, the interviews, however, were consistently guided by a loose framework of topics that I as researcher wished to cover within each interview. While acknowledging that the establishment of a truly egalitarian relationship within the interview process is extremely arduous, I did seek to ameliorate some of the inequalities through many measures.

While some interview times and locations were arranged by gatekeepers, the majority of interviews were arranged by direct contact with the research participants. Due to the nature of the research and the people involved, I was always conscious that access to participants could be closed off at any time. On some occasions, interviews were either cancelled or postponed, most of these, frustratingly, at the last moment. All participants were given the broad research questions/themes several days, sometimes weeks, prior to their interview. While most found this quite helpful and reassuring, it did have the effect that some participants felt that they would be unable to answer some questions, articulating that certain topics were not applicable to their story. At all times, I emphasised the fluid and loose structure of the interview and stressed their role in guiding the interview process also. Some participants chose not to answer certain questions prior to and some during the interview process, once again illustrating the dialectical relationship between researcher and participants.

A cornerstone of feminist research methodologies is the idea of empowering women or utilising emancipatory research processes whereby women's lives can be transformed. While this research will hopefully add important data to larger theoretical debates around women and conflict transition, I also envisaged that the research may also be of use to participants themselves. First, by documenting their experiences and stories, I would argue that this research sheds light on this overlooked section of women, which challenges the dominant narrative of women and conflict transition. And second, I have already presented some of my research findings to groups of republicans, one in Dublin and the other in Belfast. I intend to work with some of my gatekeepers upon the completion of the project with a view of presenting some of the key findings and recommendations from the work, which could add input to the growing debates regarding women and republicanism today. Some interviewees inquired to the future dissemination of the findings. Some requested any updates regarding the findings, others spoke about a possible presentation of the findings to a wide group of republicans (ex-prisoner centres and the Sinn Féin *Ard Fheis* were mentioned by some as possible venues), while others inquired as to whether it would be published in book format.

Another key method of 'equalisation' adopted during the research was through the ownership of interview data. All interviews were transcribed by me and returned to every participant for their consideration if they so wished; of the 40 interviews, 36 chose to receive a copy of their interview transcript while four declined. Participants had the opportunity to edit, modify, delete or clarify all or sections of their interview transcript. Most participants responded to acknowledge receipt of the transcript and a small number made some minor changes, mostly grammatical. Correspondence through email occurred until the participant was satisfied with an agreed final draft. This process was often arduous, time-consuming and, at times, problematic, particularly with the fact that the transfer of fluid conversation between people never 'reads well' as transcribed text. Many participants felt the need to re-phrase certain sentences that didn't appear grammatically correct. Many felt that there were times when their words sounded too 'bitter', 'happy' or 'angry'. I reminded all participants that interview transcripts always fail to capture the context and atmosphere in which they were spoken.

Maintaining the anonymity of people and organisations was a clear priority to mitigate and avoid potential harm. All materials related to the interview process were securely stored both digitally and physically in secure locations. I had sole access to these materials, including recordings, interview transcripts, interview schedule and consent forms. As a researcher, I guaranteed anonymity and confidentiality to research participants and I intend to honour that agreement. While some participants offered to use their real name, I declined and advocated that the potential harms from this far outweighed the almost nil benefit from including them.[24] Given the relatively lower numbers of women within the republican movement, I feel that it is necessary to remove any potential, no matter how small, of any harm to research participants and so it is important to state that while all names used in this thesis are fictitious in order to protect identities, it is equally as important to state that the pseudonyms chosen by the author did not duplicate any of the real names of the participants, again reducing the likelihood of exposing a participant's identity.

Organisation of the book

Feminist international relations theory argues that male consolidation of power in the aftermath of armed conflict often occurs as men gain the status of heroes in the post-war appraisals. Explorations of republican commemoration in the North of Ireland have uncovered the dominance of the male protagonist with a notable relative absence of militant republican women. Women's multiple roles and vital wartime contributions are rarely recognised or valued by male-led movements. Their exclusion from the post-war commemorative landscape is a very public and trumpeted message that when it came to times of great peril for the nation, women were not really there. When combatant women do appear in commemoration, it is only when they do so in accordance with the masculine discourse and definition of a combatant. The exclusion of women's wartime contributions that emerges in the transition period, however, is not a new phenomenon and, in fact, is a long-standing pattern of men's dismissals of women's contributions, from the battlefield to post-war memorials. Masculinised military narratives, and patriarchal understandings of what is deemed a combatant role (and what, therefore, is deemed worthy of commemorating), consistently fail to value or recognise women's multiple and vital wartime contributions.

Chapter 2 explores the ways in which republican women themselves conceptualise their roles and contributions within armed struggle. Their experiences and perspectives produce a series of narratives that run counter to the male-dominated post-war memorial landscape. Being attentive to the ways in which they conceptualise their wartime contributions not only brings their roles into view, but I argue, subverts conventional and patriarchal ways in which wartime contributions are defined. It echoes Megan MacKenzie's (2012) contention that we learn far more from 'asking and listening' about the experiences of women and girl soldiers than by relying on top-down processes. This chapter not only asks 'where are the combatant women' in post-war memorialisation but argues that combatant women's experiences, narratives, and meanings challenge existing frameworks and discourses, and therefore revolutionises the ways we define combatant and wartime roles. In other words, their struggle during conflict transition is not encompassed by simply 'adding women' to the existing picture but rather by using their unique standpoints to subvert established discourses and definitions to challenge the forces of patriarchy. The chapter begins with an exploration of the ways in which interviewees themselves define their combatant roles and experiences. Emerging from this is a rich narrative of multiple military roles that challenges and dislodges the limited, masculine definition of 'a person with a weapon'. In addition, interviewees reject the hierarchical dichotomy of fighter/supporter in favour of recognising the importance of *all* military contributions to republican armed struggle. It then moves on to examine the ways in which interviewees believe their contributions have been either diluted or erased completely within republican commemoration. The final section explores the innovative and alternative forms of commemoration by republican women in recent times. It suggests that these 'alternative' forms of commemoration accurately capture their eclectic wartime contributions at all levels of militant republicanism, bringing previously overlooked militant women onto the memorial landscape.

Feminists have long argued that mainstream forms of conflict transition are highly gendered processes, inherently male-centred, and focused towards specific concerns, particularly around issues of state security, 'good governance', and political and civil rights (Sjoberg 2010). Because gender is often either trivialised or rendered invisible, the post-war reconstruction period reflects the 'patriarchal order before the conflict' resulting in a settlement that refuses to incorporate gender issues at anything more than at a superficial and rhetorical level (Handrahan 2004: 440). Conflict resolution processes, particularly those associated with (re-)establishing formal political and civil institutions, are largely shaped by patriarchal norms synonymous with liberal, representative democracies, and furthermore, assume and require a particular gender order (MacKenzie 2012; Ni Aolain *et al.* 2011). Given this, the discourse and politics of a post-conflict 'return to normal' inherently carries with its negative implications for women's political activism (Meintjes *et al.* 2001). Furthermore, the idea that violence has neat start and end points exposes the inadequacies of those who seek to engineer a peace that deals only with the 'exceptional' violence of war. The continuum of violence resists any division between public and private domains, and, moreover, contends that the violence of armed conflict cannot be separated from other expressions of violence (Giles and Hyndman 2004).

Using the framework of a gendered continuum of violence and drawing upon the post-war experiences of republican women in the North of Ireland, Chapter 3 argues that the post-conflict moment as experienced by republican women represents not peace and security, but a continuity of gender discrimination, violence, and insecurity. While the GFA has and continues to draw plaudits both nationally and internationally as a model of conflict resolution, the everyday experiences of republican women reveal a post-war landscape enmeshed in various forms of violence, oppression, and insecurity. While issues such as the partition of Ireland represent a continuity of oppression, the post-war period has also brought an increase in other forms of violence including gender-based violence, homophobic attacks, the crippling effects of neo-liberal austerity, and the continuing struggle for women's reproductive rights. Despite unambiguous commitments to gender equality and the promotion of women within the text of the 1998 peace accord, the chapter finds a more doleful reality from the perspective of republican women. While women are making moderate but important strides forward in formal politics, paid employment, among others, the alarming increases in gender-based violence and homophobic attacks in the aftermath of the peace accord challenges the dominant declarations of a peaceful, prosperous, and secure society.

This chapter therefore endeavours to provide new insights by exploring the visions of peace and security from the perspective of former combatant republican women in Ireland. The continuum of violence indicated by republican women in this chapter is unquestionably gendered, but it is also delineated through other sources of insecurity including ongoing occupation, the vagaries of global capitalism. Engagements of combatant women with peace produces important points of comparison as well as significant points of departure with other feminist visions of peace. Their contemporary lives reveal a landscape littered with various forms of violence and conflict; from 'private' social violence to the 'public' structural violence of capitalism. Asking combatant women about their post-war visions of a just society therefore advances a series of needs, interests and concerns normally omitted by traditional approaches to peace and security. In the so-called post-conflict period, streets, homes, and bedrooms remain key battlegrounds (Cockburn 1998; Enloe 2004: 224). Rather than depicting the North of Ireland as a place at peace, primary data here indicates that decreasing levels of military violence are matched with increasing levels of gender-based violence. It is these insidious forms of violence that are identified as barriers to women's equality and a meaningful peace, but furthermore, the presence of post-war violence ensures a continuity of political and social struggles by republican women, thereby rebuking those who suggest that women's mobilisation by nationalism is simply temporal.

Chapter 4 explores the ways in which the institutionalisation of Provisional republicanism during conflict transition impacted upon the political struggles of women within the republican movement. It finds that the shoe-horning of political activism into elite, male dominated peace talks, coupled with the zealous pursuit of electoral politics, squeezed many of the political spaces created by women through the conflict years. Despite the prevailing calls within conventional approaches for women's inclusion within both institutional peace talks and the sphere of state-centric politics, the chapter suggests that the institutionalisation of political struggle can prove to be detrimental to the post-war lives of former combatant women. The chapter begins with an exploration of the changing dynamics within the republican movement during the post-ceasefire period as Sinn Féin 'professionalises' itself and its wider organisation. I then move on to explore women's experiences of the GFA negotiations, indicating a sidelining of both women and their interests as state power, elite-led negotiations, and electoral contests gain primacy. Despite the centrality of their roles and labour during the years of armed conflict, evidence here suggests a lack of direct input for republican women during the formal talks process. The lack of meaningful input within the negotiations is further compounded by the ambiguous demise of the Sinn Féin Women's Department. This previously vibrant and prolific feminist organisation appears to 'fade away' just at a time when the overall movement firmly accelerates away from its 'revolutionary struggle' towards its post-war overhaul into a constitutional political party. The analysis within the chapter suggests that the institutional re-positioning of the party required an overhaul of women's previous modes of feminist agitation to fit with its newfound mainstream departure.

Levels of post-war regression for women within nationalist movements are not unique to this book. However, it is important to move beyond the limitations of generalised narratives that propagate the post-war landscape solely as a moment of loss. Chapter 5 explores the eclectic post-war political activism of republican women, across both formal and informal spheres of politics. Despite the unequivocal commitments to gender equality in the GFA peace accord, the record of women elected as political representatives in the region between 1998 and 2016 is profoundly bleak. Notwithstanding, republican women have made significant progress within constitutional politics when compared with other political parties, and Sinn Féin is accredited with a strong record of promoting women. Furthermore, many of their elected representatives in the North of Ireland are former IRA prisoners. Notwithstanding their relative 'successes' in entering formal politics in relatively significant numbers and presence, most have also retained their grassroots, community activism, indicating the importance placed on both sites of political activism. Despite avenues and opportunities to the upper echelons of executive power, the post-war politics of republican women comprises a hybrid, or dual struggle, encompassing both formal and informal activism. The chapter finds a shared ambivalence towards institutional politics and its restrictive transformative potential among these republican women. Although they do deem it an important sphere for women, formal, parliamentary politics alone is appraised as having insufficient potential to deliver the type of change envisioned by interviewees. Moreover, this chapter finds that while the women's inclusion within electoral politics is rhetorically incorporated within the mainstream peace and security agenda, the experiences of republican women in the 'new post-conflict politics' in the North of Ireland reveals another site of post-war gender struggle. While gender equality is now exalted by the mainstream as an essential litmus test for genuinely transformed society, formal politics in the aftermath of war in the North of Ireland remains profoundly gendered in terms of barriers, norms and cultures. Given this, it is community engagement and civil society activism that is seen to provide the transformative space to address the specific issues that impact their lives and the lives of those within working-class, republican communities.

The focal point of this book is not the Irish Republican movement nor is it a text overly concerned with the North of Ireland and its on-going and ever-fragile peace process. Rather, by exploring the hitherto-overlooked perspectives and experiences of combatant women in that region, I endeavour to build upon existing international literature, and contribute important new insights and understandings to the global feminist conversation on gender, war, and conflict transition. Women's roles as combatants in non-state armed movements and their post-combat experiences are not unique to the North of Ireland; they are global issues. Due to their perceived 'unconventional' wartime roles, the analysis contained in this book reaches far beyond the parochial politics of Ireland and speaks directly to broader, global themes directly related to female combatants and post-conflict processes. While this is the story of Irish republican women transitioning from armed conflict, the content and analysis presented here offers new understandings to matters that are potentially applicable to other societies emerging from armed conflict.

Notes

1 In light of the politically loaded discourse surrounding 'the Troubles' (and most conflicts for that matter), it is important to clarify my choice of terminology. As the reader will undoubtedly have noticed even at this formative stage, I use terms such as the 'North of Ireland' (or the North) as opposed to the official title of Northern Ireland, the South instead of the 'Republic of Ireland', as well as phrases such as 'armed struggle', 'political violence'. A significant number of interviewees were concerned about this issue and did enquire if I would use their republican terminology in the writing of this book. It would have been disingenuous and undoubtedly hurtful to interviewees had I used terms such as 'terrorists' or 'terrorism'. That said, I am also mindful that those who suffered as a result of IRA actions might also be offended by my use of republican terminology. This research however, is not a moral judgement on the use of violence during 'the Troubles', nor does it seek to eulogise or legitimise the actions of armed republicans. In order to tell the story of republican women however, I decided that I would do so using their republican discourse and terminology, which largely stems from a feminist commitment to research participants to use *their* stories in order to explore *their* transitionary experiences. In order to do so, and as a mark of respect to them, I use their republican terminology and phrases throughout the entire text. This is not, nor should it be taken, as an endorsement of the political philosophy of the republican movement. It should certainly not be interpreted as a tacit approval or support for either the IRA or Sinn Féin.
2 Judy El-Bushra coined this phrase to underscore the perpetual linkages between women and non-violence.
3 Adopted in October 2000, SCR 1325 reaffirms the important role of women in the prevention and resolution of conflicts, peace negotiations, peace-building, peacekeeping, humanitarian response, and women's' role in post-conflict reconstruction and stresses the importance of their equal participation and full involvement in all efforts for the maintenance and promotion of peace and security. Resolution 1325 urges all actors to increase the participation of women and incorporate gender

perspectives in all United Nations peace and security efforts. Full text of the resolution available at www.un.org/womenwatch/osagi/wps/
4 Given that the epicentres of armed conflict existed mostly in the contested Six Counties of the North of Ireland, it is unsurprising that most of the interviews were conducted there. That said, a small number of interviews did occur in the South of Ireland.
5 The term used by many (in local communities, mainstream commentary, some scholarship, media) to denote the Provisionals is 'Provos' (or also colloquially as the Provies). Despite the passage of almost 50 years since the bitter split between Official and Provisional wings of republicanism, the term Provo has endured and remains in widespread use today
6 The breadth and scope of academic and mainstream accounts relating to all aspects of 'the Troubles' is vast. For debates regarding the roots of the conflict, see Colin Coulter's (1999) *Contemporary Northern Irish Society*, Brendan O'Leary and John McGarry's (1995) *Explaining Northern Ireland*, and Jenifer Todd and Joseph Ruane's (1996) *The Dynamics of Conflict in Northern Ireland*. For an entire overview of both 'the Troubles' and the peace process, see Fergal Cochrane's (2013) *Northern Ireland: The Reluctant Peace*.
7 The Royal Ulster Constabulary (RUC) was formed alongside the partition of Ireland and the creation of the Northern Ireland State in 1921. While many Catholics within the new Northern Ireland state were alienated and/or excluded from many positions and roles within the new state, the RUC drew its recruits and personnel largely from the protestant/loyalist community. While the force was viewed by protestant/loyalist communities as a vital safeguard against any potential threat, those within the Catholic/nationalist/republican minority saw it as a biased and repressive force of unionism. Accusations and evidence of police mistreatment and partiality of Catholics throughout the history of the state only served to exacerbate these tensions. Furthermore, the unionist government also recruited an all-Protestant militia called the Ulster Special Constabulary ('B Specials'), which acted as an auxiliary to the RUC.
8 Despite many debates, there is somewhat of a consensus that the Catholic population suffered various levels of discrimination in the North of Ireland state, particularly in the areas of housing, employment, and voting rights. While the roots of this discrimination is contested (some cite the discrimination as instigated by unionist individuals while others view as part of the state structure), undoubtedly, much of the Catholic population felt alienated from the Northern Ireland state. For more, Michael Farrell's (1976) *Northern Ireland: The Orange State*, London: Pluto Press.
9 The Ulster Defence Association (UDA) is the largest loyalist paramilitary organisation. Formed in September 1971 out of a coalition of loosely organised vigilante groups, it undertook an armed campaign lasting almost 30 years. Incredibly, it was a legal organisation for most of the conflict, despite its involvement in hundreds of killings. To mask its role in killings, it formed the Ulster Freedom Fighters (UFF) to avoid proscription of the UDA. The British Government outlawed the UFF in November 1973, but the UDA itself was not proscribed as a terrorist group until August 1992. Both the UDA/UFF was responsible for more than 400 deaths. While the organisations were involved in killing a small number of involved republicans, the overwhelming majority of its victims were Irish Catholic civilians, killed at random, in what the group called retaliation for IRA actions or attacks on Protestants.
10 The Ulster Volunteer Force (UVF) is a loyalist paramilitary group. It emerged in 1966 and is named after the original UVF of the early twentieth century. The group undertook an armed campaign of almost 30 years during 'the Troubles' with a declared intent of defending the state from Irish Republicanism. Most of its victims, however, were uninvolved Catholics. It declared a ceasefire in 1994 and officially ended its campaign in 2007, although some of its members have continued to engage in violence and criminal activities.

32 *Introduction*

11 There are some insightful accounts of women's role in militant Irish republicanism during this period, suggesting nationalist women making direct connections between national freedom and women's liberation. See Sinead McCoole's (2014) *No Ordinary Women: Female Activists in the Revolutionary Years 1900–1921*; Carol Coulter's (1993) *The Hidden Tradition: Feminism and Nationalism in Ireland*; Margaret Ward's (1983) *Unmanageable Revolutionaries*; Ann Matthews (2010, 2012) *Renegades: Irish Republican Women 1900–1922* and *Dissidents: Irish Republican Women: 1923–1941*.

12 For a thorough and comprehensive account of republican women during the conflict, see Miranda Alison's (2009) *Women and Political Violence: Female Combatants in Ethno-National Conflict*, and Theresa O'Keefe's (2013) *Feminist Identity Development and Activism in Revolutionary Movements*. For explorations of women's prison experiences see Azrini Wahidin's (2016) *Ex-Combatants, Gender and Peace in Northern Ireland: Women, Political Protest and the Prison Experience*.

13 Founded in 1914, Cumann na mBan was a female auxiliary force, providing supporting roles for the Irish Volunteers, which became the IRA in 1919. Each subsequent manifestation of the IRA since retained Cumann na mBan as an important part of armed republicanism, yet it is consistently deemed by male IRA volunteers as a supplementary role. Initially, the Provisional IRA operated along strict gender lines whereby males occupied the ranks of the IRA and females were restricted to Cumann na mBan. Stemming directly from the demands of republican women, rules barring women from the IRA were changed in the early 1970s.

14 Such actions were meted out for 'anti-social' or petty criminal behaviour in republican communities. Knee-cappings was widely used and involved shooting alleged persons in the back of the knees as punishment for her/his discretion. Tar and feather was widely use against those who fraternised with the enemy, and particularly used against women who engaged in relations with British soldiers or attended dances that were sometimes held at British Army bases. In order to maximise humiliation, the alleged 'offender' was tied to a local street lamp post and covered in tar and feathers. Sometimes hair would be shaved off, a particularly horrific experience for the victims of such attacks.

15 Like all non-state militant movements, the IRA was susceptible to informers and/or state infiltration. The punishment for such offences was 'execution'. Such actions are historical, and the shooting of alleged informers can be traced back to the IRA of 1919–1923 period and has remained since.

16 Prior to this date, all members of non-state militant groups, republican or loyalist, were categorised as Special Category Prisoners, which for all intents and purposes amounted to de facto prisoner-of-war status.

17 After five years of the No-Wash protest, republican prisoners embarked upon two hunger strikes. The first hunger strike of 1980 involved male and female prisoners and was called off in confusion about the possibility of a deal with the British. Once this deal failed to materialise, a second hunger strike commenced lasting from March to October 1981. Ten republican men died on this hunger strike and it remains, as does the entire prison protest period of 1976 to 1981, a seismic epoch in contemporary republican history.

18 Strip searching of republican women continued right up to 1992, whereby it markedly declined during the emergence of the formal peace process. That said, strip searching continues to be used by State forces today against dissident republican women.

19 Although the majority of interviewees openly disclosed their feminism or republican feminism, it is important to state that not all interviewees were feminist, with a small number even hostile to feminist politics. Given this and, of course, the contested nature of politics, undoubtedly some republican women will disagree with at least some of the feminist analysis throughout this book.

20 It is important to state that none of the participants who identified themselves as 'republican activists' detailed exactly what that role entailed. My own interpretation

of this description is that of an active support role for the IRA, including but not exclusive to communications, weapons storage, weapons transportation, intelligence gathering, reconnaissance, and look-out patrols, among others.
21 Even though it encompasses the staunchly loyalist Shankill road and other loyalist areas such as Suffolk and Blacks road on the Stewartstown road, west Belfast was, and remains, a predominantly nationalist and republican area. Given this, it was unsurprisingly an epicentre of armed actions and killings during 'the Troubles'. The Falls road stretches from Divis Street in the city centre and runs for almost three miles west where it officially ends at the junction of the Andersonstown road and Glen road. The Falls is the main arterial route through west Belfast and remains a heartland of various forms of republican activity, both political and militant.
22 Police Service of Northern Ireland. A key nationalist and republican demand throughout the peace process was the disbandment of the much-maligned RUC. In 1998 the British Government established a commission under Lord Patten, which travelled throughout the North of Ireland to gauge public attitudes, needs, and interests towards a new police force. Following Patten's report in 1999, the RUC was disbanded and replaced with the PSNI. To counter the religious imbalance, the PSNI initially used positive discrimination to attract new Catholic/nationalist recruits. That said, the PSNI retained many personnel from the RUC, engendering continuing levels of mistrust and suspicion about the partiality of the new police force.
23 Gerry Adams went 'voluntarily' to Antrim Police Station with his solicitor in a pre-arranged meeting with police officers investigating the McConville case. Upon his arrival, however, he was formally arrested and questioned for the next three days and nights.
24 This, once again, illuminates the power inequalities in the research process, where I effectively had the right to exclude their true names from their words and experiences in the findings.

Bibliography

Abdulhadi, R. 1998. 'The Palestinian Women's Autonomous Movement: Emergence, Dynamics and Challenges'. *Gender and Society* 12(6): 649–673.

Åhäll, L. and L. Shepherd. eds. 2012. *Gender, Agency and Political Violence*. Basingstoke: Palgrave Macmillan.

Aharoni, S. B. 2016. 'Who needs the Women and Peace Hypothesis? Rethinking modes of inquiry on gender and conflict in Israel/Palestine'. *International Feminist Journal of Politics* DOI: 10.1080/14616742.2016.1237457

Alison, M. 2004. 'Women as Agents of Political Violence: Gendering Security'. *Security Dialogue* 35(4): 447–463.

Alison, M. 2009. *Women and Political Violence: Female Combatants in Ethno-national Conflict*. New York: Routledge.

Anderlini, S. N. 2007. *Women Building Peace: What They Do, Why It Matters*. Boulder and London: Lynne Rienner Publishers.

Ashe, F. 2009. 'From Paramilitaries to Peacemakers: The Gender Dynamics of Community-Based Restorative Justice in Northern Ireland'. *The British Journal of Politics and International Relations* 11: 298–314.

Axelsson, S. 2015. 'Gendered Struggle for Freedom: A Narrative Inquiry into Female Ex-Combatants in South Africa'. Pp. 167–184 in *Female Combatants in Conflict and Peace*, edited by S. Shekhawat. Basingstoke: Palgrave Macmillan.

Baines, E. K. 2005. 'Les femmes aux mille bras: Building Peace in Rwanda'. Pp. 220–241 in *Gender, Conflict and Peacekeeping*, edited by D. Mazurana, A. R. Roberts and J. Parpart. Boulder, CO: Rowman and Littlefield Publishers.

Bouta, T., G. Frerks and I. Bannon. 2005. *Gender, Conflict and Development*. Washington DC: The World Bank.
Boutron, C. 2015. 'Women At War, War on Women: Reconciliation and Patriarchy in Peru'. Pp. 149–166 in *Female Combatants in Conflict and Peace*, edited by S. Shekhawat. Basingstoke: Palgrave Macmillan.
Britton, H. 2002. 'The Incomplete Revolution: South Africa's Women's Struggle for Parliamentary Transformation'. *International Feminist Journal of Politics* 4: 43–71.
Caprioli, M. 2004. 'Democracy and Human Rights Versus Women's Security: A Contradiction?' *Security Dialogue* 35(4): 411–428.
Chinchilla, N. S. 1990. 'Revolutionary Popular Feminism in Nicaragua: Articulating Class, Gender, and National Sovereignty'. *Gender and Security* 4: 370–397.
Cochrane, F. 2013. *Northern Ireland: The Reluctant Peace*. New Haven, CT: Yale University Press.
Cockburn, C. 1998. *The Space Between Us: Negotiating Gender and National Identities in Conflict*. London: Zed Books.
Cockburn, C. 2001. 'The Gendered Dynamics of Armed Conflict and Political Violence'. Pp. 13–29 in *Victims, Perpetrators or Actors? Gender, Armed Conflict and Political Violence*, edited by C. Moser and F. Clark. London: Zed Books.
Cockburn, C. 2004. 'The Continuum of Violence: A Gender Perspective on War and Peace'. Pp. 24–44 in *Sites of Violence: Gender and Conflict Zones*, edited by W. Giles and J. Hyndman. London: University of California Press.
Cockburn, C. 2007. *From Where We Stand: War, Women's Activism and Feminist Analysis*. London: Zed Books.
Cockburn, C. 2013. 'A Movement Stalled: Outcomes of Women's Campaign for Equalities and Inclusion in the Northern Ireland Peace Process'. *Interface: A Journal for and about Social Movements* 5(1): 151–182.
Cohn, C. ed. 2013. *Women and Wars*. Cambridge: Polity Press.
Confortini, C. C. 2006. 'Galtung, Violence, and Gender: The Case for a Peace Studies/Feminism Alliance'. *Peace & Change* 31(3): 333–367.
Confortini, C. C. 2010. 'Feminist Contributions and Challenges to Peace Studies'. *The International Studies Encyclopaedia*, edited by R. A. Denemark. Wiley-Blackwell and International Studies Association.
Corcoran, M. 2006. *Out of Order: The Political Imprisonment of Women in Northern Ireland, 1972–1999*. Devon: Willan Publishing.
Coulter, C. 1993. *The Hidden Tradition: Feminism, Women and Nationalism in Ireland*. Cork: Cork University Press.
Coulter, C. 1999. *Contemporary Northern Irish Society: An Introduction*. London: Pluto Press.
Coulter, C. 2009. *Bush Wives and Girl Soldiers. Women's Lives Through War and Peace in Sierra Leone*. Ithaca, NY: Cornell University Press.
Daly, M. 2000. 'Feminist Research Methodology: The Case of Ireland'. Pp. 60–72 in *(Re)Searching Women: Feminist Research Methodologies in the Social Sciences in Ireland*, edited by A. Byrne and R. Lentin. Dublin: IPA.
De Alwis, M., J. Mertus and T. Sajjad. 2013. 'Women and Peace Processes'. Pp. 169–191 in *Women and Wars*, edited by C. Cohn. Cambridge: Polity Press.
Deiana, M.-A. 2013. 'Women's Citizenship in Northern Ireland after the 1998 Agreement'. *Irish Political Studies* 28(3): 399–412.
DeLargy, P. 2013. 'Sexual Violence and Women's Health in War'. Pp. 54–79 in *Women and Wars*, edited by C. Cohn. Cambridge: Polity Press.

Denzin, N. K. and Y. S. Lincoln. 1998. *Strategies of Qualitative Inquiry*. London: Sage Publications.
DeVault, M. L. 1999. *Liberating Method: Feminism and Social Research*. Philadelphia, PA: Temple University Press.
Dowler, L. 1998. '"And They Think I'm Just a Nice Old Lady": Women and War in Belfast, Northern Ireland'. *Gender, Place and Culture* 5(2): 159–176.
El-Bushra, J. 2003. *Women Building Peace: Sharing Know-How*. London: International Alert.
El-Bushra, J. 2007. 'Feminism, Gender, and Women's Peace Activism'. *Development and Change* 38(1): 131–147.
Enloe, C. 2004. *The Curious Feminist: Searching For Women in a New Age of Empire*. Berkeley, CA: University of California Press.
Enloe, C. 2014. *Bananas, Beaches and Bases: Making Feminist Sense of International Politics*, 3rd edn. Berkeley, CA: University of California Press.
Farr, V. 2011. 'UNSCR 1325 and Women's Peace Activism in the Occupied Palestinian Territory'. *International Feminist Journal of Politics* 13(4): 539–556.
Farrell, M. 1976. *Northern Ireland: The Orange State*, London: Pluto Press.
Galtung, J. 1969. 'Violence, Peace and Peace Research'. *Journal of Peace Research* 6: 167–191.
Giles, W. 2013. 'Women Forced to Flee: Refugees and Internally Displaced Persons'. Pp. 80–101 in *Women and Wars*, edited by C. Cohn. Cambridge: Polity Press.
Giles, W. and J. Hyndman. eds. 2004. *Sites of Violence: Gender and Conflict Zones*. London: University of California Press.
Gillespie, U. 1994. *Women In Struggle*. Autumn 1994. Belfast and Dublin: Sinn Féin Women's Department.
Gubrium, J. F. and J. A. Holstein. 2004. 'The Active Interview'. Pp. 140–161 in *Qualitative Research: Theory, Method and Practice*, edited by D. Silverman. 2nd edn. London: Sage.
Handrahan, L. 2004. 'Conflict, Gender, Ethnicity and Post-Conflict Reconstruction'. *Security Dialogue* 35(4): 429–445.
Harding, S. 1991. *Whose Science? Whose Knowledge?* Milton Keynes: Open University.
Hartstock, N. 1983. 'The Feminist Standpoint: Developing the Ground for a Specifically Historical Feminist Materialism'. Pp. 283–310 in *Discovering Reality: Feminist Perspectives on Epistemology, Metaphysics, Methodology, and Philosophy of Science*, edited by S. Harding and M. Hintikka. Amsterdam: D. Reidel, Inc.
Hekman, S. 1999. *The Future of Differences: Truth and Method in Feminist Theory*. Cambridge: Polity Press.
Henshaw, A. 2017. *Why Women Rebel. Understanding Women's Participation in Armed Rebel Groups*. London and New York: Routledge.
Holstein, J. F. and Gubrium, J. A. ed. 2001. *Handbook on Interview Research*. London: Sage Publications.
Holt, M. 2003. 'Palestinian Women, Violence, and the Peace Process'. *Development in Practice* 13(2/3): 223–238.
Jacobs, S., R. Jacobson and J. Marchbank. eds. 2000. *States of Conflict: Gender, Violence and Resistance*. London and New York: Zed Books.
Jacobson, R. 2013. 'Women After Wars'. Pp. 215–241 in *Women and Wars*, edited by C. Cohn. Cambridge: Polity Press.
Jansson, M. and Eduards, M. 2016. 'The Politics of Gender in the UN Security Council Resolutions on Women, Peace and Security'. *International Feminist Journal of Politics*. (18): 4. DOI: 10.1080/14616742.2016.1189669

Karam, A. 2001. 'Women in War and Peace-building'. *International Journal of Feminist Politics* 3(1): 2–25.

Kaufman, J. and K. Williams. 2010. *Women and War: Gender Identity and Activism in Times of Conflict.* Sterling, VA: Kumarian Press.

Keenan-Thomson, T. 2010. *Irish Women and Street Politics, 1956–1973.* Dublin: Irish Academic Press.

Kelly, L. 2000. 'Wars Against Women: Sexual Violence, Sexual Politics and the Militarised State'. Pp. 45–64 in *States of Conflict: Gender, Violence and Resistance*, edited by S. Jacobs, R. Jacobson, and J. Marchbank. London and New York: Zed Books.

Krog, A. 2001. 'Locked into Loss and Silence: Testimonies of Gender and Violence at the South Africa Truth Commission'. Pp. 203–216 in *Victims, Perpetrators or Actors: Gender, Armed Conflict and Political Violence*, edited by C. Moser and F. Clark. New York: Zed Books.

Lather, P. 1991. *Getting Smart: Feminist Research and Pedagogy With/in the Postmodern.* New York and London: Routledge.

Lederach, J. P. 1997. *Building Peace: Sustainable Reconciliation in Divided Societies.* Washington DC: United States Institute of Peace.

Letherby, G. 2003. *Feminist Research in Theory and Practice.* Buckingham: Open University Press.

Lorentzen, L. A. and J. Turpin, J. eds. 1998. *The Women and War Reader.* New York: New York University.

Luciak, I. A. 1999. 'Gender Equality in the Salvadoran Transition'. *Latin American Perspectives.* 26: 43–67.

Lynch, K. 2000. 'The Role of Emancipatory Research in the Academy'. Pp. 73–104 in *(Re)Searching Women: Feminist Research Methodologies in the Social Sciences in Ireland*, edited by A. Byrne and R. Lentin. Dublin: IPA.

McCoole, S. 2014. *No Ordinary Women: Female Activists in the Revolutionary Years 1900–1921.* Wisconsin: University of Wisconsin Press.

M'Cormack-Hale, F. 2012. *Gender, Peace and Security: Women's Advocacy and Conflict Resolution.* London: Commonwealth Secretariat.

MacKenzie. M. H. 2012. *Female Soldiers In Sierra Leone: Sex, Security, and Post-Conflict Development.* New York: New York University Press.

Maillot, A. 2005. *New Sinn Féin: Irish Republicanism in the Twenty-First Century.* London and New York: Routledge.

Matthews, A. 2010. *Renegades: Irish Republican Women 1900–1922.* Cork: Mercier Press.

Matthews, A. 2012. *Dissidents: Irish Republican Women: 1923–1941.* Cork: Mercier Press.

Maynard, M. and J. Purvis, J. eds. 1994. *Researching Women's Lives from a Feminist Perspective.* London: Taylor and Francis.

Mazurana, D. and L. E. Cole. 2013. 'Women, Girls and Disarmament, Demobilisation and Reintegration'. Pp. 194–215 in *Women and Wars*, edited by C. Cohn. Cambridge: Polity Press.

McClintock, A. 1993. 'Family Feuds: Gender, Nationalism and the Family'. *Feminist Review* 44 (Summer 1993): 61–80.

McDowell, S. 2008. 'Commemorating Dead 'Men': Gendering the Past and Present in Post-conflict Northern Ireland'. *Gender, Place and Culture* 15(4): 335–354.

McEvoy, S. 2009. 'Loyalist Women Paramilitaries in Northern Ireland: Beginning a Feminist Conversation about Conflict Resolution'. *Security Studies* 18(2): 262–286.

McKay, S. and D. Mazurana. 2004. *Where Are The Girls? Girls in Fighting Forces in Northern Uganda, Sierra Leone and Mozambique: Their Lives During and After War.* Montreal: Rights and Democracy.

McLeod, L. 2011. 'Configurations of Post-Conflict: Impacts of Representations of Conflict and Post-Conflict upon the (Political) Translations of Gender Security within UNSCR 1325'. *International Feminist Journal of Politics* 13(4): 594–611.

Meintjes, S., A. Pillay, and M. Turshen. eds. 2001. *The Aftermath: Women in Post-Conflict Transformation.* London and New York: Zed Books.

Molyneux, M. 1985. 'Mobilization without Emancipation? Women's Interests, the State, and Revolution in Nicaragua'. *Feminist Studies* 11(2): 227–254.

Moser, C. 2001. 'The Gendered Continuum of Violence and Conflict: An Operational Framework'. Pp. 30–51 in *Victims, Perpetrators or Actors? Gender, Armed Conflict and Political Violence*, edited by C. Moser and F. Clark. London: Zed Books.

Moser, C. and F. Clark. eds. 2001. *Victims, Perpetrators or Actors? Gender, Armed Conflict and Political Violence.* London: Zed Books.

Mukta, P. 2000. 'Gender, Community, Nation: The Myth of Innocence'. Pp. 163–178 in *States of Conflict: Gender, Violence and Resistance*, edited by S. Jacobs, R. Jacobson, and J. Marchbank. London and New York: Zed Books.

Murtagh, C. 2008. 'A Transient Transition: The Cultural and Institutional Obstacles Impeding the Northern Ireland Women's Coalition in its Progression from Informal to Formal Politics'. *Irish Political Studies* 23(1): 21–40.

Ni Aolain, F., D. F. Haynes, and N. Cahn. 2011. *On The Frontlines: Gender, War and the Post-Conflict Process.* Oxford: Oxford University Press.

O'Keefe, T. 2003. 'Trading Aprons for Arms: Feminist Resistance in the North of Ireland'. *Resource for Feminist Research* 30: 39–64.

O'Keefe, T. 2013. *Feminist Identity Development and Activism in Revolutionary Movements.* London and New York: Palgrave Macmillan.

O'Leary, B. and J. McGarry. 1995. *Explaining Northern Ireland: Broken Images.* Oxford & Malden: Blackwell.

Oakley, Ann. 1981. 'Interviewing Women: A Contradiction in Terms'. Pp. 30–61 in *Doing Feminist Research*, edited by H. Roberts. London: Routledge.

Pankhurst, D. 2003. 'The "Sex War" and Other Wars: Towards a Feminist Approach to Peace Building'. *Development in Practice* 13(2/3): 154–177.

Pankhurst, D. 2008. 'Introduction: Gendered War and Peace'. Pp. 1–31 in *Gendered Peace: Women's Struggles for Post-War Justice and Reconciliation*, edited by D. Pankhurst. New York: Routledge.

Parashar, S. 2014. *Women and Militant Wars: The Politics of Injury.* London and New York: Routledge.

Pillay, A. 2001. 'Violence Against Women in the Aftermath'. Pp. 35–45 in *The Aftermath: Women in Post-Conflict Transformation*, edited by S. Meintjes, A. Pillay, and M. Turshen. New York: Zed Books.

Porter, E. 1998. 'Identity, Location, Plurality: Women, Nationalism and Northern Ireland'. Pp. 36–61 in *Women, Ethnicity and Nationalism: The Politics of Transition*, edited by R. Wilford and R. L. Miller. London and New York: Routledge.

Porter, E. 2000. 'The Challenge of Dialogue across Difference'. Pp. 141–162 in *Gender, Democracy and Inclusion in Northern Ireland*, edited by C. Roulston and C. Davis. London: Palgrave.

Porter, E. 2003. 'Women, Political Decision-making and Peace-building in Conflict Regions'. *Global Change, Peace and Security* 15(3): 245–262.

Porter, E. 2007. *Peacebuilding: Women in International Perspective.* London and New York: Routledge.

Power, M. 2010. 'A Republican Who Wants to Further Women's Rights': Women, Provisional Republicanism, Feminism and Conflict in Northern Ireland'. Pp. 153–170 in *Irish Women at War: The Twentieth Century*, edited by G. McIntosh and D. Urquhart. Dublin and Portland: Irish Academic Press.

Reardon, B. A. 1993. *Women and Peace: Feminist Visions of Global Security.* New York: State of New York University Press.

Reif, L. 1986. 'Women in Latin American Guerrilla Movements: A Comparative Perspective'. *Comparative Politics* 18: 147–169.

Reinharz, S. 1992. *Feminist Methods in Social Research:* New York: Oxford University Press.

Richter-Devroe, S. 2012. 'Defending Their Land, Protecting Their Men'. *International Feminist Journal of Politics* 14(2): 181–201.

Romanova, E. and Sewell, E. 2011. 'Engaging Legislation: Liberia and Chechnya'. Pp. 222–234 in *Women Waging War and Peace: International Perspectives on Women's Roles in Conflict and Post-Conflict Reconstruction*, edited by S. I. Cheldin and M. Eliatamby. New York: Continuum International Publishing Group.

Seidman, G. 1993. 'No Freedom Without the Women': Mobilization and Gender in South Africa, 1970–1992'. *Signs: Journal of Women in Culture and Society* 18(2): 291–320.

Sharoni, S. 2001. 'Rethinking Women's Struggles in Israel-Palestine and in the North of Ireland'. Pp. 85–98 in *Victims, Perpetrators or Actors: Gender, Armed Conflict and Political Violence*, edited by C. Moser and F. Clark. New York: Zed Books.

Shekhawat, S. ed. 2015. *Female Combatants in Conflict and Peace.* Basingstoke: Palgrave Macmillan.

Shekhawat, S. and Pathak, B. 2015. 'Female Combatants, Peace Processes and the Exclusion'. Pp. 53–68 in *Female Combatants in Conflict and Peace*, edited by S. Shekhawat. Basingstoke: Palgrave Macmillan.

Silverman, D. ed. 2004. *Qualitative Research: Theory, Method and Practice*, 2nd edn. London: Sage.

Sjoberg, L. ed. 2010. *Gender and International Security: Feminist Perspectives.* New York: Routledge.

Sjoberg, L. 2014. *Gender, War, and Conflict.* Cambridge: Polity.

Sjoberg, L. and Gentry, C. 2007. *Mothers, Monsters, Whores.* London and New York: Zed Books.

Smith, D. 1987. *The Everyday World As Problematic: A Feminist Sociology.* Milton Keynes: Open University Press.

Stanley, L. and S. Wise. 1993. *Breaking Out Again: Feminist Ontology and Epistemology.* London: Routledge.

Taylor, P. 1998. *Provos: The IRA and Sinn Féin.* London: Bloomsbury Publishing.

Tickner, A. 1992. *Gender In International Relations: Feminist Perspectives on Achieving Global Security.* New York and Chichester: Columbia University Press.

Tickner, A. 1997. 'You Just Don't Understand: Troubled Engagements between Feminists and IR Theorists'. *International Studies Quarterly* 41(4): 611–632.

Tickner, A. 2014. *A Feminist Voyage Through International Relations.* New York: Oxford University Press.

Todd, Jenifer and J. Ruane. 1996. *The Dynamics of Conflict in Northern Ireland.* Cambridge: Cambridge University Press.

Turshen, M. 1998. 'Women's War Stories'. Pp. 1–26 in *What Women Do in Wartime: Gender and Conflict in Africa*, edited by M. Turshen and C. Twagiramariya. London and New York: Zed Books.

Turshen, M. 2001. 'Engendering Relations of State to Society in the Aftermath'. Pp. 78–96 in *The Aftermath: Women in Post-conflict Transformation*, edited by S. Meintjes, A. Pillay, and M. Turshen. New York: Zed Books.

Wahidin, A. 2016. *Ex-combatants, Gender and Peace in Northern Ireland: Women, Political Protest and the Prison Experience. Palgrave Studies in Compromise After Conflict.* London and New York: Palgrave Macmillan.

Ward, M. 1983. *Unmanageable Revolutionaries: Women and Irish Nationalism.* London: Pluto Press.

Ward, M. 2004. 'Times of Transition: Republican Women, Feminism and Political Representation'. Pp. 184–201 in *Irish Women and Nationalism: Soldiers, New Women and Wicked Hags*, edited by L. Ryan and M. Ward. Dublin: Irish Academic Press.

Waylen, G. 1994. 'Women and Democratization: Conceptualizing Gender Relations in Transition Politics'. *World Politics* 46(3): 327–354.

2 Who fought the war?

The gendered constructions of soldiering roles in post-war commemorative processes

Introduction

At the time of field research in 2012 and 2013 there was a palpable flurry of activism among interviewees who were channelling energies into various mechanisms for recognising women's contribution to the republican armed struggle. Many of these commemorative actions were born out of a collective frustration with their perpetual invisibility in republican memorialisation. The kernel of this resurgence in emphasis on women's roles resides in 2006 and 2007, with the restoration of an executive government involving the Democratic Unionist Party[1] (DUP) and Sinn Féin. With political stability relatively secured, many republican women began to pose the important question: 'Where have the women gone?' The exclusion of women's wartime contributions that emerges in the transition period, however, is not a new phenomenon and, in fact, is a long-standing pattern of men's dismissals of women's contributions, from the battlefield to post-war memorials, as discussed in the previous chapter. Women's exclusion from commemoration during conflict transition, like Demobilisation Disarmament Reintegration (DDR) processes, is but an insidious manifestation of a more profound problem that pervades the post-war landscape. Masculinised military narratives, and patriarchal understandings of what is deemed a combatant role (and what, therefore, is deemed worthy of commemorating), consistently fail to value or recognise women's multiple and vital wartime contributions.

This chapter explores the ways in which republican women themselves conceptualise their roles and contributions within armed struggle. Their experiences and perspectives produce a series of narratives that run counter to the male-dominated post-war memorial landscape. Being attentive to the ways in which they conceptualise their wartime contributions not only brings their roles into view, but, I argue, subverts conventional and patriarchal ways in which wartime contributions are defined. It echoes Megan MacKenzie's (2012) contention that we learn far more from 'asking and listening' to the experiences of women and girl soldiers than by relying on top-down processes. This chapter not only asks 'where are the combatant women' in post-war memorialisation but argues that combatant women's experiences, narratives, and meanings challenge existing frameworks and discourses, and therefore revolutionises the ways we define combatant and wartime roles. In other words, their struggle during conflict transition is not encompassed by simply 'adding women' to the existing picture but rather by using their unique standpoints to subvert established discourses and definitions to challenge the forces of patriarchy.

The chapter begins with an exploration of the ways in which interviewees themselves define their combatant roles and experiences. Emerging from this is a rich narrative of multiple military roles that challenges and dislodges the limited, masculine definition of 'a person with a weapon'. In addition, interviewees reject the hierarchical dichotomy of fighter/supporter in favour of recognising the importance of *all* military contributions to republican armed struggle. It then moves on to examine the ways in which interviewees believe their contributions have been either diluted or erased completely within republican commemoration. The final section explores the innovative and alternative forms of commemoration by republican women in recent times. It suggests that these 'alternative' forms of commemoration accurately capture their eclectic wartime contributions at all levels of militant republicanism, bringing previously overlooked militant women onto the memorial landscape.

'I was involved': republican women and the meaning of combatant

The 'invisibility' of female combatants in the post-war period is not an innocuous oversight and has major implications for gender relations in the conflict transition period. Wartime narratives are competitive; accurately portraying women's wartime roles will affect their post-war opportunities and those for generations to come (Enloe 2004: 200). Feminist scholars of DDR programs have diligently documented the perilous losses female combatants endure because of their marginalisation in the post-war narrative. In addition, acknowledging female soldiers and women's multifarious military contributions disrupts the gendered tropes of male warriors and female victim. There is now a significant swathe of literature documenting the varied and multiple ways in which women engage in political violence during armed conflict, displacing the myth of women's propensity for peace (Lorentzen and Turpin 1998; Moser and Clark 2001; Meintjes *et al.* 2001; Jacobs *et al.* 2000). Yet, despite this vital interjection there remains significant resistance to recognising female participation in war, firmly guided normative gender stereotyping (MacKenzie 2012). In other words, the rear-view mirror assessment of wartime roles tends to promote a rather masculine vision of military roles underpinned by gendered assumptions regarding masculine and feminine roles. Often absent are the voices, experiences, and perspectives of combatant women themselves.

Landmark studies of the Irish Republican Army (hereafter the IRA) define a volunteer as a 'rank and file' member of the Army (Coogan 2000; Moloney 2002). According to the previously secret IRA internal manual, entitled *The Green Book* (1977: 3),

> Volunteers are expected to wage a military war of liberation against a numerically superior force. This involves the use of arms and explosives. When volunteers are trained ... [they] are trained to kill people. The IRA volunteer receives all his [sic] support voluntarily from his [sic] people.

This excerpt clearly defines the IRA volunteer as a sworn member of an Army whose primary role is the direct use of arms to wage war against their enemies. While there is no commonly accepted definition of a 'female combatant', the legal discourse of international DDR processes utilises a traditional notion of a combatant as a person who engages directly in armed actions using weaponry prevails (Mazurana and Cole 2013: 205).

During this research, interviewees discussed women's roles and contributions within the armed struggle. Of the 40 research participants, 31 identified as IRA volunteers and invariably recounted multiple forms of resistance activities in which they had engaged. These included 'weapons storage', 'weapon transportation', 'planting bombs', 'shooting', 'communications', 'robberies', 'bomb making', 'weapons training', 'street patrols', 'rioting', 'petrol bombing' and 'engaging the enemy in the street'. Most interviewees did not use the term 'combatant'; in fact, in some cases there was a profound disdain for the word. Republican women, like their male comrades, used colloquial expressions such as 'being involved' or 'becoming a volunteer' to describe their participation in armed struggle. Patricia is currently a Sinn Féin elected representative in the wider Belfast area and a community activist. She joined the IRA at the age of 14, was interned in the mid-1970s, and spent several years in Armagh jail. Patricia's description of her IRA roles is typical of the responses across the interviews:

> The struggle was daily life and death situations. And that went from transporting weapons from one dump to another, to robberies, to attacks in the town, incendiary devices, might be bombs, shooting operations against the British Army and things like that. So you could've had five of those operations in a day. It was quite intense and so for someone to have said to me 'a woman's place was in the home', I'd love to meet the man that had the courage to say that. There weren't any I can tell you.

In comparison to conventional understandings of soldiering and militarism, interviewees articulate a much broader and richer vision of what military involvement entails. The notion that combatant is wholly encapsulated by a 'person holding a weapon' is not only deemed erroneous by interviewees but also fails to accurately capture the realities of women's participation in armed conflict. In addition to their roles alongside their male comrades, republican women were active in other military roles within the movement. Michelle comes from the Bogside area, a predominantly Catholic/nationalist and working-class area of Derry. Her family has strong republican roots. As a self-described 'soldier', Michelle explains her contributions:

> So from 1971 onwards, I would have been involved, [in] any type of role at all really, women's action groups, internment, and then into 1972 and Bloody Sunday. I was a teenager then. I just couldn't be somebody that stood by and watch [sic] what was happening on our streets … I carried on my part in the conflict, whatever had to be done or whatever was asked of me, irrespective of the role. But this was what it was about being an active republican and this was my life.

When asked what 'these roles' comprised, Michelle described a myriad of military actions including weaponry transportation, training camps, and direct armed actions. Being an 'active republican' in the armed struggle, according to Michelle, requires far more than the role of armed volunteer. Interview data depicts a narrative of women engaged in multiple roles within the republican struggle. Michelle's description of 'doing whatever had to be done … irrespective of the role' indicates the lack of personal status attached to any particular roles by republican women. Moreover, the variety of roles occupied by women informs the ways in which they define a combatant role. Although Theresa went on to be a volunteer in the IRA right up to the late 1990s, her early activities encompassed other military roles:

> I had done a few small things, let's call it that; a few bits and stuff of carrying things from one place to another. But I wanted in [to the IRA] and I wanted to be able to do more. It so happened that I kept weapons in the house, explosives and guns. But you see there were GLs[2] held in my house, so I knew about the weapons and how to take it apart and all of that and that was another reason I wanted in there [the IRA] because I had the skill already. And then I was involved in a printing press, but I said that I'm getting involved in the 'RA[3] but they [local male leaders] wouldn't let me because of my kids. And I said sure what's the difference because I was *already* involved.

Theresa's comments are highly significant, providing significant insights into the ways in which female combatants conceptualise their involvement in armed struggle. While the prevailing masculine narrative centres on making a distinction between fighter and supporter, or what Henshaw (2016) deems combat and non-combat, republican women attempt to blur the rigid demarcation of such roles. Theresa's demands to male republicans that she be allowed join the IRA as a full volunteer are premised upon her belief that she was already involved in militarism by her other roles such as weapons storage, gun lectures and weaponry knowledge. Her frustration in asking 'what's the difference' reveals a mindset among republican women that the ring-fencing and categorising of roles into militant and non-militant did not reflect their realities. In other words, the notion of fighter/supporter is a male-imposed dichotomy, which according to interviewees denigrates and devalues women's vital wartime contributions. They are adamant that roles normally deemed 'support' were as important as the role of armed fighter.

Eileen joined the IRA in the early 1970s and remains a committed socialist republican active in many community groups in West Belfast. Eileen explains the importance she places on all military roles:

> Now yes you need guns and explosives and all that equipment, but you see without those women and those houses, it would have been impossible to carry out a war. If you're in guerrilla warfare, you don't have bases so where do you operate from? People's houses, so without those women, and those women have never been acknowledged properly for what they gave and sacrificed.

Orla grew up in a working-class, republican district of Belfast and was a young girl when the conflict erupted in 1969. She joined the IRA at the age of 16 and was arrested and imprisoned for her IRA activities some time afterwards. Today, her political activities are located in her local community centre, where she is a community worker.

> To me, if you let your house be used you're the very same as the rest of us. I mean, some people had this idea that if you weren't a Volunteer, if you weren't in jail, then you weren't good enough … maybe not good enough but if you were a volunteer you were up here (participant gestures upwards). But to me if you played a part then you were the same as everyone else. And those people in the support roles will never get the recognition, which is a shame because without them nothing could have happened. Volunteers needed safe houses, places to store weapons; without them it couldn't have happened.

Orla's extract reveals the attitude among some male republicans towards what they saw as the 'lesser' roles, which fell outside of direct combat actions. The emphasis and importance placed on these roles by republican women resonates with research on combatant women in other regions engulfed in armed conflict. An analysis of the Tupamaros National Liberation Movement (MLN), a clandestine left-wing military movement in Uruguay during the period of 1962 and 1973, found an equally eclectic set of military roles, which within women and men were active, including robberies, expropriations, kidnapping, bank assaults (Valliant *et al.* 2012: 60). In their comprehensive analysis of conflicts in South Asia, Seema Shekhawat and Bishnu Pathak (2015: 59) found that women may participate in conflicts as active fighters using arms, but also as spies, cooks, porters, radio operators, translators, medical assistants. In places such as Kashmir, women would endanger their own safety and lives by facilitating the escape of militants, feeding and accommodating militants, provide safe-houses for meetings. Some were involved in reconnaissance missions. Just as is the case in Ireland, women also acted as 'honey traps', as well as transporting weapons and explosives in their veils. The testimonies here from republican women add weight to a burgeoning global body of work, which seeks to capture women's multiple and vital contributions to military efforts in their entirety. Yet, despite

Who fought the war? 45

the immense personal risk involved, women's military roles are never deemed worthy of the standard needed to acquire the status of 'soldier'.

Cynthia Enloe (2000) reminds us that militaries, both state and non-state, do not simply rely upon a 'few good women'. Drawing on data from 72 insurgencies since 1990, Henshaw (2016) finds that while women invariably do occupy what she terms 'non-combat' roles, nevertheless, women are active participants in almost a third of all rebel groups. Jacklyn Cock's (1991) landmark study of combatant women within anti-apartheid struggles in South Africa contends that women comprised over 20 per cent of cadres in Umkhonto weSizwe (MK). Although they did occupy front-line fighter roles, like republican women, they also contributed significantly to intelligence gathering, weapons transportation, communications, weapons training, provision of safe house, among many others. In El Salvador, women constituted up to 30 per cent of the Farabundo Martí National Liberation Front (FMLN) forces, and 20 per cent of its leadership (Ortega 2015).

In their wide-ranging study of combatants in Sierra Leone, Humphreys and Weinstein (2004: 31) found that just 57 percent of combatants demobilised by turning in a weapon. Almost 75 percent of Civil Defence Force (CDF) combatants, mostly male, did not enter DDR programs due to lack of a weapon, while in the Revolutionary United Front (hereafter the RUF) just less than 50 percent faced the same problem. The rigid definition of a combatant as a 'person with a weapon' proved so problematic that the authors defined ex-combatants broadly to include any individual who lived, participated or worked with a fighting faction for at least one month (Humphreys and Weinstein 2004: 9). Furthermore, the point is strengthened when we examine the issue of child soldiers. Research, again from Sierra Leone, reveals the myriad of roles undertaken by child soldiers including looting, spying, and camp maintenance, among others. Moreover, children associated with the RUF often had access to firearms, usually owned by adult members of the group (Berman and Florquin 2005).

The picture emerging from other conflicts chimes with the data presented here and strengthens the argument that conventional definitions of a combatant are imprecise and therefore wholly inadequate for encapsulating all military labour and contributions, irrespective of gender. Departing from the rigid vision of a military role, republican women are in favour of stressing the vital contributions of *all* roles. Despite the wealth of scholarly research indicating the extent to which militaries rely upon women at all levels, conventional representations of war find validation in a gendered division of military labour which propagates the masculine front-line role while diminishing the feminine auxiliary. Perhaps the best illustration of this hierarchical distinction of 'fighter/supporter' resides in the discourse of women as the 'backbone' of the armed struggle.

'Women were not just the backbone': blurring the lines of fighter/supporter

One of the most famous wall murals in the North of Ireland is that of IRA Hunger Striker Bobby Sands[4] located on the gable wall of Sinn Féin's office on the corner of Falls Road and Sevastopol Street in Belfast. It is now a permanent memorial to this iconic republican. At the top-left hand corner of the mural is a quote from one of Sands' many prison writings: 'Everyone, republican or otherwise has his or her own particular part to play. No part is too great or too small'. The message depicts a communal (the imagined community as both local and national) resistance to British rule that involves many related and dependent cogs which sustained the functioning of the republican machine. The use of the words 'his or her' is hailed as highly significant by republican women, demonstrating the parity of roles in their collective resistance. The burgeoning commemorative landscape in the conflict transition period, however, bears little discernible resemblance to the equality of republican roles as espoused by Sands. The notion of women being the 'backbone of the struggle' (O'Keefe 2013) is a long-standing phrase within republican discourse and caused mixed emotions among interviewees. That labelling women as the 'backbone', I suggest, represents the hierarchical ordering of roles within republican memorialisation, which defines combatant roles along normative gender understandings of male/actor and female/supporter.

The emergence of the backbone discourse generated different and, at times, contrasting interpretations. The idea that 'women were the backbone of the struggle' is reproduced by a sizable minority of interviewees; who understood and interpreted the backbone label as a source of pride, arguing that the backbone of any organisation or institution represents its core structure. On this benign reading, women were therefore central and essential to the republican movement. The latter cohort, which comprised an overwhelming majority of research participants, clearly despised such a description, viewing it as degrading, pejorative, and erroneous. They argued that republican memorialisation not only largely fails to reflect women's role as front-line fighters, but increasingly their contribution is diluted and re-written solely as that of backbone supporters. Anne grew up in the Lower Falls area of West Belfast and is currently a senior Sinn Féin member in Belfast. Growing up in a staunchly working-class community, she recalls a hard yet relatively happy childhood, in which she lived in a two-up, two-down terraced house. She vividly recalls the loyalist burnings of 1969 since her family was evacuated to the relatively safer Andersonstown area for quite a while. Her father, a Protestant, and her mother, a Catholic, recalled that religion or ethno-national difference was rarely discussed. Politics in the house prior to 'the Troubles' centred mostly on socialism and trade unionism. The eruption of armed conflict in 1969 saw Anne engage in various roles including rioting, weaponry transportation, among others, and she quickly went on to become an IRA volunteer.

> There were girls involved in all of that [armed struggle], more or less written out of history. But a lot of young girls like myself, we took the same risks. I'm not being really brave here or god look at me, I'm the best rioter in the Falls. But women are not just the backbone, they're the knee bone, the hip bone, every bone of this movement. That used to annoy me about

being [labelled] the backbone; women are in this organisation on an equal footing throughout the body of this organisation, not just the backbone.

Anne's testimony is highly significant in that it depicts women as operating at all levels of the military, something widely shared by other interviewees. In addition to the lack of visibility afforded to women's role as armed activists, the issue of women's invisibility is compounded by the complete lack of attention given to other vital roles in sustaining an armed campaign. The IRA's *Green Book* makes specific reference to the status of those in 'supporting' roles:

> [armed] resistance must be channelled into active and passive support with an on-going process through our actions ... of attempting to turn the passive supporter into a dump holder, a member of the movement, a paper seller etc., with the purpose of building protective support barriers between the enemy and ourselves, thus curbing the enemy's attempted isolation policy.

From this leadership document there is a clear delineation and status between the armed volunteer and those who may act as 'dump holders'. According to the *Green Book*, those in the 'support' roles appear as merely a 'protective barrier' between the real actors, that being the IRA and its armed enemies.

Christine grew up in a family of seven children and wanted nothing other than a career in nursing. The eruption of armed conflict in 1969 saw Christine and most of her family engage in armed actions as republicans. A number of her brothers and her father spent periods of detention under internment or serving sentences in jail. Her father was previously interned in the 1950s for his part in the Border Campaign.[5] Christine was interned in 1973. Today, she is a Sinn Féin member and community activist. Christine, like so many other interviewees advocates for the recognition of these roles as valuable military contributions:

> Yes, there should be recognition and especially for those who looked after weapons, volunteers, held meetings, all these unsung heroes. There were women active and weren't caught and something needs to be done and that is actually a form of discrimination.

Christine's assertion that the lack of attention to women's multiple military roles does not represent a mere omission or blind spot but is, in fact, a form of discrimination against republican women. Gemma is currently a senior Sinn Féin officer in Belfast who previously sat on the party's *Ard Comhairle*.[6] She comes from a republican family that was consistently brutalised and harassed by the state, according to her. Gemma describes her childhood community of West Belfast as a 'war zone'. Her best friend was shot dead by the British Army in the mid-1970s, a catalyst that would lead her to join the republican movement in the 1970s. Gemma echoes Christine's thoughts:

You have all these women who never joined the IRA as such but who without the war could never have happened. These women were unbelievably brave, and it is never talked about. So there are lots of women who played those vital roles and there needs to be some sort of way of recognising them.

The theme emerging from the interview data suggests that the demands for recognising women's 'other military roles' outside that of a volunteer is an attempt to correct the erroneous and undervalued narrative of women as supplementary. Interviewees use the distinction of fighter/other roles as a statement of reality, in that both roles were different. The interview data here resonates with the findings from Dowler (1998) in which former IRA women speak inclusively of all republican military roles, rather than exclusively focusing on the 'fighter role'. Research and texts based on the testimonies of male republicans consistently reveal the narrow criteria used by men in defining a 'combatant' (for example, see Robert White's 2017 publication *'Out of the Ashes': An Oral History of the Provisional Irish Republican Movement*). During her research in Belfast in 1998, Dowler found a pervasive attitude among republican men that their role (as front-line fighters) eclipsed and superseded all other military roles. While men state that 'we [men] were the ones in the front lines … out there every night on patrol' (male republican cited in Dowler 1998: 172), interviewees in this research define IRA involvement as something far broader and eclectic, encompassing the diversity of roles women played within the republican movement. Crucially, unlike their male comrades and that of most conventional war narratives, they argued that both sites of military resistance were of equal importance to the republican struggle. While men do also occupy support roles such as porter, cooks, and communicators, Megan MacKenzie (2012) contends that their roles and the validity in claiming the title of soldier is never questioned. Though it is possible and quite plausible that one could interpret the 'backbone' label as paying homage to the integral role played by women, however, the evidence of republican women here, and elsewhere in other explorations of their experiences, indicate that this is not a view widely shared. Moreover, testimonies from male republicans appear to corroborate the argument that genuine military contributions are those that fit with the masculine conventions regarding front-line soldiering, which invariably is coded as masculine. I suggest that depicting women's support roles or 'backbone' contributions is a deliberate reworking of the post-war narrative that renders them simply as followers, bereft of agency and political consciousness; re-defining their wartime endeavours as simply an extension of their domestic roles.

Karen is currently a senior Sinn Féin elected representative and comes from Belfast. She joined the IRA in her teenage years and spent many years in jail for her republican activities. After her release in the late 1990s Karen worked in an ex-prisoners' organisation, as well as in other roles including community organising and the promotion of the Irish language.

It's important then that the role of women is not lost, and people see *all of the roles* [emphasis in the original] that women played. What I'd like to see is the acknowledgement of the women in the support network who may not have been active volunteers but all of that active support that the republican movement couldn't have survived like letting us use their homes because men didn't take those risks. These are women who were not volunteers but did provide that vital back-up support and they were almost nearly always women who did that.

Notwithstanding their use of the dichotomy of 'fighter/supporter', republican women in this book depart from their male comrades (and conventional understandings) in demanding recognition of those other roles to reduce the hierarchical lines that separate them. Connell (2005) conceived masculinity as a fluid, socially constructed, and plural concept, which within various forms of masculinity is hierarchically appraised and ranked. Hegemonic masculinities represent the idealised version of 'how to be a man'; in the realm of armed conflict, this version is invariably infused with machoism, bodily strength, courage, and leadership, among others. Hegemonic masculinity can be defined as the configuration of gender practice that embodies the currently accepted answer to the problem of the legitimacy of patriarchy, which guarantees the dominant position of men and the subordination of women (Connell 2005: 77). The soldier's body is the deliberate embodiment of an idealised masculinity, created and controlled for political concerns, infused with contradictory ideals that link violence with heroism, and the poster for normative masculine identity (Crowe 2012: 19–20). By retaining soldiering as male-only roles, combat is effectively coded as masculine. Feminist scholars have long drawn attention to the ways in which role distinction functions to privilege male power, and, explored the use of the gendered dichotomy of 'protector/protected' as a justification for waging war (Enloe 2014; Tickner 1992). The assumptions underpinning such tropes finds expression in the exaltation of male bravery while at the same time emphasising the vulnerability of the female bystander. The creation and imposition of a 'fighter/supporter' dichotomy is also deeply problematic for two reasons. First, it fails to adequately reflect the wartime contributions of republican women, which are spread across a vast array of roles. And second, the separation and hierarchical ordering of 'soldiering' and 'supporting' roles are highly gendered and invariably reifies and privileges the male narrative of war. Such a depiction places woman in the corridors and backrooms of the battlefield. The prevailing masculine definition of a combatant enforces a dichotomous classification that categorises women as supplementary parts of the armed struggle. At the heart of such hierarchical ordering is the notion that supportive roles, and therefore women's roles, are not 'real' forms of combat. Instead, interviewees blur such categorisation by emphasising the importance they place on *all* military roles. Republican women reject such categorisation as elitist and instead articulate a valuing of roles within the entire military struggle.

Feminist IR theory contends that male consolidation of power in the aftermath of armed conflict often occurs as they gain the status of heroes in the post-war appraisals, presenting positions of authority (Enloe 2014: 121). The reassertion of traditional masculine and feminine roles in the post-war phase is often the point of significant losses for women (Ni Aolain *et al.* 2011: 41). Patriarchy sustains itself by privileging particular forms of masculinity while simultaneously keeping women in subordinate roles (Enloe 2014). It is clear from the data that republican women use the fighter/supported distinction in the same ways their male comrades do. The call for the broadening of the combatant definition by interviewees, however, is the distinct point of departure that separates them from their male comrades. Despite the centrality of women's labour to the sustainment of militaries, their contributions are often minimalised or trivialised (Sjoberg 2014: 41). Yet, militarism remains a vital sphere for the performance and evaluation of masculinity, and so masculinised visions of militaries have an ideological stake in confining women's roles to the periphery (Enloe 2000: 40). Given that conventional forms of soldiering are often used to validate expressions of masculinity, and vice versa, non-direct combatant roles, or supportive roles largely undertaken by women (though it must be stressed, not exclusively), are not deemed a valid expression of normative masculinity, and therefore remain marginalised and devalued. The evidence here from republican women resonates with the global feminist conversation, which uncovers a myriad of inter-related roles vital to the maintenance of non-state military movements. The conventional vision of a combatant is therefore partial; it sees only the top of the pyramid while largely excluding the many layers that undergird those fighters on the front lines, both male and female. Examining the experiences of combatant women not only bringing their lives into view, it also produces a more accurate account of women's wartime military contributions. Doing so, I suggest, also challenges the rather limited prevailing definition of a combatant. The data and discussion advanced here concurs that the dominant notion of combatant fails to reflect the realities of republican women's wartime experiences. The evidence here strongly suggests that the persistent conflation of combatant with the handling of a weapon is a rather limited and inadequate definition. By taking the perspectives of republican women seriously, I argue that we acquire a broader spectrum of vision to encapsulate *all* military roles involved in the waging and sustaining of armed conflict. The persistent construction of 'combatant' as a person with a weapon diminishes women's multiple and vital wartime contributions, projecting a masculine post-war narrative that the 'real' actors in armed conflict are mostly male. Taking the lives of combatant women as a starting point quickly exposes the gendered and patriarchal assumptions that underpin such narrow definitions.

'A lesser species of revolutionaries?' Women and armed struggle

Most existing research indicates that women's involvement within the IRA was 'the result of a combination of female insistence and male recognition of the necessity of having some militarily trained women' (Ward 1989: 259).[7] While women did, for the most part, fill support roles, interviewees resolutely assert that all ranks of militant republicanism were populated with female recruits. All interviewees felt that they played an 'equal role' alongside their male comrades within the IRA. As one interviewee remarked to me, 'the nearness of death is a great equaliser'. Geraldine is from Belfast. She is a former member of the IRA and is currently a Sinn Féin activist. As a child her earliest memories is the burning of her family home, which was situated in a predominantly protestant/ loyalist part of Belfast. Although Geraldine does not recall political discussions in her home as a child she was keenly aware of the republican history in her family. Her mother was a prominent republican from Donegal as was her father who hailed from the city of Derry. Both parents were 'active' in the republican campaigns of the 1940s. During the recent conflict, Geraldine's family were heavily affected by the violence. All four of her brothers joined the IRA. Her husband, also a militant republican, died in a republican feud in the latter years of the conflict. She joined the IRA in the early 1970s at the age of 16 and was interned twice.

> To be honest, during the struggle and the Brits on the streets, man and woman was equal ... but any time at all and whatever you were going out to do ... I always remember being treated as equal as any volunteer in the movement.

During her interview, Eileen was never reticent about speaking frankly and criticising the republican movement. Here though, she herself believes that men and women were equal within the ranks of the IRA:

> Well when you there in the streets and you were a volunteer operating, we were treated the same, that's how I felt. So you weren't treated any differently when it came to do anything on the streets. I never felt that women were left to make the tea; I always felt like an equal within the movement.

The sentiments expressed above were widely shared by most interviewees. Ostensibly, they felt they played an equal role alongside men. This is not to suggest, however, that the republican movement was some feminist utopia immune from the pervasive forces of sexism and patriarchy. On the contrary, a feminist analysis of the interview data indicates a perpetual struggle waged by women to be included as armed activists within the IRA. According to interviewees, women had to struggle to be involved as volunteers within the IRA in the formative years of the conflict, where they consistently encountered a patriarchal wall of reluctance among the male-dominated leadership and membership.

CHRISTINE: At the start it was the women looking after the men because they were looking after the barricades and keeping the area safe. So the women made the tea and all of that. But with regards to when the [British] Army came in, then women got involved, you know rifles went into prams. When more men were arrested women took over and in many respects women were at the forefront of the campaign because the majority of men were being arrested so it was women who led a lot of the departments, were very much involved, like you always had girls in the street for scouting and carrying and taking away but from the '70s women played a real part but there was still that sense among the [male] volunteers that women should really keep their own place. Like [*sic*] they're good for carrying stuff but in the end, it wasn't like that, women became fully trained and well trained.

Christine's recollections reveal a common theme across most interviews, showing that the inclusion of women within the IRA stemmed from a logistical requirement for the 'reserve army' to fill the depleting ranks in the aftermath of continuing losses due to arrests. It suggests that the shift in thinking among the leadership (and the wider membership) regarding women's role in the IRA resides not in an ideological awakening towards gender equality but more with the resource demands in a period of accelerating and intense armed conflict. In addition to the use of the reserve army, interviewees describe their resistance to such exclusion, by demanding their role in the IRA.

PATRICIA: Women were encouraged to go into the *Cumann na mBan* and the thing about that which bothered me, and no disrespect to them but they had their own structure different to the IRA structure. I was as able and equal as any man. And if I'm going to die carrying a gun then I'm not going to die carrying a gun for a male comrade, or I am not going to be arrested for carrying a gun and serving ten years after *he* had shot somebody with it. If I go to jail or if I die, then it'll be under my own probation to be a very active member.

Interviewees depict an organisation that adhered strictly to very patriarchal definitions of masculine and feminine roles within a militant movement. The male leaders were reluctant revolutionaries when it came to women's emancipation and so the armed struggle represented a site of perpetual struggle for republican women to be acknowledged and accepted as equal participants. While initial responses from interviewees described little or no difference between men and women within the ranks of the IRA, very quickly their recollections revealed congenital formations of patriarchy within the movement. Linda recalls an astonishing IRA meeting from the early 1970s:

We had a lot of debates internally. The republican movement that I joined was a very male-dominated movement and we had a lot of battles. I remember being at one meeting where somebody mentioned a motion where any woman that got pregnant, she was to be dismissed immediately. So I just got up and said 'what do you mean she's to be dismissed, if she still wants to be in the republican movement then that's her choice' … now if she wanted to stay in or take a leave of absence then that's fine too. But you see here was I saying, 'what about the volunteer that got her pregnant, is he getting dismissed?' ... so you were fighting this war but also the war with the Brits. But you knew the undercurrents of the men were very old fashioned. Some men regarded the women, because of the split between the IRA and *Cumann na mBan*, as a kind of lesser species of revolutionaries and things like getting women on the same training camps as men or going on the same operations as men, women had to fight for that, had to prove themselves so that was always in there.

Despite women's success in entering the male-dominated realm of armed conflict, overt sexism and patriarchal norms attempted to strictly limit women's political mobility. It is clear from Linda's comments, and the testimonies from others, that women's reproductive role coupled with the gendered division of domestic labour was utilised as a mechanism to curtail women's agency. The interview data indicates that they were hard fought for and won by the demands of women themselves. Although a committed republican, Emily recalls the IRA as a very male-dominated organisation, and 'the fact that women got to play a part in the struggle was only because women fought to play a part and it wasn't straight forward'. Siobhan is currently a Sinn Féin activist who also works as a councillor in Derry city. She grew up on the Creggan estate, a working-class area of small, terraced houses built to meet the growing demands for housing in the 1940s and 1950s. Although her family had no republican history, the eruption of the armed conflict would see Siobhan along with many of her brothers and sister engage in armed actions, many of them entering jail on multiple occasions.

At the start, there was some thinking around that women had a certain life span and the thinking was that women will join the IRA when they are young and single. They will meet a man, marry, have children and then they'll leave the IRA. So the thinking was that women have a certain life span so what's the point in training them up so women ... em (sigh) ... but when I got to 18 that wasn't our notion and were sort of saying 'No, we're as good as the next man', plus the fact, if someone went out and took a shot and shot a Brit or an RUC[8] (Royal Ulster Constabulary) man and you were arrested taking the weapon away then you were getting charged with that killing.

Siobhan's extract echoes Linda's and that of many others regarding the value placed by men on women's 'mothering' role. References to the 'life span' of revolutionary women suggests that men saw women's inclusion as a temporary affair, all of which would be brought to a satisfactory conclusion when these rebel women 'realised their real true role': marriage and motherhood. It indicates that regardless of their contribution to armed struggle, there remained a virulent patriarchal attitude among many male republicans that women's 'true' role in the national project was mothering. Given the centrality of women's reproductive role within nationalist ideology (Yuval-Davis 1997), the use of mothering to temper 'rebel women' is hardly surprising. Many non-state struggles from Latin America, including El Salvador, Guatemala, and Nicaragua, revealed similar instances in which pregnancy saw women labelled as 'failed combatants' while equally commended for 'producing more revolutionaries' (Chinchilla 1990; Ibanez 2001). The male expectations of combatant women is one that never strays too far from the domestic, private realm, re-enforcing the perpetual links between women, motherhood and the home. Despite women's presence at all levels of state and non-state militaries, there remains a virulent understanding that their combatant roles are both arbitrary and temporal.

Republican women's struggle for full inclusion within the IRA is distinctly like other non-state militaries. In the Eritrean People's Liberation Front (EPLF), women had to overcome major barriers of exclusion from its membership ranks, despite their vast contributions through arms transportation and military reconnaissance (Henshaw 2016: 49). There are three main reasons why republican women broke through the male-only citadel of the IRA. First, republican women themselves demanded to be included as full and equal members at all levels of the republican armed struggle. At local and national levels, women organised and lobbied the republican leadership to drop its long-standing ban on women as IRA volunteers. Second, between 1969 and 1971 the ranks of the IRA were quickly depleting due to hundreds of arrests and lives lost in combat, thus creating a logistical need to replenish the declining number of volunteers. And third, the inclusion and participation of women within the ranks of non-state liberation movements is symbolically important in terms of its claims regarding legitimacy and equality. In other words, republican women's entry into the armed campaign was not a given and something that was hard fought for by the women themselves, despite the revolutionary rhetoric of non-state nationalist movements. During the wartime years, the IRA was not only a site of armed struggle but also a site of gender struggle. And so long before we arrive at the commemorative actions in the transition period, republican women had waged a long-standing struggle for inclusion, recognition and equality within the republican movement. Interview data clearly indicates that the battle for recognising and valuing women's contributions in post-war commemoration is, in fact, a continuity of struggle by women against sexist and patriarchal norms within the republican movement.

Republican commemoration and the 'invisibility' of women

Commemoration plays a significant and deeply influential role in the shaping of collective memories and dominant narratives of wartime roles and events (Rolston 2003). It is, however, as much a process of forgetting as it is remembering (Forty and Küchler 1999).

> State formations, political parties or movements, and other social agents are all involved in constructing versions of the national past and national

identity, selecting from or reworking the repertoire of stories and symbols to fashion effectively useable public memories for their particular ends and purposes

(Ashplant *et al.* 2000: 16)

In other words, commemoration is never an objective mirror accurately representing the past; architects of memorialisation are motivated and informed by specific political ambitions as they 'imagine the nation' (Anderson 1983). While various forms of republican memorialisation existed during 'the Troubles' (typically parades, murals, and a small number of plaques), the transition period under examination here witnessed a rapid increase, with a high percentage of memorials for every one of the 294 IRA volunteers who were killed in the conflict (McDowell 2008: 345). Contemporary republican commemoration is prolific, manifested in monuments, murals, republican plots in cemeteries, ceremonies and annual commemorations, parades, wreath laying, graveside orations, sporting events, festivals, song and music (Graham and Whelan 2007). The vast number of murals, memorials and plagues, indicates the value afforded to the use of prominent public spaces by republicans (and loyalists also) to tell their version of the war. Many memorials list IRA volunteers and civilians who died at the hands of the 'British State' constructing a vision of oneness and unity between the armed IRA and the community on behalf of which they vowed to fight for (McDowell 2007).

Despite this spirit of collective resistance where 'everyone has a part to play',[9] republican commemoration has traditionally privileged certain military roles over others. Often, the male protagonist dominates the commemorative landscape with a notable relative absence of militant republican women (Graham and Whelan 2007; McDowell 2007; O'Keefe 2013). Such a gender-blind vision of wartime participation led to significant levels of frustration among interviewees who felt that their contributions were not accurately reflected in the vast majority of commemorative projects. Theresa voices her frustration at the lack of recognition:

> Did we not count? *Do we not count?* I just feel there have been too many women who are just forgotten about or who have not ever been recognised or given any recognition for all the work she [*sic*] done. If you were active you stayed away from these big do's [social functions], you avoided the limelight if you like. So I'm a wee bit resentful, but that resentment comes from the fact that I know so many, so many brilliant women who never received recognition nor ever will get that recognition.

Siobhan echoes those sentiments, indicating the androcentrism that pervades republican commemoration:

> There has been (interviewee sighs) how would you say this ... I need to be very diplomatic here. There have been a lot of books written about the

[republican armed] struggle, and sometimes if you listen to some of our [commemorative] songs and I think if I hear the words 'son, father, husband' once more then I'm going to squeal because you'd nearly think that women played no role at all in the IRA.

Both extracts are typical of the responses across most interviews, all of whom are linked by a profound sense of frustration, resentment and in some instances anger. Irish rebel songs or ballads as indicated by Siobhan play a significant role in republican commemoration. Their importance is augmented by the fact that these songs are prominently performed at social functions and pubs in republican areas. Lorraine Dowler's extensive research in West Belfast in 1998 found vast levels of frustration among republican women at the male dominance and bias within songs and ballads. Of the 74 republican songs analysed by Dowler, she found just four referred to women's roles in armed struggle. Echoing the experiences of interviewees here, Dowler's research reveals similar anxieties regarding the erasure of women's stories from the republican struggle. Most interviewees here are consistent in stating their belief that the leadership was doing its best to include women within its commemorative work. Despite such affirmations, there is a common theme of resentment and frustration at the lack of attention to women's wartime contribution. This is particularly noticeable across the interviews when examining the ways in which the prison protest is now recalled in commemorative format.

The prison protests of the late 1970s and early 1980s remains a dominant focal point for republican commemoration. Although republican prisoners, both male and female, were incarcerated in various jails across Britain and Ireland, the focus of the prison protest resided in the H-Blocks of Long Kesh,[10] which housed male inmates, and Armagh jail, which housed female inmates. A first hunger strike involving both men and women collapsed in December 1980, a second hunger strike in 1981, which lasted for more than eight months, resulted in the deaths of ten men in the H-Blocks. The twentieth anniversary of the hunger strike in 2001 witnessed a plethora of acts of republican memorialisation regarding the prison protests, and today remains a prominent feature in the republican commemorative calendar. Many local commemoration committees were formed in 2001 across Ireland to commemorate the Hunger Strikes, mostly populated by male ex-prisoners. The Falls Cultural Society produced many elaborate memorials to the IRA's 'D' company, which operated in the Lower Falls area close to Belfast city centre. The Conway Mill project is another that engaged in Irish cultural events but is 'equally bound up in Sinn Féin party politics' (McDowell 2007: 731). Many local '81 committees[11] engaged in tree planting ceremonies, mural painting and sporting events. The Upper Springfield '81 Commemoration Committee engaged in large-scale acts of commemoration including (unofficially) renaming streets and roads after some of the hunger strikers. Again, this group also comprised mainly male ex-prisoners. These efforts to 'republicanise' West Belfast also included the erection of new statues and the opening of new memorial gardens (McDowell 2007: 731). Interviewees are deeply frustrated at the lack of attention given to their prison struggles in Armagh contrasting sharply with the immense focus on men's. If the Hunger Strike commemorations of 2001 endeavoured to 'republicanise' West Belfast, then the data here indicates that such memorialisation also masculinised the landscape of West Belfast.

Edel is a lifelong republican and lives in West Belfast. Edel's family has no republican history and her engagement with republicanism was very much a self-guided journey. She joined the republican movement in the late 1980s, although she was already politicised in terms of feminist and socialist politics through her time at university. Although stating that she still supports the Sinn Féin party electorally, she is no longer a formal member of the party. She works as a full-time community activist in West Belfast.

> There was an event recently on women's contribution to the prison protests and [named female speaker] was speaking and then there were two [named male speakers] but she gave a lovely ten minutes speaking [sic] about the comradeship in Armagh and what happened there. But then the rest of the two hours was the [two male speakers] experience of the prison protests. No gender balance at all ... I was livid at the end of it and I couldn't voice this anger because I felt it would diminish the stories of the male speakers or the deaths of the Hunger Strikers. When I said it [male domination at event] to some people on the way out of the event, nobody else had noticed. To me it is glaring, and it glares that there is something missing ... a whole section missing that is not acknowledged.

At the time of interview Gemma had recently attended the national hunger strike rally and was shocked at the dearth of attention given to women's contribution:

> Women's stories haven't been told and even when you look at the Hunger Strikes you need to keep reminding people that three women were on Hunger Strike. At the recent national rally for the Hunger Strike in Monaghan, the speakers never mentioned women once, not once, not their role in the Hunger Strike or the war and so there has been a complaint put into the *Ard Comhairle* over that. So no, women are not getting the recognition.

The pattern across all interviews contradicts their earlier assertions that women were equal to men when it came to the ranks of the IRA. Their struggle for recognition in commemoration is not new but merely represents a new terrain of patriarchal resistance to women's military participation. Bernie works for Sinn Féin as a constituency worker as well as being involved in several local community groups in Belfast. Like so many other interviewees, Bernie's family biography bears the scars of armed conflict. Bernie was interned in the early 1970s. She was released in the mid-1970s but found herself back in Armagh jail because of her IRA activities. Bernie was involved in the prison protests of the late 1970s and early 1980s during her time in jail.

> Women have just been wiped out of history and even with regards to the Hunger Strike and that. Some people are making documentaries or writing books about it, and it's like Armagh didn't exist and that can be very frustrating. I know we were only on it [hunger strike] for 19 days and I cannot take away how long the men were on [it], but sometimes it gets a wee bit frustrating because it's like 'were we not in Armagh and were women there not on Hunger Strike?'

Bernie's thoughts resonate with material from of other interviews, suggesting critical levels of awareness regarding their 'invisibility' in commemoration, something particularly lucid when it comes to the prison protests. The perennial question among most is 'were we not in Armagh on the protest also?' The dominant narrative within republican commemoration suggests that women were not really there during the war. All interviewees agreed that republican acts of memorialisation during the conflict transition period do not reflect their experiences or contributions in a meaningful or accurate way, even though most also stated that 'the movement was doing its best' to include women. The data here regarding the exclusion of women within commemoration indicates that while all interviewees state that they played an 'equal' role alongside the men, the memorial landscape in the transition suggests that this view was not shared by the vast majority of men. It appears that the struggle for women to be recognised and included within commemoration in the transition period is, in fact, a continuity of their wartime struggle to be recognised and included as 'equals'.

The example of the Hunger Strikes perfectly illustrates the deliberately subdued stories of women's experiences in Armagh when contrasted with the amplified male narrative of the H-Blocks. The interview data here substantiates existing research that argues that women's wartime contributions are rarely considered worthy 'celebrating'. Wall murals have played a prominent commemorative role in republicanism from the hunger strike period onwards. An analysis of over 500 republican and nationalist murals in 1996 revealed that just six referred to armed republican women (O'Keefe 2013: 102). It is reasonable to conclude that republican commemoration in the past 15 years eagerly pays homage to a war fought by male combatants. Interview data here substantiates existing research that argues that there is a dominant masculine image prevailing in republican commemoration (Graham and Whelan 2007; McDowell 2008). The image of the male militarist literally looms large. In Derry city cemetery a ten-foot high black marble stone statue was erected in 2001 to commemorate the twentieth anniversary of the Hunger Strikes. The figurative sculpture depicts a masked man in military uniform, wearing dark glasses and a beret brandishing a gun. This caused much annoyance and offence to many republican women who felt their contribution to the prison protest, and by extension to the overall struggle, was omitted (McDowell 2008: 343). The towering statues represent a vision of combatants as militarised masculinity (Graham and Whelan 2007). This trend continued with similar statues erected in republican strongholds throughout the North of

Ireland in 2001, despite the disquiet and protestations expressed by republican women.

It is important to state at the juncture that I am not suggesting that all republican women are absent from republican memorialisation. The Price sisters, Marian and Dolours, were both given life sentences in London in 1973 for their part in an IRA bombing campaign, the very first Provisional IRA bombs in England of 'the Troubles'. Anecdotal evidence suggests that the two sisters were, in fact, the team leaders for that bombing campaign (O'Keefe 2013). Mairead Farrell was shot dead by the British army (SAS)[12] in Gibraltar in 1988 during an attempted bomb attack on British military targets there, specifically a weekly British military parade. Mairead had previously spent time in Armagh jail for her part in a bomb attack on the Conway Hotel on the outskirts of West Belfast. Dorothy Maguire and Maura Meehan were shot dead by the British Army in the Lower Falls on 23 October 1971. At the time of their deaths, they were engaged in 'Hen Patrols',[13] scouting streets for the presence of state forces to warn active republicans in that area. As the British Army entered Clonard Street, just off the Falls Road, the women attempted to warn republicans by sounding the horn of their car. The British army responded and shot both women dead. Other *Cumann na mBan* volunteers such as Anna Parker and Anne Marie Pettigrew were killed when the bombs they were transporting for IRA volunteers exploded prematurely (Brady *et al.* 2011).

When examining this cohort of republican women, it is interesting to see the ways in which some are prominent in republican commemoration while others are barely visible. Mairead Farrell is relatively prominent in public memorials such as murals, quotations, and her name is often placed alongside the names of other prominent republicans such as Bobby Sands during commemorative speeches and political speeches. This is somewhat similar in the case of the Price sisters. Although they parted their ways with the mainstream republican movement due to ideological differences,[14] they remain widely 'celebrated' for their 'successful'[15] bombing operation in London, despite their arrest and imprisonment.

The cases of others however, such as the volunteers of *Cumann na mBan* who also lost their lives, remain largely invisible. It appears that when women do come into view within male-led republican commemoration, they are those who were acting in accordance with the roles traditionally associated with being a 'combatant'. Those in roles deemed as 'non-combat' or support structures who also gave their lives barely elicit a mention. It suggests that when female combatants are included, they are included on men's terms and conditions; tacked on to a format that adheres to a masculine definition of militarism, and is situated within an established commemorative discourse. Republican commemoration reflects the long-standing view that women's contribution is valued only when it fits into the patriarchal vision of combatant. Commemoration is therefore a reflective manifestation of a much broader trend which sees women's contribution appraised positively by men only when it occurs on their terms and definitions.

In addition to the formal processes of commemoration, interviewees describe other informal instances of male domination in the post-war narrative. Anne states that 'men have this primal thing to be recognised, to be applauded, to be promoted', sentiments widely shared across most interviews. Sara McDowell (2007) asserts that commemoration is deeply enmeshed within spatial politics, arguing that the republican movement is preoccupied with territory and space within its many forms of commemoration. A key theme across most interviews are the ways in which public space, typically bars and clubs within republican communities, are dominated by what the interviewees term as 'men's loose talk', again reinforcing a masculine conceptualisation of male heroics and acts of valour during 'the Troubles'. Ruth, a former IRA volunteer and now both a Sinn Féin and Community activist, describes the 'loose talk':

> We see it at republican functions, the loose talk from men is unbelievable and you'll never find a woman doing loose talk about what she did during the war. Part of the problem is that women tend to do what they do and then they move onto the next job. And men are more able to talk about what they did, and a lot of women don't. There are women living in houses with their children and grandchildren and they probably did more in the war than some of these men who are doing the loose talk. And it is these women that we want to draw out because their role and their contributions need to be marked and need to be recorded. If you were to listen to what's being said in the bars and that, sure you'd think it was only men who fought the war.

The term 'loose talk' was a colloquial phrase used by republicans during 'the Troubles' to describe how careless conversation in bars and clubs about republican activity could easily be intercepted by undercover British state agents. It is interesting to hear the phrase now being used by the women to describe this informal storytelling. It is a theme present throughout most interviews:

CHRISTINE: A lot of the men sit around tables, shooting their mouths off about what they say they did in the struggle.
ANNE: I think women's contributions needs to be continuously recorded because there are thousands of women out there who have a story, but men will come forward and have no problem blowing their own trumpets.
BERNIE: You see men have no problem talking about themselves, while women aren't full of themselves.

Commemoration is as much about power relations in the present (and future) as it is about recalling the past. Interview data suggests and substantiates existing research, that the male-led commemorative project is deeply imbued with masculine concerns regarding the pursuit of personal status or positions of power (O'Keefe 2013). The dominance of the male narrative sequesters important public realms within republicanism, such as clubs, bars, and social functions, transforming them into masculinised spaces. In doing so, spatial control is exerted along gender lines, which invariably re-enforces the notion of a male public and a feminine private. Dowler (1998) argues that public arenas such as pubs, social functions, and nationalist drinking clubs remain male-dominated in ways that depict the public realm as a masculine space. Kelly is a life-long member of the republican movement, although she deliberately avoids stating if she was a member of the IRA or not. Throughout her interview, Kelly recounts her involvement in street rioting, street agitation such as civil disobedience and protests, as well as activism in Sinn Féin, among others. She currently works as a manager in the community sector in Belfast and she also works for Sinn Féin, as well as being a part-time councillor in social services. Her father was a former British Army soldier. While her family had no republican or nationalist history prior to the eruption of armed conflict in 1969, her sisters and brothers joined the republican movement during the armed conflict.

> It is very still much a male-dominated organisation [so] that you have to keep going 'where's the women?' From my experience, men find it easier to talk about their achievements even within the republican movement. So men would boast and joke about what they did in the war where the women don't.

Theresa O'Keefe suggests that there is a pervasive link between hegemonic masculinity and men's endeavours for personal glory and hero status. Collective hero-worship as a memory work for societies in transition, sustains the nation by reminding its members of their place within it and the assorted roles they are expected to perform (O'Keefe 2013: 100). She argues this status is not afforded or sought by women themselves. Eileen, an ex-prisoner who now works solely in community activism states her frustration:

> So I really like that thing that Bobby Sands says about everyone having their own part to play so I hate this attitude, especially among the men. They love to boast about what they did, and you'd think only the men fought the Brits. They didn't, it's only women don't boast about it, women did it because it was the right thing to do. They didn't do it and then go out and herald it, 'look at me, aren't I great'.

Commemoration is often cited as a type of 'symbolic warfare' or 'war by another means' (Graham and Whelan 2007; McDowell 2012). According to McDowell, memorialisation not only constitutes war by other means, it also serves to reproduce the wartime gender order/regime where it is men who decide who, what, where and when to commemorate (2008: 340). It is clear that much of republican commemoration was guided by a rigid adherence to a narrow, masculine definition of combatant, exalting the male protagonist and recasting women as 'supporters'. The male-led commemorative processes consistently endeavour to push women's roles to the background, effectively dismissing their vital wartime contributions as supplementary.

The daily reality for military movements across the globe, both state and non-state alike, is their overwhelming reliance upon the military labour of women and men. Despite this reality, the post-war commemorative milieu facilitates the erasure of women's contributions by fashioning soldiering duties which adhere to normative masculine visions and conceptualisations. Gender power, however, is socially, culturally, and symbolically constituted, and sustained through the hierarchical ordering of masculinities and femininities. The cultivation of militarised masculinity through gendered discourses, symbols, and practices predisposes the commemorative landscape to a narrow vision that invariably produces a distorted history of women roles during armed conflict. The function of post-war appraisals, such as commemoration, is to airbrush any lingering vestiges of femininity from the war record and project a mythical narrative that re-secures the realm of soldiering as a masculine space only. In other words, the tendency to conflate soldiering solely with men and manliness draws sustenance from gendered role distinctions, which positions men at the vanguard of armed actions while simultaneously deposing women. Conventional narratives of war magnify and value those activities typically associated with normative masculinity and its culturally assigned behaviours. Therefore, women's multiple roles are often invisible, but furthermore, many other roles that men undertake that fall outside what is broadly termed as direct combat, are also missed. In other words, traditional, male-dominated approaches to war and conflict transition are wholly inept for yielding an accurate account of what women and men do in times of war. The often-neglected standpoints of combatant women mean that understandings of war and militarism remain partial and incomplete. Listening to the experiences and perspectives of combatant women not only corrects the distorted male-saturate narrative, but also furnishes a more accurate account of the ways in which non-state military movements sustain themselves over vast periods of time.

The issue at stake here extends far beyond the field of post-war commemoration; the dearth of women in post-war memorialisation is, in fact, the manifestation of a long-standing struggle by republican women to be recognised for their wartime contributions. Feminists consistently argue that the struggle against patriarchy is a daily one; its omnipresence requires a relentless struggle of resistance by women always. The struggle by republican women to alter the commemorative landscape is not something unique to the conflict transition period. In fact, it represents a continuum of cultural violence, and hence also a continuity of political struggle to have their voices, activism and interests as part of the republican agenda, from the front lines of battle to the recollection of history in conflict transition. Just as they had previously resisted sexist and patriarchal attitudes within the republican movement during the conflict, the realm of commemoration in conflict transition sees republican women reorganising to ensure that their wartime contributions are recognised and valued.

Re-writing themselves back into history

To reinforce the agency of interviewees it is important to document the many ways they have responded to *and* resisted their exclusion within mainstream republican commemoration. During the conflict years, particularly in the late 1980s, women established multiple spaces to ensure recognition of their contribution to armed struggle as well as articulating positions on other political and social issues. Republican women were writing and publishing their own stories in magazines such as *Women's News*, a Belfast feminist magazine, *The Captive Voice*, a republican prisoners' production, and a short-lived yet incredibly powerful publication *Women In Struggle*, which was published by the Sinn Féin Women's Department. *The Captive Voice* ran many articles and editorials relating to women's issues, including the use of pornography by male prisoners, domestic violence, and the exploitation of women, all of which are indicative of the tone of debate on-going within the republican movement (Power 2010: 159). In the aftermath of the 1994 IRA ceasefire, the Falls Women's Centre produced a video documentary entitled *What Did You Do in the War Mammy?* based on interviews and testimonies from female Volunteers. In contrast with the prolific and sizable output of republican women during the years of armed conflict, the period leading up to and immediately after the 1998 peace accord was marked by a discernible absence of women's voices.

In 2012 and 2013 however, there was a reinvigorated effort, reflected in the burgeoning commemorative activism by interviewees at the time of fieldwork, as stated in this chapter's introduction. Much of this activism, a prolific output of various projects, began in 2006 when republican women began to re-organise to counter their lack of visibility within republican commemoration. The Irish Republican History Museum, which contains many references and exhibits of women's wider contribution to the struggle, opened in West Belfast in 2007 and was the culmination of years of work by former prisoner Eileen Hickey. Another of her initiatives in documenting women's history culminated in the 2011 publication of *In the Footsteps of Anne*, a vast collection of personal testimonies of female ex-prisoners. The book covered the stories of women located across a myriad of eclectic military roles. In 2007, the Women's Garden of Remembrance opened in the grounds of the Roddy McCorley Society, a prominent republican club located on the Glen Road in West Belfast. The memorial garden's significance cannot be overstated. Roddy's remains the epicentre of much republican activism, both informally as a social club and formally through acts of commemoration, press conferences, and exhibitions, among others. The use of such a prominent public republican space for the women's garden of remembrance presents a huge victory for republican women. The garden is also used as a focal point for women's commemorations and other events such as International Women's Day.

In addition to the activities described above, republican women are now organising across Ireland to ensure that future commemoration relating to the prison protests captures as many experiences and perspectives as possible. At the time of writing, vast efforts were underway to create a digital database for all republican women ex-prisoners.

BERNIE: We do not have a comprehensive data base [for female ex-prisoners] and so what we done is sent out a wee survey thing to as many as possible. So we had an idea to contact as many women as possible and get their feedback and see if anything could be done for them.

Ruth is currently a Sinn Féin activist and community activist in the Falls area of West Belfast. She also served previously as a local elected representative. Ruth was born and reared in West Belfast and comes from what is traditionally described as a republican family. Her father was interned in the 1940s and her mother was also a senior republican. Both parents spent some years of the early 1950s 'on the run'. With five brothers and three sisters, she recalls a happy childhood mixed with a strong sense of republican identity, reflected in her family upbringing where Irish language was widely spoken and pictures of republican martyrs from previous IRA campaigns hung proudly on the walls of the family home. Ruth joined the IRA in the early 1970s.

I'm involved in a focus group [female ex-prisoners], because even in 2012 there is not even a database of female prisoners, nothing. And part of that, statistics don't exist for the women nor no in-depth study done on the women as there has been on the men. That's why the focus group was set up. Basically we were told that if the women's story is to be told, then we're the only ones that are going to tell it. But within a few weeks we received over 450 names and I feel women are crying out for this and so many tales are to be told. My own thing that I want is a definitive thing like a library, living history type.

While the idea of compiling a database on female prisoners and the establishment of female ex-prisoner's groups initially started in Belfast, the research reveals similar endeavours in Derry and other cities and town on both sides of the Irish border.

MICHELLE: We've started this women's ex-prisoners' group here in Derry. Well we formed it about two months ago after I got a phone call to come up to the women. Like in the office next door, all the photos in the room are all of men so I left them a note saying 'was there no women in the struggle?' so we formed this group to make sure that the women's role was being recognised.

LINDA: We worked on the book of women ex-prisoners and we talked to everyone, and you were conscious and explaining yourself as you were taking the stories and we knew that there were hundreds of women out there. Like a big, detailed, extensive oral history could be what is needed. Do one with women and then one with men or whatever but that would be a fascinating look at the whole conflict as opposed to just one particular group in society. But there shouldn't be any hierarchy about who gave the most, because it was a big movement of people and there are lots of people out there sitting silently, forgotten about. Some people were very emotional because this was the first time they'd ever told anyone about their experience, you know, like stories of strip searches and we're being given this story and they're upset so it was difficult at times. For some people it came out easily while for others it didn't. But women had the power to write their own stories.

In addition to these efforts, interviewees also described the ways in which they are attempting to highlight *all* of women's wartime contributions. In 2014, new wall murals emerged capturing women's roles as armed fighters, their roles in *Cumann na mBan* (both located in Derry) and, equally as important, other roles such as that of providing safe houses and weapons storage. In 2012, a mobile exhibition entitled *Women In Struggle*, which documented women's multiple contributions to the republican struggle toured towns and cities across Ireland. At the entrance to the Irish Republican History Museum in West Belfast, a large stone plaque lists all those women, both IRA and *Cumann na mBan*, who lost their lives in the armed conflict. These recent efforts indicate a willingness to act in order to bring in view the entirety of women's roles.

All interviewees argued that these 'new' forms of commemoration not only corrected their exclusion as volunteers but that they were also processes capable of bringing women's other militant labour into view. Street drama and plays are gaining increasing importance in articulating women's stories and experiences. *Unbroken*, the story of IRA volunteer Mairead Farrell began touring Ireland in 2013. According to Cynthia Enloe, most masculinised war museums don't have much to say about widows. They have even less to say about the wives of male soldiers, banished from the murals and display cases (2004: 204). Republican women countered such exclusion with a play entitled *Just A Prisoner's Wife*, which documents the struggles and sacrifices of women whose partners were incarcerated, and continues to tour Ireland periodically.

GEMMA: But there are improvements and last week we had a play called Just a *Prisoner's Wife* written by women and it gave people a whole new perspective and you can get it out that way, women's story that is and you had male prisoners saying that they never thought of it like that.

In June 2012 I attended an innovative audio and visual exhibition in West Belfast called *Captured Voices*, which documented the experiences of republican women during state raids on their homes and the incarceration of their loved ones because of the conflict. The use of mechanisms runs parallel with the commemorative endeavours of combatant women in other armed struggle. In Colombia, combatant women there formed the Collective of Female Ex-Combatants in 2001, some ten years after the first wave of demobilisation. The

Collective issued their founding document, which defined female combatants as *all* women who participated in political tasks, organisational, logistics, military and solidarity activities to support political and military organisations. It sought to recover the hidden histories of women's participation in guerrilla groups (Ortega 2015: 238). It did so by engaging in unconventional ways such as theatre, film documentaries, academic studies, among others. The use of drama, story-telling, and exhibitions are alternative commemorative mechanisms for combatant women which allow for a more accurate encapsulation of women's multiple wartime contributions; a more inclusive and broader type of commemoration. In addition to their own semi-autonomous memorial activism, republican women are also having some success in re-shaping commemoration within the broader republican movement. In recent years there has been a marked increase of awareness within the broader republican movement regarding women's role in armed conflict. The recent centenary of the foundation of *Cumann na mBan* in 1914 added fresh momentum to this on-going burst of commemorating women. Across Ireland (and some in Britain) events such as lectures, commemorative parades and new wall murals marked this important milestone. The relatively high level of attention to *Cumann na mBan* by the overall republican movement is in marked contrast to its previous neglect throughout the previous four decades. The moderate success of women in shaping the contemporary commemorative spectrum and agenda are indicative of the political agency and mobility among republican women as they continue through conflict transition. The recent centenary of the Easter Rising in 2016 saw this surge in women's commemorative actions continue unabated. On March 8 2016, International Women's Day, several events occurred across Ireland to recognise women's multifarious contributions to Irish republicanism, from 1916 to today. *Tar Anall*, an ex-prisoners' group in Belfast held an event entitled 'It's Our Story Too', in which a commemorative quilt was unfurled, detailing the names of republican women throughout the decades. On the same day in Dublin, Sinn Féin held a large march and commemoration at the GPO on O'Connell Street, one of the key sites during the hallowed republican armed rising in 1916. Moreover, many of the murals that have dominated public spaces in republican communities throughout 2016 foregrounded women and their diverse roles within republicanism.

Much of the work around commemorating and recognising women's contribution to the armed struggle stems directly from women themselves. They are spurred into action out of a sense of deep frustration at their lack of visibility within the overall movement. Whether this is a fleeting moment or the turning point towards a more serious effort by the republican movement to recognise women's various contribution remains to be seen. The interview data, coupled with their increasingly eclectic and prolific forms of memorialisation, I argue, displaces the masculine definition of combatant and expands our spectrum of vision of military roles in times of armed conflict. Moreover, it brings combatant women into view in a way which accurately reflects their realities and experiences. Their commemorative emphasis on *all* roles disrupts the male-imposed 'fighter/supporter' dichotomy and ultimately challenges the erroneous narrative that in times of war, it is men who are the real actors.

Conclusion

The role of feminist scholars is to make visible hidden experiences to theorise the role of gender in war and conflict transition. Soldiering and militarism remain primary vehicles through which men display their masculinity; the conflation of armed combat and manliness has endured. An examination of the lives and experiences of combatant women however, challenges such easy associations. Often the front line, visible, combatant role is but the tip of the iceberg or the top tier of a military pyramid. It is demonstrably evident that the exalted front-line combatant reaches the top of that pyramid by standing on the shoulders and backs of those positioned in so-called peripheral roles. Like the typical patriarchal household, military movements exhibit a clear gendered division of labour, governed by cultural norms and expectations regarding appropriate masculine and feminine roles. Given the high proportion of women within the non-combat roles, the glorified (typically male) front-line fighter is facilitated and enabled by women's low-status 'domestic' labour within non-state militaries. All around the reified position of 'front-line soldier' are roles that are vital to the sustainment of all military movements. While these roles are occupied by women and men, it is the gendered classification of these roles that renders women invisible while simultaneously heaping glory and reward on the male-dominated post of front-line soldiering.

Given the centrality of gender to feminist scholarship, the issue with prevailing, androcentric definitions of military contributions and combat roles goes beyond their imprecision. Bringing the lives and experiences of combatant women into view not only corrects the distorted narrative of war, but also uncovers the centrality of gender to the constitution of masculine power and status within conflict transition. Irrespective of women's roles as front-line fighters, and despite the fluidity of composition regarding women and men's wartime roles, the discursive and cultural practices within commemorative revisions reaffirm soldiering as a thoroughly masculinised zone. Though the contributions and labour of women – from unpaid domestic labour, prostitutes, active combatants – are essential to the production and reproduction of all militaries (Basham and Catignani 2018), the masculine myth of male heroics continues to wield significant power, shaping public consciousness, mainstream academic approaches, governmental and international organisations' policy positions on conflict resolution.

Women's multiple roles and vital wartime contributions are rarely recognised or valued by male-led movements. Their exclusion from the post-war commemorative landscape is a very public and trumpeted message that when it came to times of great peril for the nation, women were not really there. When women do appear in commemoration, it is only when they do so in accordance with the masculine discourse and definition of a combatant. The hierarchical distinction between 'fighter and supporter' re-enforces the trope that it is men who are the real heroes of the battlefield. The data contained in this chapter challenges such a distinction by calling for recognition of the importance and value of all women's military endeavours in their entirety. By doing so, I suggest, they are effectively subverting the patriarchal definition of a combatant by blurring the highly gendered lines of distinction between fighter/supporter in favour of a far broader understanding of the multiple ways in which women militarily contribute to national armed struggles.

The recent output of republican women's commemorative activism demonstrates how innovative mechanisms of memorialisation are capable of encapsulating and valuing women's multiple militant roles of resistance. While this chapter clearly indicates the ways in which women are marginalised, both during and after war, it also documented the ways in which combatant women react and resist such reversions. The post-war commemorative battles waged by combatant women is constitutive of the cultural violence which occurs when language and symbolism are utilised as a means of attaining male power and while simultaneously diminishing the reality and value of women's wartime contributions. The attempts to sequester the 'combatant role' as masculine and male demonstrates the salience of gender in understanding processes of power and domination in post-war scenarios. The struggles contained in this chapter are not exclusive to the period of transition as such, but are, in fact, a continuity of struggles against sexist and patriarchal attitudes that date to the very birth of the Provisional republican movement. Conflict transition is, in fact, a new tier of patriarchy that republican women have a long-standing history of resisting. This chapter reveals that while it is useful to ask, 'where are the women', it is not enough to simply 'add women' to prevailing wartime narratives. The actions of the women in this research suggests that the resistance to women's marginalisation resides not in 'adding' their views within existing frameworks and discourses, but by struggling to alter prevailing definitions through their unique perspectives and actions.

Notes

1 The DUP is currently the largest unionist political party in the North of Ireland. The kernel of the party resides in the Protestant fundamentalism of its founder and long-time leader the Rev. Ian Paisley. Founded in 1971, Ian Paisley led the party for 37 years. With strong links to the Free Presbyterian Church, the party was widely viewed as an extremist unionist party with a high percentage of evangelicals among its membership and support base coupled with its uncompromising stances on the conflict, links with the South of Ireland, its visceral opposition to other more liberal unionist parties, and its social conservatism on matters such as abortion and marriage equality. While certain loyalist paramilitary members have cited the firebrand speeches and actions of Ian Paisley as key motivating factors in their decision to engage in violence, Ian Paisley has never been linked directly to any paramilitary groups. That said, key members of the party, including leading figures such as Ian Paisley and Peter Robinson, established a Third Force, also known as Ulster Resistance in 1986 and some members of the group were involved in bringing assorted arms and weaponry to

the North. After a number of arms seizures in 1988 and 1989, the group faded. It is important to unequivocally state that Ian Paisley and Peter Robinson have always denied any knowledge or hand in any illegal arms, and no charges were ever brought against them. At the time of the GFA and right throughout the peace process, the DUP roundly rejected the entire project as nothing more but an 'appeasement process' for terrorists. In the 2004 elections, the DUP overtook the more moderate Ulster Unionist Party as the largest unionist party, and, remarkably, entered into a power-sharing government with Sinn Féin in 2007 following the St Andrew's Agreement the previous year. While traditionally a peripheral and largely a 'party of protest' the last ten years have witnessed a broadening out of its membership and some of its previously rigid policies and standpoints.

2 Stands for Gun Lectures, which in the early days of 'the Troubles' were held in houses of IRA members or sympathisers in cities and towns in the North.

3 'The 'RA' is colloquial shorthand for the IRA, used extensively within working-class republican communities.

4 Bobby Sands led the second hunger strike of 1981 and was the first of ten men to die on hunger strike in that year. Already a well-known and revered republican, his election as a Westminster MP during his hunger strike in a by-election for the constituency of Fermanagh-South Tyrone in April 1981 propelled him and the cause of the Hunger Strikes onto the global political stage. The Hunger Strikes are widely accepted as a watershed moment in the broader armed conflict, but, moreover, Bobby Sands remains an iconic figure for the Provisional republican movement.

5 Officially called Operation Harvest, the IRA's Border Campaign (Dec 1956–Feb 1962) was a series of relatively large-scale attacks on military and infrastructural targets in the North of Ireland. By 1961, the campaign cost the lives of eight IRA members, six RUC members, and four republican supporters. The two states on the island of Ireland responded with widespread internment and after a series of disastrous attacks, coupled with little public support, the IRA called off Operation Harvest in 1962. Considered a military failure by many, republicans in the aftermath of the campaign turned their attention to political and social issues such as housing conditions, with a distinct departure towards socialist and some would suggest Marxist standpoints.

6 This is Gaelic or Irish for the party executive or ruling body.

7 Explorations of gender and women within the IRA is beyond the scope of this chapter. For a more comprehensive study, see Miranda Allison's *Women & Political Violence* and Theresa O'Keefe's *Feminist Identity Development and Activism in Revolutionary Movements*.

8 The Royal Ulster Constabulary (RUC) was formed alongside the partition of Ireland and the creation of the Northern Ireland State in 1921. While many Catholics within the new Northern Ireland state were alienated and/or excluded from many positions and roles within the new state, the RUC drew its recruits and personnel largely from the protestant/loyalist community. While the force was viewed by protestant/loyalist communities as a vital safeguard against any potential threat, those within the catholic/nationalist/republican minority saw it as a biased and repressive force of unionism. Accusations and evidence of police mistreatment and partiality of Catholics throughout the history of the state only served to exacerbate these tensions. Furthermore, the unionist government also recruited an all-Protestant militia called the Ulster Special Constabulary ('B Specials'), which acted as an auxiliary to the RUC.

9 This is a famous quote from the highly revered republican Bobby Sands, who died after 65 five days on Hunger Strike in 1981.

10 Long Kesh is located a few miles South-West of Belfast, near the city of Lisburn. It was a former RAF base, but its Nissan huts were used as an internment camp and jail by the State in the initial years of the conflict. In 1976, the H-Blocks were opened on the same site, which was then renamed the HMP Maze by the British Government, a title that republicans (and some Loyalists) reject.

11 During the prison protests of the late 1970s and early 1980s, relatives and supporters of the prisoners established local Relatives Action Committees locally throughout Ireland under the overall banner of the National H-Block/Armagh Committee in order to agitate and organise public support for the prisoners. The first RAC was established in Easter 1976. In 2001, republicans attempted to mirror the structural organs of the 1981 model in order to commemorate the hunger strikes of 1981. These commemorative committees were established in localities within towns, cities, and villages right across the island of Ireland. Deemed by republicans as a 'year of commemoration', 2001 witnessed hundreds of diverse local events to remember the hunger strikers culminating in a national rally in Casement Park in West Belfast in August 2001.

12 The SAS (Special Air Services) is an elite unit of the British Army. Although formed during the Second World War as a regiment, thereafter the unit was widely used for clandestine activities, including what the British Army describes as 'covert reconnaissance, counter-terrorism, direct action and human intelligence gathering'. In the North of Ireland, the SAS gained a fearsome reputation among republicans stemming largely from the SAS use of lethal firepower in order to counter militant republicanism. The 1980s, in particular, would see a sharp rise in the so-called 'shoot to kill' incidents in which IRA members would be killed by the SAS in disputed circumstances. The charge levelled at the British by republicans was that it effectively used the SAS as judge, juror, and executor.

13 In the early 1970s the British Army began night-time incursions into republican areas, some of which were designated by locals as 'No-Go' areas for state forces. For the most part these incursions were for house raids and arrest operations and became known as 'Duck Patrols'. In reaction, groups of republican women began patrolling the streets in order to alert the community and active republicans of the presence of state forces. They became known as 'Hen Patrols'.

14 Marian and Dolours were given two life sentences and immediately embarked on a hunger strike for repatriation to a prison in the North of Ireland. They endured 167 days of forced feeding by the prison authorities. Upon their release in the early 1980s, Marian was relatively inactive politically but did emerge in the 1990s as a vociferous opponent of Sinn Féin. In November 2009 she was arrested and detained in connection with the killing of two British soldiers at Massereene Barracks, outside of Belfast. She was charged with inciting support for an illegal organisation. She endured daily strip searches, among other brutalities, sparking a widespread campaign for her release. All charges were eventually dropped in 2012. Her supporters described the entire episode as a convenient form of internment and state abuse. Like her sister Marian, Dolours emerged as a formidable opponent of Sinn Féin in the 1990s. She was a regular contributor to *The Blanket*, an online journal that heavily criticised Sinn Féin. It is widely known that Dolours' mental health suffered, undoubtedly caused by the many years of abuse during her hunger strike, among other issues related to the conflict. She died in January 2013 at her home, evidently as a result of the toxic effect of a mix of prescribed sedative and anti-depressant medications.

15 I use the word 'successful' to denote the ways in which IRA volunteers would appraise this operation and in no way should this be interpreted as a way of disregarding the pain caused to the hundreds who suffered horrific injuries and the man who suffered a heart attack directly as a result of the bombs. This operation, in particular, is still hailed as a heavy blow against the British by republicans, despite the capture and jailing of the bombing team.

Bibliography

Anderson, B. 1983. *Imagined Communities: Reflections on the Origin and Spread of Nationalism.* London: Verso.

Ashplant, T. G., G. Dawson and M. Roper. eds. 2000. *The Politics of War Memory and Commemoration.* London: Routledge.

Basham, V. M. and S. Catignani. 2018. 'War Is Where the Hearth Is: Gendered Labor and the Everyday Reproduction of the Geopolitical in the Army Reserves'. *International Feminist Journal of Politics* 20(2): 153–117.

Berman, G. and N. Florquin. 2005. *Armed and Aimless: Armed Groups, Guns, and Human Security in the ECOWAS Region.* Geneva: Small Arms Survey.

Brady, E., E. Patterson, K. McKinney, R. Hamill, and P. Jackson. 2011. *In the Footsteps of Anne: Stories of Republican Women Ex-Prisoners.* Belfast: Shanway Publications.

Chinchilla, N. S. 1990. 'Revolutionary Popular Feminism in Nicaragua: Articulating Class, Gender, and National Sovereignty'. *Gender and Security* 4: 370–397.

Cock, J. 1991. *Colonels and Cadres: War and Gender in South Africa.* London. Oxford: University Press.

Connell, R. W. 2005. *Masculinities.* Cambridge: Polity Press.

Coogan, T. P. 2000. *The IRA.* London: Harper-Collins.

Crowe, L. 2012. 'Masculinities, Pain and Power: Gendering Experiences of Truth Sharing in Northern Ireland'. Pp. 19–38 in *Gender, Agency and Political Violence*, edited by L. Åhäll and L. Shepherd. Basingstoke: Palgrave Macmillan.

Dowler, L. 1998. '"And They Think I'm Just a Nice Old Lady": Women and War in Belfast, Northern Ireland'. *Gender, Place and Culture* 5(2): 159–176.

Enloe, C. 2000. *Manoeuvres: The International Politics of Militarizing Women's Lives.* Berkeley and Los Angeles: University of California.

Enloe, C. 2004. *The Curious Feminist: Searching For Women In A New Age of Empire.* Berkeley, CA: University of California Press.

Enloe, C. 2014. *Bananas, Beaches and Bases: Making Feminist Sense of International Politics*, 3rd edn. Berkeley, CA: University of California Press.

Forty, A. and S. Küchler. eds. 1999. *The Art of Forgetting.* Oxford: Bloomsbury Academic.

Graham, B. and Y. Whelan. 2007. 'The Legacies of the Dead: Commemorating the Troubles in Northern Ireland'. *Environment and Planning D: Society and Space* 25: 476–495.

Henshaw, A. 2016. 'Where Women Rebel'. *International Feminist Journal of Politics* 18(1): 39–60, DOI: 10.1080/14616742.2015.1007729

Henshaw, A. 2017. *Why Women Rebel. Understanding Women's Participation in Armed Rebel Groups.* London and New York: Routledge.

Humphreys, M., and J. M. Weinstein. 2004. 'What The Fighters Say: A Survey of Ex-Combatants in Sierra Leone'. Retrieved 11 December 2016. www.columbia.edu/~mh2245/Report1_BW.pdf.

Ibanez, A. 2001. 'El Salvador: War and Untold Stories: Women Guerrillas'. Pp. 117–130 in *Victims, Perpetrators or Actors: Gender, Armed Conflict and Political Violence*, edited by C. Moser and F. Clark. New York: Zed Books.

Irish Republican Army. 1977. *The Green Book.* Retrieved 11 December 2016. https://tensmiths.files.wordpress.com/2012/08/15914572-ira-green-book-volumes-1-and-2.pdf.

Jacobs, S., R. Jacobson and J. Marchbank. eds. 2000. *States of Conflict: Gender, Violence and Resistance.* London and New York: Zed Books.

Lorentzen, L. A. and J. Turpin. eds. 1998. *The Women and War Reader.* New York: New York University.

MacKenzie. M. H. 2012. *Female Soldiers In Sierra Leone: Sex, Security, and Post-Conflict Development.* New York: New York University Press.

Mazurana, D. and L. E. Cole. 2013. 'Women, Girls and Disarmament, Demobilisation and Reintegration'. Pp. 194–215 in *Women and Wars*, edited by C. Cohn. Cambridge: Polity Press.

McDowell, S. 2007. 'Armalite, the Ballot Box and Memorialisation: Sinn Féin and the State in Post-conflict Northern Ireland'. *The Round Table: The Commonwealth Journal of International Affairs* 96(3993): 725–738.

McDowell, S. 2008. 'Commemorating Dead 'Men': Gendering the Past and Present in Post-conflict Northern Ireland'. *Gender, Place and Culture* 15(4): 335–354.

McDowell, S. 2012. 'Symbolic Warfare in the Ethnocratic State: Conceptualising Memorialisation and Territoriality in Sri Lanka'. *Terrorism and Political Violence* 24(1): 22–37.

Meintjes, S., A. Pillay and M. Turshen. eds. 2001. *The Aftermath: Women in Post-Conflict Transformation.* London and New York: Zed Books.

Moloney, E. 2002. *A Secret History of the IRA*. London: Penguin.

Moser, C. and F. Clark. 2001. eds. *Victims, Perpetrators or Actors? Gender, Armed Conflict and Political Violence*. London: Zed Books.

Ni Aolain, F., D. F. Haynes and N. Cahn. 2011. *On the Frontlines: Gender, War and the Post-Conflict Process.* Oxford: Oxford University Press.

O'Keefe, T. 2013. *Feminist Identity Development and Activism in Revolutionary Movements*. London and New York: Palgrave Macmillan.

Ortega, L. 2015. 'Untapped Resources for Peace: A Comparative Study of Women's Organisation of Guerrilla Ex-Combatants in Colombia and El Salvador'. Pp. 232–249 in *Female Combatants in Conflict and Peace*, edited by S. Shekhawat. Basingstoke: Palgrave Macmillan.

Power, M. 2010. 'A Republican Who Wants to Further Women's Rights: Women, Provisional Republicanism, Feminism and Conflict in Northern Ireland'. Pp. 153–170 in *Irish Women at War: The Twentieth Century*, edited by G. McIntosh and D. Urguhart. Dublin and Portland: Irish Academic Press.

Rolston, B. 2003. 'Changing the Political Landscape: Mural and Transition In Northern Ireland'. *Irish Studies Review* 11(1): 3–16.

Shekhawat, S. and B. Pathak. 2015. 'Female Combatants, Peace Processes, and the Exclusion'. Pp. 53–68 in *Female Combatants in Conflict and Peace*, edited by S. Shekhawat. Basingstoke: Palgrave Macmillan.

Sjoberg, L. 2014. *Gender, War, and Conflict*. Cambridge: Polity.

Tickner, A. 1992. *Gender In International Relations: Feminist Perspectives on Achieving Global Security.* New York and Chichester: Columbia University Press.

Valliant, G., M. Kimmel, F. Malekahmadi, and J. Tyagi. 2012. 'The Gender of Resistance: A Case-Study Approach to Thinking About Gender in Violent Resistance Movements'. Pp. 55–76 in *Gender, Agency and Political Violence*, edited by L. Åhäll and L. Shepherd. Basingstoke: Palgrave Macmillan.

Ward, M. 1989. *Unmanageable Revolutionaries: Women and Irish Nationalism.* London: Pluto Press.

White, R. 2017. *'Out of the Ashes': An Oral History of the Provisional Irish Republican Movement.* Newbridge, Kildare: Merrion Press.

Yuval-Davis, N. 1997. *Gender and Nation*. London: Sage.

3 Gendering the post-conflict narrative

Introduction

Feminists have long argued that mainstream forms of conflict transition are highly gendered processes, inherently male-centred and focused towards specific concerns, particularly around issues of state security, 'good governance', and political and civil rights (Sjoberg 2010). Because gender is often either trivialised or rendered invisible, the post-war reconstruction period reflects the 'patriarchal order before the conflict' resulting in a settlement that refuses to incorporate gender issues at anything more than at a superficial and rhetorical level (Handrahan 2004: 440). Conflict resolution processes, particularly those associated with (re-)establishing formal political and civil institutions are largely shaped by patriarchal norms synonymous with liberal, representative democracies, and furthermore, assume and require a particular gender order (MacKenzie 2012; Ni Aolain *et al.* 2011). Given this, the discourse and politics of a post-conflict 'return to normal' inherently carries with it negative implications for women's political activism (Meintjes *et al.* 2001).

Furthermore, the idea that violence has neat start and end points exposes the inadequacies of those who seek to engineer a peace that deals only with the 'exceptional' violence of war. The continuum of violence resists any division between public and private domains, and, moreover, contends that the violence of armed conflict cannot be separated from other expressions of violence (Giles and Hyndman 2004). In every militarised society, war zone and refugee camp, violence against women and men transcends the simple diplomatic dichotomy of war and peace. While the continuum of violence highlights political, economic, and social forms of violence effecting women and men, a gendered continuum of violence demonstrates how gender links violence at different points on a scale reaching from the personal to the international; from the domestic home to the manoeuvres of tank columns (Cockburn 2004: 43). Furthermore, gender relations penetrate and shape the political, economic, and cultural forms of violence, and so therefore, any attempt to tackle violence of whatever sort or source must be attentive to gender relations and their power imbalances.

Using this framework, and drawing upon the post-war experiences of republican women in the North of Ireland, this chapter argues that the post-conflict moment as experienced by republican women represents not peace and security, but a continuity of gender discrimination, violence, and insecurity. While the Good Friday Agreement (hereafter the GFA) has and continues to draw plaudits both nationally and internationally as a model of conflict resolution, the everyday lives of republican women reveal a post-war landscape enmeshed in various forms of violence, oppression and insecurity. Though issues such as the partition of Ireland represent a continuity of oppression, the post-war period has also brought an increase in other forms of violence including gender-based violence, homophobic attacks, the crippling effects of neo-liberal austerity, and the continuing struggle for women's reproductive rights. Despite unambiguous commitments to gender equality and the promotion of women within the text of the 1998 peace accord, the chapter finds a more doleful reality from the perspective of republican women. While women are making moderate but important strides forward in formal politics, paid employment, among others, the alarming increases in gender-based violence and homophobic attacks in the aftermath of the peace accord challenges the dominant declarations of a peaceful, prosperous, and secure society. Despite the substantial tide of optimism among many in the aftermath of the agreement, the policy, practices and discourse of the ensuing peace process has failed to produce substantive changes for women, where gender equality remains a subsidiary aspiration (Cockburn 2013; O'Keefe 2012, 2013).

Feminist scholarship debunked many of the universalising myths regarding women's experiences of war and peace by diligently highlighting the heterogenous experiences among women. While these approaches provide a major contribution to how peace and security are conceptualised away from the needs of the state towards the needs of people, there remains a pressing gap in addressing how combatant women conceptualise peace and security. Laura Sjoberg argues that a critical reformulation or redefining of traditional notions of security occurs through explorations of new or previously neglected subjects, including combatant women (2010: 4). Recognising and exploring the experiences and needs of overlooked groups such as female soldiers and combatants adds new insights to on-going debates regarding human security as well as highlighting the limitations of anchoring approaches in highly generalised or universal accounts. This chapter therefore endeavours to provide new insights by exploring the visions of peace and security from the perspective of former combatant republican women in Ireland.

'No link to England': republicans at peace?

Given the deeply polarised conditions that envelop most post-war regions, including northern Irish society, women do not represent a homogenous bloc, and so being attentive to the differences as well as the similarities among women needs to be foregrounded. The depiction of women's insecurity as constituted by intersecting forces of patriarchy, imperialism, and neo-liberal capitalism problematises not only the male-dominated conventional approaches to peace and

Gendering the post-conflict narrative 75

security. but also delineates a complex and often conflicting set of needs, interests and experiences. The substantial and various forms of insecurity experienced by republican women since the declaration of peace in 1998 adds important testimonies to those of combatant women in other regions, and I suggest, provides the basis for expanding feminist endeavours to dislodge conventional understandings and moreover, construct a genuinely inclusive feminist vision of peace and security. Any attempt to generalise about war is bound to demean the experiences of individuals caught up in it (El-Bushra and Mukarubuga 1995). In the field of peace-building and post-conflict social reconstruction, 'there are huge risks in over-generalising and thereby failing to understand the dynamics of power inherent in each situation. We need a definition of peace which encompasses the *totality* of women's needs and interests' (El-Bushra 2007: 143–144).

After 30 years of armed conflict, which claimed the lives of over 3700 people, the GFA signed in April 1998 marked a formal end to the violence that had characterised the conflict up to that point. The centre-piece of the GFA was a political framework in which the two polarised ethno-national blocs would share institutional power-sharing within political apparatus which adhered largely to a consociation democracy. The 10th of April 2018 marked the calendar date 20 years on from the GFA. Even though power-sharing between nationalists and unionists remains suspended, the 20th anniversary provided an opportunity to invite the key players from the 1998 talks to critically reflect on the agreement and its effectiveness to deliver peace. Former US president Bill Clinton spoke at a series of events in Belfast and Dublin and, once again, he reaffirmed his belief that the 1998 peace accord was a

> work of genius that's applicable if you care at all about preserving democracy ... because it called for real democracy, majority rule, minority rights, individual rights, the rule of law, the end of violence, shared political decision-making, shared economic benefits, shared special relationships.
> (Kelly 2018)

It was, of course, an overwhelmingly male-dominated series of events and public engagements in which peace and security were presented as gender-less, universal, and objective. The substance of Clinton's assertion was a firm belief that the North of Ireland is at peace, and has largely been so for the last 20 years, a view predicated on the notion that the absence of military actions and the establishment of formal democratic institutions denotes the presence of peace. Over two decades on from the signing of the GFA, acts of politically motivated violence that were once commonplace have become rare. While a great deal has undoubtedly changed for the better, the reality of post-war life in the North of Ireland indicate a society riddled with various forms of political, economic, and social forms of violence. Despite its many critics, the Irish peace process and the GFA is still held in high esteem by many and is often cited as a prudent model of conflict resolution, so much so that some have argued for its application to

76 *Gendering the post-conflict narrative*

other regions embroiled in armed conflict (Coakley 2008; McGarry 2001). While the merits of such claims are widely contested within academic literature, there is broad consensus that the peace process and GFA is a success story for Sinn Féin and Provisional republicanism (Bean 2007; Maillot 2005; Frampton 2009). However, republican appraisals of the peace process thus far, have been largely male.

When asked if the North of Ireland is a place at peace, all research participants were unequivocal in answering 'no'. Despite the many claims, by senior republicans, international political figures, mainstream commentators, and some academics, that the North is a society making steady progress through a successful conflict transition, the republicans here offer a rather different appraisal. Anne, a former IRA prisoner who now works solely for Sinn Féin typifies most of the responses:

> Well, there are no soldiers on the ground and that's what we were used to. So peace to me means a 32 county all Ireland. Now that hasn't happened yet but peace to me has no link to England so it's confusing to say the North is at peace.

As republicans, interviewees state that they fought an armed struggle with the objective of removing a British imperial presence in Ireland to create a unified all-Ireland nation-state. While the predominantly male republican leadership talk of a society at peace, there appears to be a profound disconnect between that and the narrative expressed here:

NIAMH: Nothing has changed, they're not away, the Brits are not away. The struggle, albeit now a political struggle, is still there and remains until they go. So it's very important that, and I have no intentions of stopping, it is important that young people get in and fulfil the roles and carry on until the Brits are gone.

Niamh's extract illustrates the widespread contention among interviewees that the 'Brits', representing British occupation and the partition of Ireland, remain and that this fundamentally contradicts the notion of a society at peace. Interview data indicates a distinction between ending armed actions against the British state and ending the struggle against occupation. For interviewees, a genuine end to war can only be brought about by eradicating what they see as the source of Ireland's problems. In other words, the core principle for peace is British withdrawal, not silencing weapons. Cathy was born and reared in a large town close to the Irish border. She comes from a republican family and in her teenage years joined Sinn Féin during the 1980 and 1981 Hunger Strikes. She is the chair of the local Sinn Féin *cumann*[1] as well as being involved in several community groups. She also volunteers for a local organisation that provides vital services for people with special needs. Her thoughts here are typical of those elicited from others interviewed:

> I was always more interested in getting the British out of our country as opposed to wanting peace so that goal of getting them out and staying out is still there because we haven't achieved that yet. So that is what peace means to me and we can't have peace until we get the Brits out. So there is potential for conflict to start again and that is why you have these dissident groups. So let's remove the British and then we can get on with other issues around social justice, redistribution of wealth and justice and fairness for all, equality for all.

Republican women interviewed tend to collapse the struggle for peace into the struggle for a British withdrawal from Ireland: the two are inextricably linked. Peace is visualised as an outcome that can only be achieved through the removal of British jurisdiction over the North of Ireland. Conventional tropes tend to designate women's peace activism as 'apolitical', motivated by some innate desire of 'just wanting peace' (Anderlini 2007: 59). Defying the gender stereotype enforced by dominant narratives, the collective priority for republican women is not 'peace' for the sake of ending armed violence, but peace via the establishment of a new anti-imperial reality. Cathy's description that she was 'always more interested in getting the British out' is emblematic of the fact that interviewees conceptualise imperialism as the antithesis of a genuine peace. For most interviewees, peace is conditional on the end of imperialism, as opposed to the end of armed actions. Republican women do not necessarily want to end violence for the sake of violence, they want to end occupation.

The universalising tendencies within conventional approaches to war and peace typically homogenise women as a unitary group while simultaneously positioning them as 'outsiders' to the conflict. Such approaches assume they are neither representatives of warring parties nor members of other groups involved in war (Jansson and Eduards 2016: 7). These tropes typically find clear expression in the persistent conflation of women with peace and/or victimhood, so much so that the 'women and peace' hypothesis remains a dominant conceptual frame in which the role of gender in conflict zones is analysed (Aharoni 2017). While women's pursuit of peace and non-violence creates spaces for mobilisation, activism, and the pursuit of social justice, theoretically the idea that shared gender indicates a shared meaning of peace is highly problematic. It neglects the historical and cultural specificities that shape women's identities, needs, and interests, and assumes that women primarily interpret or construct their political identities in a one-dimensional way, that being through gender, without taking seriously their ethnic, national, racial identities. The deliberate positioning of women as 'outsiders' to the conflict is premised on a myth that women do not have an interest or stake in ethno-national politics. While women (and, of course, men) do often oppose violence, there are others who support or are directly involved in armed actions to resist various forms of oppression. Based on reductive gender stereotypes, it is often assumed that women apparently have 'softer' and more peaceful qualities (McLeod 2011: 600). In her assessment of Palestinian women, Sarai Aharoni (2017) criticises the liberal conflation of 'gender equality with peace' as a configuration which presupposes peace as a common aspiration and interest to *all* women. Such an assumption obscures the specific political and social contexts within which political violence is used, and moreover, silences the contradictory needs and concerns of women such as military occupation (2016: 4). Given their republican politics, the statements above are unsurprising but they are nevertheless powerful in that they conceive of 'peace' in a manner which again positions them as 'outsiders' within the outsider category. Conventional approaches, which accentuate women's unified partiality for peace and opposition to violence, neglect the ways in which experiences of occupation and imperialism delineates a particular standpoint on peace and equality.

There is palpable confusion and discomfort, even among those interviewees most supportive of the republican leadership, in accepting the prevailing discourse of a 'society at peace' given that the North retains a British presence for the foreseeable future. This is perhaps most pronounced when dealing with the issue of policing. Even though Sinn Féin signed up to accepting the Police Service of Northern Ireland (hereafter the PSNI)[2] in 2007, interviewees have huge difficulties accepting the PSNI, whom many see as no different to the force it replaces, the much-derided Royal Ulster Constabulary[3] (hereafter the RUC). For many, policing in the North still retains the vestiges of imperial links and the PSNI remains a partial force of unionism:

GEMMA: There is a lot of difficulty in the peace process [for republicans] too; the ceasefire, great, the GFA was great ... I could live with that but there were other things. Handing over the [IRA] weapons ... (pause three seconds) ... I remember crying over it. Policing, policing which was a *huge* issue (emphasis in the original), I was tortured over that, but I knew from earlier in the talks that the policing thing was going to happen no matter what. Emotionally the second phase of the struggle [peace process] was more difficult ... the decommissioning, the policing ... and we lost a lot of people over that issue. Like even now I sit in meetings with the police and I feel like a traitor, like I'm doing something I shouldn't be doing.

SIOBHAN: See if people rang the RUC, or the PSNI now as they like to call themselves, and they didn't respond and all that then we'd be onto them. So we are saying to people, 'look if we want to live into a normal society then we're going to have to have a police service as opposed to a police force'. So there is still a lot of mistrust and it is changing slowly. I staff the [Sinn Féin] centre on a Thursday night and there's people coming in looking for republicans to sort this or that out and we're having to say no we can't do that, you'll need to ring the police and people saying 'no way, don't trust them'. But it is going to take a long time to achieve a real impartial police force.

Siobhan's extract provides an insight into the republican appraisal of the 'new' police force. Like so many republicans, Siobhan sees little or no difference between the PSNI and the much-despised RUC. When asked to elaborate on

Gendering the post-conflict narrative 79

why she continues to call the police the RUC she replies, 'because nothing has changed, it's the same people using a different name'. Bernie explains that 'there are still plenty of peelers[4] who are on a war footing, who don't like change, don't want change'. Many republicans continue to view the police as hostile, partial, unionist, and ultimately part of British imperialism in Ireland.

ORLA: I mean we get people in here [community centre] every day with lots of complaints about anti-social behaviour or whatever and the answer given to them is 'go to the peelers' and they go 'I wouldn't phone the peelers' … it's odd. I don't think the message is getting out there. People are just expected to have blind faith in them [the republican leadership]. So it's a hard pill for people to swallow.

The resistance to engaging with the PSNI as described by both Orla and Siobhan, and others, indicates how large sections within working-class nationalist/republican communities, continue to regard the police with mistrust and disdain, undoubtedly a residual effect of 'the Troubles' (Jarman 2004: 430; Maillot 2005). Despite the resounding declarations of a new dawn for the North of Ireland within the mainstream discourse, in many respects, the fundamentals of the conflict remain unchanged.

In addition, on-going issues around growing sectarianism and (often violently) contested issues regarding parades, flags and emblems appear rooted in the historical legacy of British imperialism. Orla, a former IRA prisoner who now runs a community centre in a working-class community in Belfast:

Have a look around this community and you tell me where the peace is. We're surrounded by so-called peace walls, held to hostage, and hemmed in during hundreds of Loyalist marches every year, people are losing their jobs, benefits, services are being cut, women are coming to us with issues of domestic abuse, alcohol abuse. Now the British Army are off the streets and Sinn Féin are in power and that's great … but there are still issues on the ground with the new police, real issues with that new force. So really, on a ground level, what has really changed for the people of this area in the last 15 years? What peace? I don't see it.

This extract is tightly packed with multiple and overlapping issues and represents the archetypical narrative that runs right through most interviews when exploring the peace, or lack thereof. A genuine peace process according to them involves far more than the cessation of 'conventional' armed violence and a negotiated settlement at a formal level. The vision of peace here is a broad one, encompassing macro historical processes of imperialism right down to the immediacy of domestic and gender-based violence on an everyday level. Orla's reference to being 'hemmed in by so-called peace walls' refers to the segregation of residential homes, particularly in Belfast city. Housing segregation illuminates the widening divisions in the North more than any other.

LINDA: Has anything really moved on? Look at the peace walls ... where is the community and peace between Catholics and Protestants? Because if we were really in a post-conflict society, then you wouldn't have these peace walls and people who live there would tell you that if those walls came down tomorrow, they'd be tortured on both sides.

Previous research indicates that 35–40 per cent of Catholics and Protestants live in communities divided along ethno-national/sectarian lines (Hughes *et al.* 2007). The physical division between opposing traditions appears to adhere to lines of social class, with disadvantaged working-class areas significantly more likely to be highly segregated than more affluent areas (Shirlow 2001). Research on segregated communities reveals daily experiences of fear, anxiety, suspicion, and a sense of threat among residents, transforming physical barriers into psychological barriers among citizens of the North (Hughes at al. 2007; Shirlow 2001). Alarmingly, despite the announcements from the upper echelons of the political classes regarding a society at peace, residential segregation has increased since the signing of the GFA in 1998 (Hughes *et al.* 2007). In the aftermath of the 1994 ceasefires, interface and communal violence increased significantly, with some claiming it as the worst rioting period since the early 1970s (Jarman 2004: 421).

Republican women maintain that issues of growing sectarianism, like many of Ireland's political and social ills, stem from the partition of the country. These ongoing issues only serve to augment their belief that a true and lasting peace can only occur within a united Ireland, free from what they see as 'imperial interference'. The data and discussion advanced thus far indicates the pitfalls of homogenising women's visions and meanings of peace within ill-informed conventional approaches. Conventional discursive and cultural representations of women and peace fabricates a narrative that peace and the ending of armed actions is in the interest of all women (Aharoni 2017: 314). Consequently, it distorts our view of women's realities in conflict zones by ignoring the processes and structures that shape the myriad of roles women undertake in times of armed conflict. While often women do work to end armed actions, it is important to be attentive to the reality that women are also engaged in armed groups to resist various forms of oppression. If the diversity of roles, needs, identities, and interests of women during times of war is accepted and acknowledged, then it surely follows that there exists a diversity of security concerns among women after war. While gender as a variable and power relations can and do produce differences between women and men in conflict zones, cross-cutting social and political cleavages such as nationalism invariably produces areas of convergence. Just like their male comrades, republican women have a vested interest in ending imperialism and occupation as key preconditions for a genuine peace. In her field work in Palestine and Israel, Aharoni (2017) finds that women's vision of peace is invariably shaped by structural conditions, economic vulnerability, and ethnic discrimination. Women's experiences of war, their ethno-national identities, class position, and, of course, their gendered lives determine their visions of peace and security. While the ending of imperialism as an essential pre-condition for a genuine peace is unsurprising, the post-war everyday lives of republican women also reveal other forms of violence and insecurity.

'Despair and the dole': positive peace in the context of neo-liberal capitalism?

In addition to the faith placed in liberal representative democracy, proponents of the dominant liberal peace model remain wedded to the 'virtues of free-market enterprise, private finance initiatives to bolster public services and foreign direct investment' (Nagel 2018: 404), a belief that unfettered, free-market enterprise are the most effective mechanisms for delivering 'peace and prosperity' for all. When asked to describe what a genuine peace looks like, all research participants articulated an anti-capitalist, pro-equality and social justice vision of a positive peace. The voices of Irish republican women resonate with the feminist contention that peace is not simply the absence of armed actions, but the elimination of 'other' threats such as poverty, political exclusion, economic marginalisation, and the threat of violence from men (Jansson and Eduards 2016).

Joanne was born and still lives in a small, rural village close to the Irish border. Hailing from a strong republican family, armed conflict and political debate was a familiar feature of her household life. The political talk in her house is critical of both the political establishment in the South and in the North. In the early 1990s she was elected as a local councillor but resigned due to the conflicting demands of her paid job, her children, and the demands of constituency work as a councillor. She remains a committed republican and member of Sinn Féin.

> Peace first and foremost means that people are not killed, and nobody is going to prison. I would like to see a united Ireland but there is no point in having a united Ireland if it is going to be run like the Twenty-Six Counties. Because I feel that the government there disgusts me, and it is not right with people living on the breadline. James Connolly's vision of an Ireland that is equal, for men, women and children being treated properly because that is so important, that is real peace.

Here, Joanne is concerned first and foremost with ending 'occupation'. The latter part of this extract links that national struggle with a socialist one, particularly her reference to republican socialist James Connolly. Peace is the ending of partition, but it also means the radical transformation of peoples' material living conditions. Many interviewees exhibit a critical awareness regarding the transformative potential of a united Ireland as a political starting point, not an end. There is no evidence in the data of 'blind faith' in the idea that a united Ireland represents the elusive panacea required to address Ireland's many political and social ills. Removing the yoke of imperialism therefore represents formative steps in a broader political struggle towards creating a society in which the most marginalised must feel the benefits of a genuine peace. Here, the data is theoretically consistent with the idea of positive and negative peace. In simple and succinct terms, Galtung (1969) states that while the latter refers to the absence of direct and observable violence, the former denotes the eradication of structural violence such as poverty and cultural violence, which allows such violence to be rationalised or normalised. Structural violence occurs when social and economic conditions inflict pains, suffering and death as a direct outcome of the unequal distribution of resources (Galtung 1969). The pioneering definition of a positive peace, therefore, expands the very narrow definition of violence solely as direct violence to include what is considered 'normalised violence' and this appears to be the definition most commonly held by the republican women. According to Bronagh:

> What's the point in having a united Ireland if people live in poverty, live with injustice, I couldn't see myself being happy with a united Ireland while people were still living in slums in this city. It is also about harmony and social justice and that is all about people living in peace. That is what peace means to me, you know.

According to Emily, 'peace has to have some indication as to how the lives of the masses has changed for the better; while people are being harassed and exploited, you can't call that a peaceful society'. When asked to elaborate further, she clarifies that 'harassment by the peelers and exploitation as workers by the capitalist system'. Eileen outlines her frustrations at the lack of peace for working-class people:

> Peace is about changing society and we need to try and change things that'll improve peoples' quality of life and what you have now are these myths that things are better now. Look at all these young people going to school, battling through all of that, going to university and what have they got at the end of it all? Despair and the dole. Suicide is increasing and will get worse. People were led to believe that you can get money from anywhere and this whole Celtic Tiger[5] nonsense. Look at all the bankers, where governments bailed out banks and enforced cuts on people. So what is peace? The North certainly is not at peace, I don't think so. Yes, there are no troops on the streets, you don't have street battles going on everyday but to me there's more to peace than just ending armed struggle.

Colin Coulter (2014) argues that the official narrative of the North of Ireland as a post-conflict prosperous and progressive society, fails to square with the hardships and realities of daily life for many. Eileen, like so many other interviewees, endure and experience a rather different social and political world than that described by the elite architects of peace, uncovering the partiality and myths which undergird the mainstream discourse. While the removal of the 'British presence' in the North is unsurprisingly a pressing concern, advanced capitalism and the salience of social class remains prominent among interviewees. The 'violence' of global capitalism, seen most overtly in the wielding of cuts to vital services and in state funding of failed banks, remains a prominent and daily source of women's insecurity. The vision of peace articulated here requires far more than the measures of increasing women's visibility or the active participation of a select few within existing institutions. On the contrary, a significant number of republican women believed that existing political institutions and structures are complicit in the 'post-war violence' by virtue of their role in the administration of austerity and vast levels of inequality.

LINDA: I would love peace to have meant that we were sitting here in an Ireland that was trying to deliver some sort of socialist politics. That is what I see as peace, that we are all in to try and make life better for everyone in this country, that's what I'd love to see in peace.

JANETTE: Even when we do get a 32 county republic we're going to have to realise that it's Angela Merkel and the IMF that is running the show now and that uniforms and guns are not going to be as important as pounds and euros. I mean, look at the state of the South of Ireland and that can be very depressing. Now people are looking at banks as the new enemies; they don't need uniforms, they just wear suits. So when you look at citizens bailing out banks, why did that happen? So now it's like more than Brits out, it's also big business out and all these people and all of what is happening with our brothers and sisters in the developing world.

It is interesting to see how some interviewees depict transnational capitalism as similar in effect to the British army, that being a foreign force of oppression and occupation. Once again, interviewees are critically aware that the goal of a united Ireland is meaningless if the capitalist system of inequality and austerity prevails; removing the British from the North of Ireland does little to disturb the powerful position of banks or bodies such as the IMF. While their formative meaning of peace is viewed within a strictly nationalist ideological outlook, their conceptualisation of a genuine peace is also shaped by a class perspective. Republican women see the exploitation of capitalism, unemployment, economic austerity as the anti-thesis of a genuine peace.

The current global crisis in capitalism has inflicted devastating austerity cuts on services and provisions that are vital to working-class communities. The 'war on women' campaign in the United States has highlighted the ways in which violence against women is exacerbated by austerity economic policies, disproportionately impacting on women located in areas of socio-economic disadvantage (True 2015: 563). As the current crisis of global capitalism continues, the last ten years of devastating austerity under the auspices of male-dominated global, macro-economic policies, are fundamentally premised on the exploitation of women's labour through low-paid, low-status precarious work (Rai and Waylen 2013). Republican women here connect the daily personal struggles of women in working-class communities to national and global forces of neo-liberal capitalism. Many interviewees see these cuts not only as class based but also gender based:

> LINDA: Particularly now with this right-wing Tory government and you have Sinn Féin implementing right wing conservative politics. You have these austerity cuts coming in and we already have high levels of poverty here and high levels and instances of abuse, suicide. All the things that go with a community coming out of conflict-so now we're going to get hit with these huge measures which are aimed straight at the poor. We are going to have a lot of women sitting out there because women do bear the brunt of a lot of the economic burden for the family still. And this will have a serious knock on effect on what women are going to need so I think the various Women's Centres are going to be even busier in the coming years.

Latest research from Women's Resource and Development Agency (WRDA) found that nearly half of full-time female employees in the North were employed in public administration, education, and health, compared with just 23 per cent of men. Overall, women accounted for almost two-thirds of the public-sector workforce. Attacks on workers' terms and conditions have also had a gender dimension, as 37 per cent of women worked part-time, compared with just 8 per cent of men, meaning most of all part-time employees were women (Hinds 2011). It is women who are mainly on zero-hour contracts, with zero sick pay and zero holiday pay. Under the guise of 'returning to growth' or the 'road to recovery' the British Government has for the last ten years driven an accelerated agenda of devastating austerity, with a strategy of reducing the national deficit by a 3:1 ratio of public spending cuts to tax revenues. Given women's prominence in public sector employment in the North of Ireland, coupled with the wholesale funding cuts to services such as childcare, healthcare, dedicated domestic violence, it is women, and particularly working-class women who are shouldering the weight of austerity (Molan 2012). Feminist scholars have long highlighted that the security of the state often comes at the expense of citizen's insecurity (Sjoberg 2014). Even though working-class women benefited least from the so-called boom years of capitalism, the 'security' and well-being of the national economy is built upon the insecurity of women.

Class and gender oppression work together rather than separately (Whitworth 1994: 27). The state utilises gender and the gender division of labour with regards to austerity to serve its own needs. In Latin America, Safa (1990) finds that austerity programs at the behest of the IMF, have deeply devastating impacts on children and women, whereby state subsidies for basic foods are eliminated, government cuts in social services such as health and education reinforce the need for collective action (1990: 356–357). Cynthia Enloe's (2004) examination of the IMF's austerity measures reveals their gendered nature and outcome. She argues that a government's ability to maintain its legitimacy depends at least on the capacity of families to tolerate those measures, specifically on the capacity of women to stretch their budgets, to continue to feed, clothe and care for their families. This may include severe domestic financial management as a well as travelling abroad as foreign domestic servants, often with the requirement that a significant proportion of their salaries be repatriated back to the home country.

In other words, the politics of austerity is not only class based but also deeply gendered. Interview data concurs with existing research conducted in other 'post-conflict' regions such as South Africa where participants involved in peace-building emphasise the meeting of basic needs such as food and shelter as opposed to the security of the state (McKay and Rey 2002). Peace based upon social justice is rooted in the immediacy of fulfilling human needs (Porter 2003: 257). Formal declarations regarding the North as a 'society at peace' generates a narrative that the current dispensation is universally beneficial for all, yet the evidence here suggest that a genuine 'peace' involving social justice has yet to yield any discernible results in the lives of working-class, republican communities.

In addition to insidious forms of fiscal austerity, the lack of a genuine 'peace dividend' is expressed by many. Eileen who joined the IRA in Belfast in the 1970s vents her frustration at the lack of 'peace dividend' for those communities who need it most:

> When I think of peace I think of something better for the people on the ground and when I look around I don't think it has. They talk of the peace dividend and you look around working class areas of Belfast and Derry. How has life improved for them? It hasn't. Peoples' lives in some regards have gotten worse. Have a look at the Falls today; it is being destroyed by anti-social behaviour and government cuts and lack of investment. For a real peace, you have to [be] actually making improvements to peoples' lives. What we have here is a manufactured peace.

Liberal peace has dominated both national and international approaches to resolving armed conflict, a peace which seeks to export a particularly Western vision of peace and security while reinforcing the privileged positions of elites (Mac Ginty and Williams 2009). The tenets of liberal peace are premised on representative democracy, secure borders, primacy of the individual, law and order, ownership of private property, and, of course, an unbending belief that the unfettered forces of the capitalist market will ensure peace, security, and prosperity for all (Duffield 2014; Mac Ginty 2015; Mac Ginty and Williams 2009). A key component of the formal peace process was the notion of a peace dividend as mentioned by Eileen and others. New-found economic prosperity for the masses would be the key ingredient within the elite-devised recipe for peace. In rather basic terms, when political violence ended, the 'mess of the war' would be swept up, presenting a blank canvass for global capitalists and multinational firms to design a new post-ceasefire economic landscape. According to Colin Coulter (2014), neoliberal economics was a fundamental girder that underpinned the mainstream discourse and approach to 'selling the peace' in the North of Ireland, particularly to those in working class communities. It was essentially a political promise of economic rewards for the abandonment of political violence, that being 'substantial inward investment and job creation' (O'Hearn 2008: 102). During the formative years of the peace process and throughout the negotiated settlement, the strategy to assuage republican or unionist fears of 'political sell-out' was quite simple; what is lost politically would be adequately compensated for financially.

> EDEL: There are whole swathes of society that are at peace. The areas that were disproportionality affected by the conflict, there is a micro conflict there and that is very worrying. There hasn't been the economic regeneration of West and North Belfast. Unemployment rates in Ballymurphy[6] are the same today as they were in 1994 so something has failed there, seriously failed ... social infrastructure is just as poor as it was back then as well. So you know, we [republicans] weren't particularly strategic at those because we were focused on early release of prisoners, policing, all those big things that have traditionally taken the focus while social and economic rights did not.

Edel's comments regarding the lack of peace for those who endured the worst of the war is shared by many other interviewees. In common with other regions blighted by armed conflict, those areas which endured the worst of the violence tend to benefit least from the peace. West and North Belfast remain the poorest parts of the North of Ireland where poverty is markedly concentrated (Horgan 2006). It is unsurprising that the so-called peace dividend 'has accrued not to the poorest sections of society in the six counties but rather to those who already enjoyed considerable privilege' (Coulter 2014: 767). Those areas blighted most by social deprivation are also those which endured the burden of the armed conflict. Current statistics puts West Belfast as the area of highest unemployment in the North, followed very closely by North Belfast. Unemployment claimant percentages put West Belfast at 9.6 per cent, doubling that of the more affluent South Belfast. Statistics indicate that the number of people in the region earning less than £7.50 per hour rose from 170,000 to 195,000 in the decade to 2011 (Coulter 2014: 767).

The much promised 'peace dividend' has failed to make significant changes in the lives of those in the most marginalised communities. The primary focus of the elite architects of peace was on the security of the state and related matters, while social and economic issues were left to the fickle market forces of neo-liberalism. Given Sinn Féin's declared socialist ideology and their stated opposition to austerity, their central role in the Stormont Government has done little to over-turn or resist neo-liberal austerity. For instance, in 2012 the North of Ireland's Finance Minister, Sinn Féin's Máirtín Ó Muilleoir advocated (and continues to advocate) for the lowering of corporate tax from 20 per cent to match the South of Ireland's 12.5 per cent tax, despite the unanimity among left-wing groups, political parties, and organisations demanding an increase in the tax contributions from Ireland's multi-national corporations. Considering this, it suggests that the real issue at stake perhaps, is not the personnel (male or female) charged with steering the state but with the actual institutions themselves. Despite their commitments to an anti-austerity agenda, Sinn Féin in government appears either incapable or unwilling to alter the administration of capitalist economic policies. A genuine peace according to republican women is the overhaul of the existing capitalist structures to redistribute the wealth from the few to the many. According to those interviewed, a genuine peace can only exist when the communities who bore the brunt of the armed conflict experience the same services and opportunities afforded to those more affluent communities in the North. This, of course, presents many contradictions given their party's role in government alongside the centre-right Democratic Unionist Party (DUP). Given the crippling levels of austerity meted out over the course of the last ten years, Sinn Féin stand accused by their opponents of espousing socialism while simultaneously embracing capitalism and austerity by their role in the North of Ireland Government.

Notwithstanding these contradictions, the grim reality of social deprivation in the wake of state-led austerity is cited as a specific barrier to a genuine peace. Cutbacks in funding public services are viewed as direct targets against the working-classes and working-class women.

SIOBHAN: When it [community centre] first started [in 1996] there were 50 people coming through it a year, this year we've had 670 referrals through the doors. A lot of them are people impacted by the conflict and now it's under threat at the minute from funding cuts. The end result will be to re-traumatise those who have already been traumatised. It's going to cause more division … and this is only one part of it, there are lots of other things I see. You know so, what's changed?

When I asked Siobhan to elaborate on what she means when she asks, 'what's changed' she replies that 'it is like one type of conflict has replaced another'.

KELLY: How can you have peace if there isn't enough funding for counselling, not enough funding for the health of people, and education and they have to be the key things for looking after people; housing, health and education, I think they should be the focus for politics.
FIONA: You have to have equality and we didn't have that when we were growing up. So it is more than just having no violence or no war. We need to make the quality of our peoples' lives much better because if we don't what's the point? So peace is not just the absence of violence, it's about adding on to our society and building a better society for our young people.

While those in positions of state power decree that austerity is a necessary measure, republican women view it as a form of violence and a tenacious obstacle to a genuine peace. One of the key tenets rooted in top-down, liberal peacemaking has been the virtues and ability of free market economies to provide employment, security and wealth distribution in an equitable way that reduces the risks of a return to armed actions. Despite the passage of 20 years since the

GFA, the propensity of its chief architects to exalt its virtues contrasts with the reality of 'post-conflict' life in the North of Ireland where neo-liberal capitalism is not only incapable of tackling rising rates of poverty, gender job segregation, escalating mental health, but is itself a source of conflict. To be sure, the material peace dividend is not a myth, but its discursive representations as universal is certainly a work of fiction. There is, of course, much evidence of growing inward investment, rising consumption and a thriving tourist industry but the spoils of peace are unevenly distributed. The evidence however, consistently demonstrates that the areas and the persons who suffered the most during the conflict have benefited materially least from the peace. Conventional security approaches, dominated by the schools of realism and liberalism, hold that security threats are invariably those which are external to the state. State-centric constructions of security frames external threats as solely 'military threats', and therefore excludes the possibility that states may be the actors that threaten the security of their own citizens (Shepherd 2008; Sjoberg 2014; Tickner 1992; Wibben 2011). Architects of such frameworks endeavour to associate security solely with the interests of the state, thus trivialising and normalising forms of economic violence and insecurity. Positioning global capitalism as a source of insecurity challenges the state-centric security logic which endeavours to normalise such sources of insecurity by excluding it from the discourse and agenda of conflict transition. While unquestionably austerity was felt by all regions of the UK and Ireland during the latest crisis in global capitalism, the pernicious effects of economic austerity were acutely felt in the North of Ireland where the economy relies heavily on the public sector and central funding from the UK Government (Nagel 2018). Moreover, the unresolved scars of armed conflict serve to exacerbate the impact of austerity in the region.

Conceptualising women's equality

Gender-based violence

The UN Security Council released a world-wide statement on International Women's Day on 8 March 2000, which declared that: 'Peace is inextricably linked with equality between women and men'. The statement then goes on to affirm that

> the equal access and full participation of women in power structures and their full involvement in all efforts for the prevention and resolution of conflicts are essential for the maintenance and promotion of peace and security. If women are to play an equal part in security and maintaining peace, they must be empowered politically and economically, and represented adequately at all levels of decision-making, both at the pre-conflict stage and during hostilities, as well as at the point of peacekeeping, peace-building, reconciliation and reconstruction.
>
> (United Nations 2000)

Gender equality is cited as a fundamental principle of Provisional republicanism (Maillot 2005; Power 2010). For most interviewees, the path to peace and women's rights is cited as the eradication of gender-based violence, the increased provision of services to meet women's needs and interests and the right to access reproductive health care. When asked to describe gender equality in relation to peace, women's formal participation within institutional politics was largely absent among interviewees. While republican women do see women's role in formal politics as important, most articulated such a view in the context of their continuing activism (Chapter 5), not in the context of conceptualising women's equality and peace. In addition, not a single interviewee referenced the widely hailed 'gender equality' provision with the GFA. Breda joined the IRA in Belfast in the early 1970s and eventually ended up 'going on the run'. She relocated to the South of Ireland where she remains a full-time Sinn Féin and community activist. Her community activism focuses on providing essential services to the young and elderly in a working-class community.

> Peace to me is equality for all, including women. The North is getting there but it's not at peace. There is peace as such in terms of that [*sic*] you're not being stopped and searched, not stopping at barriers. There is still people being stopped by the police and homes being raided but compared to the scale before, it is way, way down. So the Brits are gone off the streets, but you need equality among the people, men, and women, and certainly that's not there at the minute.

A belief is expressed in the interview data that women achieving equality is a pre-condition for a meaningful peace. Joanne, a former elected representative, articulates her views:

> Look at what happened after the British left the South of Ireland. Nothing really changed [for women], they changed the name and they changed the crown to a harp. De Valera[7] was supposed to be this big revolutionary and he did serious damage to women in this country, him and his cronies. So I do see gender equality as part of the whole peace thing because there is no use in talking about equality if everyone is not going to benefit from it. And there is such inequality for women in this country.

Joanne's comments show how interviewees see the end of partition as falling short of achieving peace unless women's equality is a fundamental outcome. The ending of partition does not automatically produce women's equality and so the eradication of patriarchal oppression remains a firm pre-condition to a just and peaceful society.

When asked to describe women's equality and women's rights, interviewees made little reference to their position within formal political structures and instead projected a vision of equality as an eradication of gender-based violence, the provision of vital services and access to full reproductive rights.

SANDRA: To have peace you have to have women's equality and so you need to have certain services as a minimum. In order for women to access equality we have [here in the Women's Centre] childcare, advice units, which helps around benefits, housing, domestic violence, and we work around immigration also. We also do a whole array of education courses and delivering computer courses. We are also community advocates around issues of suicide, among many other issues. That, to me, is how you pursue equality for women.

Many Women's Centres in Belfast provide essential services, space, and refuge for women, particularly those in working-class communities. Republican women, including many in this research, are deeply embedded in these centres, dealing with vastly increased levels of violence against women in the so-called 'post-conflict' period. In general, the term 'post-conflict' refers to the period when predominantly male combatants have ceased to engage in 'official' war (Handrahan 2004; McLeod 2011). Feminists reconceptualise 'post-conflict as a period of continued violence and insecurity for women' (McLeod 2011: 599), where they remain socially, politically and economically marginalised and exposed to various forms of physical violence, which paradoxically appears to increase in the aftermath of war (Cockburn 2013; Karam 2001; Kelly 2000; Krog 2001). Gender-based violence, domestic violence, increasing homophobia, and restriction on women's reproductive rights remain key sources of women's insecurity in societies emerging from armed conflict.

Drawing upon a constructivist view, I use the term gender-based violence to examine various forms of increasing violence in the aftermath of armed conflict. There are several reasons for this. First and foremost, gender-based violence offers a broad category in which various forms of violence against men can be included. Laura Sjoberg (2014) convincingly argues that gender assumptions regarding actor/victim in conflict impinges upon our reality of men and women's experiences of war and precludes violence inflicted upon men. Second, the constructivist view allows for a fluidity and multiplicity of roles and experiences. Imposed binaries such as victim/protagonist or power/powerless are often gendered and serve to conceal the variety of men and women's experiences of war. Rigid and often imprecise dichotomous labels and categories circumvent the breadth and diversity of roles. For instance, undertaking a fighting role within a military is assumed to preclude one from also being a victim. In conceptual terms, combatant women clearly defy the gendered conflation with victimhood but, nevertheless, it is assumed their combatant role also defies other experiences. Finally, it allows for examination of violence against LGBT persons or those deemed to fall short of their normative gender identity (Shepherd 2008). Such an approach shifts the analysis away from reductive essentialist approaches and instead, positions post-war gender violence as constitutive of power relations.

In the North of Ireland, the aftermath of the 1994 ceasefires witnessed an escalation of varied forms of violence against women, indicating that the formal declarations of a peace displayed all the hallmarks of an androcentric peace. The prevailing narrative of a post-war society making steady progress belies the violent reality of women's daily lives in the North. While 'progress' on the de-escalation of military violence certainly holds weight, interview data depicts a far bleaker landscape for women.

SIOBHAN: In most regions where there has been protracted conflict, domestic abuse and suicide rates increase dramatically. People feel dislocated and that's a problem here today; alcohol addiction, domestic abuse. Our abuse rates went through the ceiling [after the 1994 military ceasefires], all types of abuse, physical, sexual, neglect. It's frightening.

SANDRA: So conflict is still there; domestic and sexual violence against women has not decreased since the ceasefires and GFA.

For all the official rhetoric regarding a new peaceful dispensation, the data here indicates that in the aftermath of war, violence against women undermines the very notion of a society as 'post-conflict'. In the North of Ireland, violence specifically (though obviously not solely) directed against women and girls – rape, trafficking, abuse in the home – appears to be growing rather than diminishing with the 'peace' (Cockburn 2013: 163). The prevailing narrative of a post-war society belies the violent reality of women's daily lives in Northern Ireland. Statistics from Women's Aid Federation Northern Ireland 14,714 women and 14,356 young persons and children received refuge since 1999. On average, the PSNI respond to a domestic incident every 19 minutes. According to the latest PSNI reports, in August 2016 domestic abuse incidents have increased year on year since 2004/2005 except for two years.[8] The period of 2015–2016 is the highest level recorded since 2004/2005 with 13,078 domestic abuse crimes recorded; an increase of 1430 crimes on the previous 12-month period. The latest figures covering 2015–2016, show 738 women currently living in refuge in Northern Ireland with a further 267 women unable to access refuge due to lack of provision. Domestic violence accounts for 13.4 per cent of all reported crime to the PSNI. Threats to women are often depicted as 'stranger danger'; the hyperbole depicting the dangers of the public realm (dark alleys; consumption of alcohol in public spaces), conceals the 'private hell' for many women. The reality is that male current partners and ex-partners account for over 80 per cent of domestic abusers in Northern Ireland. Sandra who runs a Women's Centre in Belfast states that despite the advent of the peace process, their work load has increased significantly in the post-ceasefire years.

SANDRA: Well today I am the centre manager here in [named organisation] and we have over 20 members of staff and we work with women around domestic violence, sexual violence and to enhance women's lives and to make women's lives better and so we provide multiple services'.

LINDA: Things haven't changed all that much, especially for women. Women are still victims of domestic abuse, victims of violence, women are still

> struggling to get equality in this society, it's all still there. People are talking about this new era [for women]; it's not there for a lot of people ... maybe you see some high profile women who are in [formal] politics but what about all those other women out there.

The so-called 'post-conflict' landscape depicted here is enmeshed with various forms of gender-based violence. Linda's reference to 'some high-profile women' indicates her belief that a numerical increase of women within institutional politics is largely superficial, and projects a façade that the position of women is improving. Such moves may be empowering for the individual involved but does little to disturb the doleful daily experiences of gender-based violence.

The presence of structured gendered inequalities and pervasive gender-based discrimination in a society remains a promising line of inquiry for understanding the causes and utility of widespread gender-based violence (Davies and True 2015: 502). A 2012 UN report found that levels of sexual and gender-based violence are most likely to occur in conditions of women's general subordination, their precarious economic conditions resulting from a lack of security from the State, and the existence and acceptance in culture that women's bodies are objects that belong to men (Ki-Moon 2012). I am not suggesting that the State is actively complicit in acts of gender-based violence; there are, however, compelling comparative case-studies from other regions also emerging from armed conflict which demonstrates the linkages between transformations in gender relations at a macro level and the potential for conflict in intimate partnerships. In her comparison of peace processes in the North of Ireland and Chiapas, Melanie Hoewer (2013) found that while the former prioritised state-centric concerns such as power-sharing government, the latter recognised indigenous women's autonomy, reversed neo-liberal socio-economic processes. In contrast to the North of Ireland, Chiapas macro peace process was informed equally by female and male perspectives, and in doing so created the conditions necessary for challenging community traditions and masculine power, leading to a significant decrease in gender-based violence. In addition, Tripp's (2015) comparative work on various peace processes in Africa found that those which incorporated women's rights, such as reproductive rights, bodily integrity, and gender-based violence had clear and observable benefits for women's post-war lives when contrasted with those who excluded both women as participants and a women's rights agenda.

The documented experiences of women's exposure to various forms of violence in the aftermath of armed conflict, here in the North of Ireland and globally, undermines the very essence of terms such as 'peace process', 'conflict resolution' or 'post-conflict'. According to John Brewer (2010), terms such as 'post-conflict' are now widely interpreted as being too vague and inadequate. Brewer argues for the use of a 'post-violence' society, for those regions transitioning from communal violence. Given the global pattern of increased post-war gender-based violence, and the inextricable links between conflict resolution and gender power, the question begs; post-violence for whom? The daily reality for many women in the North of Ireland suggests that conventional definitions of violence, peace, conflict, and post-conflict are entirely inept for the purposes of examining gender relations both during and after armed actions.

Given this, the transformation of women's lives and the eradication of patriarchy requires far more than the 'some high-profile women' within formal politics. Republican socialist feminist Bernadette McAliskey stated in 1994 that

> when the [British] government are talking about guaranteeing an end to violence, they are talking about the IRA handing over the weapons ... they are not talking about making it a criminal offence for a man to beat his wife
> (Connolly 1995: 15)

It appears that dominant, masculine forms of conflict resolution consider men as security threats only when armed with weapons. The narratives here present points of commonality with existing feminist theorising of peace, echoing the argument of Cynthia Cockburn (1998) with regards to the violence which permeates every aspect of women's lives. Women's equality and rights are promoted here as the provision of services at a community level to tackle the scourge of gender-based violence. It highlights the vast disconnect between a select few women in positions of institutional power and the harsh reality of everyday struggles of working-class women.

Homophobia

Violence and armed conflict do not come to an end because of a negotiated peace agreement. Rather, new forms of violence and social conflict manifest and erupt in other spheres (Jarman 2004: 420). Despite the much-lauded South African constitution, gender-based violence is widespread with a rape occurring on average every 26 seconds. Verbal, physical and sexual violence inflicted, however, is not considered a security risk or concern. To include such violence within conventional approaches to peace and security would require critical questioning of the prevailing gender order in each society. These are not individual acts; they are gendered acts and enabled by a post-war gender regime enmeshed in normative gender assumptions and heterosexual practices. The prevailing gender order embeds normative gender roles and heterosexual practices as part of a framework which enables and sanctions various forms of gender-based violence. Research spanning more than two decades reveals extremely high rates of gender-based violence in South Africa, including intimate partner violence and sexual abuse and violence against girls and women (Jewkes and Abrahams 2002; Abrahams *et al.* 2013). The rape and murder of lesbians have become common, everyday features of the violence waged against women in contemporary South Africa. Despite the formal equality established in the post-apartheid constitution and the legalisation of same-sex marriage, corrective rape continues to target working-class women living in black townships (Mieses 2009; Carter 2013).

In addition to the other forms of violence explored, the North has also witnessed an increasing level of violence against minority groups in society. Homophobic incidents have generally increased year on year since 2006.

LINDA: Women who are lesbian have to hide their identity a lot because things aren't still very good here for the lesbian and gay community and these women are dealing with the issue of being a woman and the issue of being a lesbian and there is a huge issue around this and it's not being highlighted and that is still here; social stigma and prejudice are still there.

JANETTE: Well, I think there is an awful lot of violence due to anger and drink and drug taking; there is violence against gay people, but people are more likely to stand up against this. In my organisation you come across horrific stories and you now realise how endemic these things were in society.

In 2014 there were 293 homophobic incidents of which 194 were reported to police as homophobic crimes. Between July 2015 and June 2016 326 homophobic attacks were recorded, representing the highest ever recorded since date collection first began in 2004. Latest statistics for the year of 2017 have witnessed a slight decrease with 264 recorded homophobic attacks. The dominance of the Christian church teachings in the North tends to be a source of multiple difficulties for the LGBT community. Despite the calls for feminists to remain critically attuned to the different needs and interests of women in the aftermath of war, many current approaches have little to say about women's sexuality. The conservative nature of northern Irish society ensures that the everyday lives of LGBT citizens are far from peaceful. Yet, prevailing feminist approaches fail to address these important fissures among women. It appears that the overwhelming objective of many feminists is to accentuate the points of commonality between women at the expense of sidelining important points of difference, producing a limited vision of peace. While ostensibly such approaches are predicated on obtaining unity among women, it nevertheless has the effect of marginalising those who do not fit with the prevailing prescription.

LINDA: It's still a huge issue and suicide is a massive issue … also another thing that you don't see highlighted either is suicide within the lesbian and gay community, and so the Falls Women's Centre will work with women who are lesbian because they have to hide their identity.

While largely absent from the prevailing feminist discourse on peace, republican women in the Falls Women's Centre, among others, work daily with women who suffer because of their sexuality. There has been some progress with the establishment of the Equality Commission in the wake of the GFA accompanied by a raft of anti-discrimination legislation. The LGBT community is a strong and vibrant part of life in the North, yet the dominance of religious conservatism remains a problem. In addition to homophobic attacks, violence of various kinds has increased against other minority groups in the North. The PSNI have adopted the definition for racially motivated incidents as recommended by the Stephen Lawrence enquiry as any incident deemed to be racist by the victim. The broad parameters produce a wide scope with the 'Hate Motivation Crime' covering racial, sectarian, faith/religious, transphobic, homophobic, and disability incidents. In 2004, racists incidents were recorded at a figure of 813 and racist crimes at 633 incidents. Racist incidents for the year ending 2016 stand at 1221 while racist crimes for the same year stand at 853. Nearly two-thirds of the increase in both incidents and crimes is concentrated in Belfast.

Reproductive rights

Elisabeth Porter (1994) argues that 'reproductive rights affirm equality as an extension of the principle of bodily integrity, and self-determination'. In addition to eradicating gender-based violence, unsurprisingly many interviewees cite women's reproductive rights as a fundamental part of women's equality. It is important to state that a sizable minority of interviewees opposed abortion on what they described as a 'moral' principle. Some interviewees such as Eileen simply declared that she 'had big, big problems with it'. Cathy stated that she 'was fed up with feminists within Sinn Féin banging on about abortion. When they get up to speak at the *Ard Fheis*,[9] that's when I go for my tea break'. In October 2016 Anne Brolly, a high-profile member, quit the party after it changed its policy in 2015 to allow terminations in cases of fatal foetal abnormality. Anne Brolly became a leading member of a new republican lobby group Cherish All Children Equally.[10] Some of the internal tensions within the Republican Movement were brought to the surface recently when the state in the South of Ireland held a referendum to Repeal the 8th amendment to the state's constitution, which acknowledged the 'right to life of the unborn' as 'equal to the right of the mother'. The 8th amendment meant that abortion was prohibited but for extreme instances such as the immediate threat to the life of the woman. The referendum was held on 25 May 2018 and was passed with a significant 2:1 majority in favour of repealing the 8th amendment. In the referendum Sinn Féin adopted a position in favour of repeal and campaigned for a Yes vote to repeal the 8th amendment, which will pave the way for the state to liberalise Ireland's restrictive abortion laws. Several high-profile republicans, including political representatives, openly challenged the position adopted by the party. At the party's annual *Ard Fheis* held in June 2018, just shortly after the referendum, the party's grassroots membership voted to reject a motion that would allow party member 'freedom of conscience' when voting on any future abortion legislation. Speaking afterwards, the party's northern leader Michelle O'Neill stated that 'we are all pro-life, but this is legislating for women who find themselves in crisis, who find themselves in very difficult circumstance'. Women's right to choose, reproductive health care, and full bodily autonomy are core feminist principles and demands. The statements from Sinn Féin, while a positive shift in position, is still a long way from the feminist belief in a woman's right to choose as the cornerstone of equality.

The historical and on-going tensions regarding abortion are an important caveat to any suggestions that the Provisional republican movement is wholly conducive or receptive to feminist politics. Its membership remains what it has always been; a broad church ranging from social conservatives to pro-choice feminists, and the resignation of Anne Brolly, among others is indicative of the internal battles which rage within it around such matters. Most interviewees however, see women's right to choose as a fundamental part of their gender equality vision. Elaine, a senior Sinn Féin member typifies the sentiments of many:

> Sinn Féin has a very, very strict line on abortion and it's something that I really, really can't get to grips with accepting in any way and I will not rest until it is changed. Because I see the choice issue and being pro-choice as a fundamental part of gender equality, and gender equality is a fundamental part of republicanism, so I don't really see how anyone can define it in any other way.

Others describe their activism for women's choice as an important part of their political standpoint.

LINDA: Even before the issue was raised in the party, I was already active at university on pro-choice issues but a lot of those [male republican] activists didn't get involved. They should've been asking themselves 'am I pro-choice here or not' because it is a big woman's issue.

EDEL: I was a feminist first really and was involved in feminist politics. And, of course, the conflict was still on-going here and so I became interested in both the conflict and republicanism and I eventually joined Sinn Féin. And it was the Women's Department that gave us an outlet for [feminist] issues, especially issues around choice.

Most of the interviewees who demand women's reproductive rights state that they themselves would not choose to have an abortion but that the issue at stake is the right for women to have a *choice*. Here many interviewees saw the importance of linking women's struggle for reproductive rights with the republican national struggle.

SIOBHAN: Now I don't agree with abortion, but I do believe that everyone has a right to self-determination. I've no right to shove my opinions down on top of someone else. You can't push your morals on other people.

JANETTE: A woman does have the right to choose. We're not for or against abortion but women have a right to choose what they do with their own bodies. But if you say that a woman has to bear a child, like if someone was raped or if you're in a position not to have another child such as living in a violent home or mental instability, well I wouldn't deny the option of an abortion to someone else or the right to decide that for themselves. I might not choose to do it, but I shouldn't force my opinions onto somebody else. Now if you have to carry a child to completion every time you conceive then it's almost like rape of another form. You know, 'you must have this child'. It's almost like sharia law or something.

Approximately half of the interviewees stated that they personally did not agree with abortion but did argue that women as self-determining individuals had a right to choose if to access medical treatment for a termination. Many described the lack of choice for women as being like that of an 'enforced pregnancy'. Others described women's lack of choice as akin to the state or others were enforcing laws or regulations upon women's bodies as 'simply another form of occupation or oppression'. Interviewees believed that a woman's right to choose is inextricably linked to self-determination and liberation, and that the denying of a right to choose was another form of oppression.

So, while many personally disagreed with the idea of an abortion for themselves, they framed abortion as a self-determination issue which goes to the heart of the Irish republican struggle. According to Aoife, the issue of choice is quite simple; 'you could be totally opposed to abortion and that is fine but don't impose that upon me or other people'. If rape and sexual violence are accepted as deliberate acts of violence in wartime, it surely follows that women's bodily autonomy sits at the heart of any basic definition of peace and security. The dearth of attention to reproductive rights stems from the dominance of traditional security concerns such as institutions of governance, sovereignty, and demilitarisation (Thomson and Pierson 2018). While it has no universal or agreed definition, broadly, reproductive rights refer to a broad spectrum of which abortion is central, alongside contraception, maternal care, among others (Thomson and Pierson 2018). The vast attention afforded to rape and sexual violence by conventional approaches to war and peace is in stark contrast to the dearth of attention to women's reproductive rights as a security issue.

Continuum of violence; continuum of struggle

While nationalism as a social construct or 'imagined community' (Anderson 1983), seeks to homogenise differences under the discourse of a broad horizontal comradeship based on equal membership, Western-based feminist explorations diligently illuminated the role of gender as a central constitutive force in its construction and ideological sustenance, concurring that 'all nations depend on powerful constructions of gender' (McClintock 1993: 43). Within nationalist discourse women's perceived vulnerability and biological reproductive capability is employed and exploited both symbolically and practically (Alison 2009), whereby women are designated as biological and cultural reproducers of the nation (Yuval-Davis and Anthias 1989), while also identified as symbolic bearer of the nation's honour and identity such as 'Mother Ireland' or 'Mother India' (Ashe 2006), as well as icons of the nation to be defended or the 'booty or spoils of war' (Bracewell 1996). Nationalism, therefore, amounts to an institutionalisation of gender differentiation, which is firmly grounded in essentialist concepts of masculinity and femininity, leading McClintock to caution that 'all nationalisms are gendered, all are invented, and all are dangerous' (1993: 62). On this analysis, women's participation within nationalist movements therefore is a futile endeavour as the eradication of patriarchy in anything other than rhetoric remains an unlikely outcome. Cynthia Cockburn, among others, advocates against the synthesis of feminism and nationalism because once anti-imperial movements gain power they quickly 'shed their socialist and feminist ideologies that were present during conflict upheaval' (1998: 42). Anne McClintock also warns against viewing nationalist movements as a panacea to women's emancipation, as feminist nationalists are frequently told by their male comrades to 'hold their tongues until the revolution is over' (1993: 77); promises of a more gender-equal society after the war ring hollow whereby once conflict has ended, pre-conflict gender norms quickly re-establish themselves and 'feminist nationalists find themselves once again under the thumb of institutionalised patriarchy' (Nagel 1998: 253).

Notwithstanding the importance of their contributions, such approaches often assume a single common relationship between gender and nation and obscure the complexities involved (Vickers 2006). Pettman (1996) argues for the need to differentiate between dominant nationalisms (used by states and/or imperial powers to dominate others) and anti-colonial nationalisms (grassroots anti-imperial movements). Others highlight the variants of feminism and nationalism using a cultural relativism framework that places women at the centre of knowledge while contextualising women's experiences to their culture, arguing that feminism and nationalism can co-exist in social movements within certain cultures (West 1997). The relatively large and burgeoning body of case-study research on the experiences of women within non-state nationalist liberation movements indicate women's politicisation, agency, mobilisation, and often, the development of a feminist consciousness alongside their nationalist identities, thus indicating the heterogenous nature of nationalism and women's experiences within them (Åhäll and Shepherd 2012; Alison 2004, 2009; Chinchilla 1990; Coulter 2009; Henshaw 2017; MacKenzie 2012; Moser and Clark 2001; O'Keefe 2013; Parashar 2014; Shekhawat 2015; Sjoberg 2010). In other words, women's associations with nationalisms vary significantly and so, it is important for feminist scholars to identify which kinds of nationalisms produce positive results for women (Vickers 2002: 249). Despite this body of theoretical and empirical work documenting women's experiences as nationalist activists, feminist critics of nationalism cite the post-war moment as the period in which nationalist women once more find themselves under the thumb of patriarchy. That nationalist women face regression in their political fortunes at the end of armed actions is not in dispute. The focus on combatant women's losses reinforces conceptual linkages between femininity and victimhood and obscures the reality that experiences of victim, loss, and regression should not and does not preclude agency to resist, subvert and challenge.

The breadth of diversity of women's experience within variants of national projects highlights the shortfalls and imprecision of theories which rest upon generalisations and universalisms. The universalising tendencies within these narratives are premised upon an assumption that first, nationalist women simply heed the calls from their male comrades to demobilise and return to pre-conflict roles, and second, overlooks the development of a feminist consciousness by nationalist women which is demonstrably carried over into the post-war period where they experience new and existing forms of oppression and insecurity. Despite the gendered and often patriarchal nature and outcomes of nationalism, literature from across the globe clearly indicate the role of nationalism and anti-imperial struggles as springboards to propel women to new levels of political consciousness. Combatant women's acquisition of political consciousness and revolutionary mobilisation can and does nurture a feminist and often socialist standpoint that transcends their political objectives beyond nationalism and nation-building, as demonstrated throughout this chapter. The data here also suggests a striking similarity in the motivations for their wartime mobilisation and the motivations behind their contemporary activism.

Research on women's grassroots activism in other regions reveals how their own personal experiences of class discrimination, racism or state marginalisation provides the initial political consciousness that motivates their subsequent political organising (Naples 1998; Safa 1990). Furthermore, combatant women in other regions, such as the Tamil Tigers in Sri Lanka (Alison 2009; Davenport 2007; Gowrinathan 2017) and Palestine (Aharoni 2017; Farr 2011) also identify collective marginalisation and state repression as key sources of women's mobilisation and commitment to armed resistance. All interviewees here stated that their wartime mobilisation was motivated by an obligation to resist injustice, state violence and oppression, and protect themselves, their families and community from attack. Republican women's post-war struggle for the betterment of their communities today represents a continuity of political consciousness stemming from their wartime experiences of injustice. When asked about the motivations behind their wartime activism, very few spoke about theological republicanism, citizenship, Irish nationalism, or the creation of new structures of governance, but rather, cited the existence of discrimination, injustice and oppression by the state. When asked about the motivations for their contemporary political activism, participants stressed that same sense of wartime obligation, of seeking justice, of righting wrongs, of 'needing to do something for their communities'. Given the high levels of post-war violence in their communities, they viewed their current activities as a direct continuation of their wartime activism.

FIONA: Well, I think the conflict has been so much a part of my life for so long and it has shaped my whole life. You can't grow up as a child in a situation and then join the republican movement, be involved in a conflict as a participant, go to prison, come back out, get involved in all the things and it not to have an impact on you personally. It shapes the person that you are today, but I have to say that for me, even when I look back on things now, I think that for me, the driving force is for now to bring about a social justice that never was here before.

PATRICIA: Well, I think there is still a struggle, there are major issues that still need to be addressed. I'm all for the people, with the people and to the people; it's always been my politics. Because of the injustices that I witnessed [during the armed conflict], and we're still experiencing injustices today, and I hope that my contribution will still go a long way in addressing some of those issues. A phone call from the housing executive telling me of an available house for a young mother [constituent], then that makes my job very worthwhile and that is the same things that motivated me throughout the 1970s; by the people, with the people and for the people. So when the war ended I simply said, 'where's the next tier of struggle?'

Very few interviewees spoke of becoming involved in armed republicanism as a derivative of nationalist or republican ideology. Right throughout the data are striking and recurring similarities between wartime and post-war motivations, that being the existence of injustice and oppression. Analysing these factors is important for enhancing understandings of the post-war agency of combatant women in the context whereby their primary method, that being armed actions, has ended. Demobilisation, Disarmament, and Reintegration (DDR) processes continue to function as a primary reference point for many feminist explorations of combatant women in the aftermath of armed actions. While these clearly represent important avenues of feminist enquiry, a disproportionate focus on DDR means that the continuity of consciousness and agency of combatant women is under-researched and less well-understood. In the case of republican women here, the ending and demobilisation of armed republican struggle does not equate with a demobilisation of political activism. Moreover, being attentive to the continuity of struggle underscores the central link between a plurality of violent sources (before, during and after war) and the post-war consciousness and capacity of republican women to challenge it. Throughout this chapter, republican women are critically aware that the 1998 peace accord does not remove all sources of violence and insecurity. Understanding that combatant women can and do develop a broad agenda for political struggle alongside their nationalist goals not only challenges those narratives which assume a return to pre-conflict roles, but signifies their willingness and ability to challenge other forms of injustice and social harms not directly related to republicanism or armed struggle. Furthermore, many interviewees cited their decision to join the republican movement as a moment in which they were 'liberated' from normative, gender assigned roles. There was a shared belief that many would not be involved in political activism today had it not been for their role in armed republicanism. Orla is a full-time community activist in Belfast and believes that, had she not been an active republican, she would have spent most of her life within an unpaid domestic role.

Well I probably would not be doing what I'm doing today. The woman that runs this centre got in contact with me to see if I could help out because I couldn't be doing with sitting around doing nothing when I got out of jail.

So I did a business studies course [in jail] and got involved that way. Before going inside [jail] I was a factory worker but inside [jail] was where you got an education and decide what you were going to do when you got out. The girls I knew in jail are great and doing a great job as politicians or community workers. I would imagine the women in it [political activism] today are there because of the roles and experiences of the conflict. Their past has certainly helped them to where they are today.

It appears that despite the obvious hardships involved, jail also yielded improvements in personal circumstances such as level of education (Alison 2009; Corcoran 2006; O'Keefe 2013). Her decision to join the republican movement 'liberated' Orla from a life time of monotonous factory work or unpaid domestic labour to a position today where she is employed in a role that has meaning for her and the people she serves in the community. Despite the obvious pain, trauma and loss of 'the Troubles', most interviewees stated that their current role exists solely because of their involvement in armed struggle. 'Deirdre', who joined the IRA in the 1970s, now works as a community activist around drug abuse prevention. She states that her current activism is directly linked to her conflict role:

> Yes, women were politicised [during the conflict] and even myself, had I not been involved in armed struggle, there is no way I would be doing what I'm doing today because I wouldn't have the political or social conscience. And my role today is all about challenging injustices and wrongs, to challenge inequality, irrespective of what type because we are more in-tune with noticing and confronting inequalities.

Deirdre's words exemplify the connection felt by these republican women between the post-war violence and injustice today and the injustice that motivated their involvement in armed conflict. In addition, their empowerment through armed conflict ignited a political appetite and consciousness that they were determined to continue after armed actions had ended.

EILEEN: Republican women who were fighting on the streets with the men and who did the same activities as the men, they fired a gun as the same as a man and planted a bomb the same as a man, so women then saw 'well if I can do that the same as a man, then I can go into politics the same as a man, or maybe better' ... so it gave them that sense they valued themselves more, maybe they weren't valued by other people more, but it gave us a sense of 'I can do this and I'm not afraid to do anything'.

The sense of 'I can do this' indicates a sense of personal empowerment that carries over into other spheres of political struggle.

ANNE: So going into [Belfast] City Hall, people standing up and speaking but to me it's just another arena of struggle. So as a republican woman, I am involved in a continuation of that same struggle, that struggle justice and equality.

SIOBHAN: To me, it was still a struggle, but we had just moved from being an armed struggle into a political struggle and it was just making that cross over. You were still on the side of the struggle, but rather than putting your energy into military operations you were putting energy into political activities and working towards a more peaceful and political resolution. But I just saw the armed struggle ending and politics as another site of struggle as opposed to the armed struggle and that's it.

In addition, it is interesting to note how their declared motivations are consistent with those described in other research on community activism, which states that women who themselves experience multiple forms of marginalisation, develop both a political consciousness and sensitivity to all kinds of injustice and discrimination (Naples 1998: 117), their activism usually infused with ideals of solidarity and reciprocity. Eileen, who joined the IRA in Belfast in the early 1970s, and who now works solely in the community sector, stated that her actions within armed republicanism were informed by the pursuit of equality and justice, which continues to inform her contemporary activism:

So my politics today is about equality for all no matter what you have materially. So equality in terms of employment and education and as a socialist and as a republican my politics is like a duty for me to give something back to the people, irrespective of who they are or of their views on the conflict.

HELEN: Involving myself in the war was a last choice. So it [joining the IRA] was never a personal journey of growth. It was always about what I could do and contribute towards improving our community. Some cynics out there say that people [today] on welfare are scroungers, that old people stash their pensions under their pillows or that there is no hunger out there well let me tell you, we do community audits and when I knock on the door, poverty answers and that is what gets me out of bed in the mornings.

There was a profound sense of obligation, or as Eileen describes it, a 'duty', motivating their contemporary roles, one that they consistently linked back to the same sense of obligation in taking up arms or supporting the use of armed struggle on behalf of their communities during 'the Troubles'. While the struggle is primarily framed by the republican movement as a fight for national independence and self-determination, for interviewees here, peace and equality also means education, resisting austerity, and challenging the subordinate position of women. Many feminist studies on gender and nationalism depict a deeply problematic relationship and often for women, a regressive one in the aftermath of war. While nationalism is undoubtedly a gendered construct, the data here indicates that women's wartime empowerment is not merely an aberration. The notion that most nationalist combatant women return to pre-conflict roles in the post-war period does not stand up in the face of the overwhelming evidence here. The interview narratives demonstrate that wartime political consciousness raising and mobilisation, can be successfully carried forward into other political realms outside of the national struggle, thus motivating women's continuing activism in pursuit of a genuine peace and equality. The transition phase from revolutionary nationalism to state-building nationalism however, invariably furnishes a post-war landscape that falls far short of nationalist women's expanded political objectives. The end products of nationalism – sovereignty; structures of governance; borders – are incapable of recognising let alone eradicating all sources of women's insecurity. Therefore, the establishment of such nation-state structures should not be interpreted as the end of women's struggles. The contradiction between feminist exponents of nationalism's post-war regressive tendencies and the relatively sizable body of evidence arguing to the contrary is indicative of the fact that the vexed relationship between women and nationalism in the post-war moment remains under-theorised and less understood.

The shift from broad-based, collective national mobilisation during wartime to the often elite-driven, technocratic state-building in the aftermath typically proves to be detrimental to women's rights and a shift towards more conservative norms (Al-Ali and Tas 2018), and is an issue that will be explored in depth in the next two chapters. For this chapter however, it is important to highlight the theoretical links between the post-war continuum of violence and nationalism's inability to recognise, let alone challenge many of these sources of insecurity seriously. While nationalism, in all its varieties, may well posit the creation of an independent, post-colonial state as the teleological 'end of struggle', feminist nationalists (as well as those male comrades of a more leftist perspective) view the construction of a nation-state as the first of many steps in the creation of a truly egalitarian society. Western feminist critics of nationalism are limited by their unidimensional analysis of nationalist movements, that being a top-down perspective that privileges the ways in which male leaders position women to the detriment of ignoring the agency, and therefore the resistance, of nationalist women themselves (O'Keefe 2013). Theresa O'Keefe's analysis of republican feminism indicates that it emerged partly as a reaction to patriarchal forces within the republican movement, made meaningful because of nationalism's patriarchal tendencies. Following on from this, women's agency in nationalist movements is defined as the capacity to determine and to act, not only as a means of resistance but also as a means of subverting their domination by using the practical and ideological space within nationalist movements to insert their own needs and interests. While feminist critics unquestionably furnish an important part of the gendered nature of nationalist movements, the neglect of combatant women's agency as a direct response to continuing forms of post-war violence means we have a distorted view of combatant women. The gender continuum of violence, injustice, and insecurity ensures that many nationalist women reject the fiction of peace and security, and so retain their wartime capacities by channelling them into post-war struggles for a genuine peace. As former combatant women, their plural understandings of violence – physical;

direct; cultural; structural – is central to understanding the links between post-war sources of insecurity and the demonstrable capacity of combatant women to recognise, root out, and resist these ubiquitous forms of violence. Considering the overwhelming evidence here, and that of combatant women in other regions, there is a pressing need to shift attention away from generalised narratives, which overwhelmingly measure the post-war lives of combatant women through a top-down prism. Rather, the experiences and practices of armed conflict cultivates a political consciousness that does not simply 'de-mobilise' alongside the ending of armed actions. On the contrary, their wartime activism and high degree of agency mutates from practices of armed struggle to practices of peace-building, that being the pursuit of social justice, equality and the removal of all sources of insecurity.

Conclusion

The narratives of combatant women provide a nuanced perspective on the multifarious and intertwined layers of patriarchy, global capitalism, and imperialism, which form the basis of insecurity among working-class, republican ex-combatants in the post-war period. The strength of using the standpoint of republican women in which to conceptualise peace is that it is rooted in their everyday material and social worlds. Their understandings of peace, security, and equality are profoundly shaped and informed by their daily activities and experiences. In addition, recognising the multiple standpoints of women shifts the emphasis from singular, generalised narratives often associated with 'womenandpeace' (El-Bushra 2007), towards a more accurate and richer depiction of women in their diversity of political struggles. What emerges here is a feminism that does not see 'men' as sole source of oppression. The type of peace envisioned by republican women is mosaic and demonstrably underlines the ways in which identity, both collective and individual, shapes constructions of peace and security. While they do, of course, make specific reference to issues of imperialism and ending the partition of Ireland, they are, of course, equally concerned with conceptualising and achieving peace that is relevant in the everyday lives of working-class republicans.

Given the significant role of influential international players, particularly the United States and the EU, it is unsurprising that the nascent peace process of the 1990s developed into and reflected the norms of liberal peace-making. The North of Ireland is, of course, a much better place than it was 30 years ago, and it would be churlish to dismiss the achievements of the peace process. There is ample evidence of peace and prosperity, but it is unevenly spread. A genuine transformation of conflict via grassroots relationships was eclipsed by zealous pursuit of elite, top-down governance and the expansion of its capitalist economy, producing a certain *type* of peace and security. The prevailing ethno-national prism in which violence and peace is viewed has privileged certain forms of violence over others. While the on-going peace process has been largely successful in managing ethno-national antagonisms, it has been at the expense of neglecting other sources of conflict and violence. The peace that prevails in the North of Ireland masquerades as universal, normative, and equally beneficial for all. Its ability to garner legitimacy is based on the propensity to conflate the absence of military violence as the presence of peace.

Of course, the findings here are not something unique to this study. The data, unsurprisingly, echoes the voices of combatant women in other regions, as well as chiming with post-colonial feminist approaches to women's oppression, where feminism is intertwined with the politics of nationalism, socialism, ecofeminism as well as challenging everyday sexism and patriarchy (Mohanty 1988; Spivak 1988). In her research on combatant women in El Salvador and Colombia, Luisa Ortega (2015) contends that female ex-combatants tend to have broad conceptual understandings of peace as not simply the ending of armed hostilities but with processes of political and social transformation. There, ex-combatants spoke of human rights, corruptions, gender, ethnic and class discrimination, reproductive rights, gay rights. Like nationalist women active in other regions such as Palestine (Farr 2011) and Iraq (Gibbings 2011), republican women situate gender within, not separate to, their other struggles against global capitalism and imperialism. The argument here does not suggest that all women do not suffer under patriarchy. On the contrary, exploring the differences *between* women allows for a richer excavation of patriarchy in all its many manifestations. Oppressive masculinity and other sources of women's insecurity however, come in all forms and guises, including neo-liberal capitalism, homophobia, gender-based violence and imperialism, among others. By exploring the lives of republican women, we uncover alternative visions of peace which many prevailing approaches fail to grapple with.

Despite the dubious claims consistently linking feminism with peace, conventional processes and narratives continue to converge around women deemed to be acting in accordance with the archetypal role as 'bridge-builder' or innate peace-makers. For reasons that are self-evident, the outcome is the reification of those women who wage peace and the marginalisation of those who wage war. The elite-driven architects of peace processes and conflict transition throughout the world cling to a construction of womanhood rooted in peace and non-violence, much to the detriment of those who do not fit the idealised version of femininity, such as combatant women. Consequently, conventional approaches to conflict transition that overlook or omit the multiple sources of women's insecurities underestimate the complexities and multiplicity of women's roles in armed conflict. Neglecting the post-war needs and interests of combatant women begets a vision and strategy for peace and security that, at best, has only partial relevance to the daily lives of differentially positioned women.

The continuum of violence indicated by republican women in this chapter is unquestionably gendered, but it is also delineated through other sources of insecurity including ongoing occupation, the vagaries of global capitalism. Engagements of combatant women with peace produces important points of comparison as well as significant points of departure with other feminist visions of peace. Their contemporary lives reveal a landscape littered with various forms of violence and conflict; from 'private' social violence to the 'public' structural violence of capitalism. Asking combatant women about their post-war visions of a just society therefore advances a series of needs, interests and concerns normally omitted by traditional approaches to peace and security. While the post-war period is often referred to as a time of 'de-militarisation', the fact remains that masculinity and patriarchy remain the dominant force (Enloe 2004). In the so-called post-conflict period, streets, homes and bedrooms remain key battlegrounds (Cockburn 1998; Enloe 2004: 224). Rather than depicting the North of Ireland as a place at peace, primary data here indicates that decreasing levels of military violence are matched with increasing levels of gender-based violence. It is these insidious forms of violence that are identified as barriers to women's equality and a meaningful peace, but furthermore, the presence of post-war violence ensures a continuity of political and social struggles by republican women, thereby rebuking those who suggest that women's mobilisation by nationalism is simply temporal. The next two chapters seek to explore how republican women politically organised to pursue their vision of peace and equality over the course of the last 20 years of the peace process.

Notes

1 *Cumann* is the Gaelic (Irish language) word for branch, association or local unit.
2 Police Service of Northern Ireland. A key nationalist and republican demand throughout the peace process was the disbandment of the much-maligned RUC. In 1998 the British Government established a commission under Lord Patten, which travelled throughout the North of Ireland to gauge public attitudes, needs, and interests towards a new police force. Following Patten's report in 1999, the RUC was disbanded and replaced with the PSNI. To counter the religious imbalance, the PSNI initially used positive discrimination to attract new Catholic/nationalist recruits. That said, the PSNI retained many personnel from the RUC, engendering continuing levels of mistrust and suspicion about the partiality of the new police force. Despite the changes to policing structures, the new PSNI fell far short of republican demands and it was not until January 2007 that Sinn Féin signed up to accept the PSNI as a legitimate police service. It must also be acknowledged that the disbandment of the RUC was a major source of loss for many within the Protestant and unionist community, who believe that the RUC had fought to protect the people from decades of IRA violence.
3 The Royal Ulster Constabulary (RUC) was formed alongside the partition of Ireland and the creation of the Northern Ireland State in 1921. While many Catholics within the new Northern Ireland state were alienated and/or excluded from many positions and roles within the new state, the RUC drew its recruits and personnel largely from the protestant/loyalist community. While the force was viewed by protestant/loyalist communities as a vital safeguard against any potential threat, those within the catholic/nationalist/republican minority saw it as a biased and repressive force of unionism. Accusations and evidence of police mistreatment and partiality of Catholics throughout the history of the state only served to exacerbate these tensions. Furthermore, the unionist government also recruited an all-Protestant militia called the Ulster Special Constabulary ('B Specials'), which acted as an auxiliary to the RUC.
4 'Peeler' is a colloquial republican name given to members of the RUC and now the PSNI. Peeler refers to a member of her majesty's constabulary, that being a police officer. The name is derived from Sir Robert Peel who founded the Royal Irish Constabulary in 1814 and developed the Metropolitan Police Act in 1829, which proved

to be the foundation for the modern police force in Britain. The continuing use of the term by republicans indicates their linkages between imperialism and the local police in the North of Ireland.
5 The term 'Celtic Tiger' refers to the economy of the Republic of Ireland from 1994 to the financial crash of 2008. It represented a time of unprecedented economic growth largely predicated on the neoliberal tenets of attracting Foreign Direct Investment, tax cuts, tax incentives for the wealthy, and vast speculation on property. Though the economy was presented by many as a 'boom' in which all citizens shared the spoils of wealth, there were many dissenting voices cautioning against it, including economists, sociologists, and some media commentators. While widely lauded at home and abroad, the Celtic Tiger model has been subject to much criticism in the wake of the global capitalist crash.
6 Ballymurphy is a working-class housing estate in West Belfast. Located at the junction of the Whiterock and Springfield roads, this small network of houses was a major epicentre of violence during 'the Troubles'. It was (and remains) a major source of recruits for armed republicanism as well as being the site of many British Army killings. In August 1971, 11 civilians were killed by the British Army over a two-night period in the immediate aftermath of the introduction on internment. Some of the most exalted republican dead hail from the area, which are commemorated in the scores of wall murals which adorn the gable end of houses there. It is also the childhood home of Sinn Féin leader Gerry Adams
7 Although born in New York, Eamonn De Valera was a prominent political figure in twentieth-century Ireland. Having participated in the 1916 Easter Rising, his death sentence for his role was commuted to prison after a petition from the United States Government due to his citizenship there. He was elected president of the first Dail in 1919, a revolutionary underground government. After the war of Independence in 1921 he rejected the Anglo-Irish treaty as a political sell-out. He would eventually leave Sinn Féin and establish a new political party, Fianna Fail, in 1926. He would be elected Taoiseach in 1932 and would dominate political life until the early 1960s. As a devout Catholic, De Valera and his governments were heavily influenced by Catholic teachings and were particularly regressive on the position and role of women in Irish society.
8 Notwithstanding the shocking levels indicated here, it is also important to bear in mind that the increases of reported incidents may be linked to the Sinn Féin acceptance of the PSNI in 2007.
9 Gaelic (Irish language) for annual meeting or conference for Sinn Féin.
10 The title of the group is highly significant. 'Cherishing all the Children of the nation equally' is a direct quote from the hallowed 1916 Proclamation, which declared an Independent sovereign republic during a failed rebellion in Easter of that year. The Proclamation document remains revered in the pantheon of Irish nationalism and Irish republicanism. It is read aloud at both state and non-state commemorations of the rebellion each Easter throughout the breadth of Ireland.

Bibliography

Abrahams, N., S. Mathews, L. J. Martin, C. Lombard, and R. Jewkes. 2013. 'Intimate Partner Femicide in South Africa in 1999 and 2009'. *PLoS Medicine* 10(4): 1–8.

Åhäll, L. and L. Shepherd. eds. 2012. *Gender, Agency and Political Violence*. Basingstoke: Palgrave Macmillan.

Aharoni, S. B. 2017. 'Who Needs the Women and Peace Hypothesis? Rethinking Modes of Inquiry on Gender and Conflict in Israel/Palestine'. *International Feminist Journal of Politics* 19(3): 311–326.

Al-Ali, N. and L. Tas. 2018. 'Reconsidering Nationalism and Feminism: The Kurdish Political Movement in Turkey'. *Nations and Nationalism* 24(2): 1–21.
Alison, M. 2004. 'Women as Agents of Political Violence: Gendering Security'. *Security Dialogue* 35(4): 447–463.
Alison, M. 2009. *Women and Political Violence: Female Combatants in Ethno-national Conflict.* New York: Routledge.
Anderlini, S. N. 2007. *Women Building Peace: What They Do, Why It Matters.* Boulder and London: Lynne Rienner Publishers.
Anderson, B. 1983. *Imagined Communities: Reflections on the Origin and Spread of Nationalism.* London: Verso.
Ashe, F. 2006. 'The Virgin Mary Connection: Reflecting on Feminism and Northern Irish Politics'. *Critical Review of International Social and Political Philosophy* 9(4): 573–588.
Bean, K. 2007. *The New Politics of Sinn Féin.* Liverpool: Liverpool University Press.
Bouta, T., G. Frerks, and I. Bannon. 2005. *Gender, Conflict and Development.* Washington DC: The World Bank.
Bracewell, W. 1996. 'Women, Motherhood and Contemporary Serbian Nationalism'. *Women's Studies International Forum* 19: 25–33.
Brewer, J. D. 2010. *Peace Processes: A Sociological Approach.* Cambridge: Polity Press.
Carter, C. 2013. 'The Brutality of "Corrective Rape"'. Available at http://archive.nytimes.com/www.nytimes.com/interactive/2013/07/26/opinion/26corrective-rape.html (last accessed 13 July 2018).
Chinchilla, N. S. 1990. 'Revolutionary Popular Feminism in Nicaragua: Articulating Class, Gender, and National Sovereignty'. *Gender and Security* 4: 370–397
Coakley, J. 2008. 'Has the Northern Ireland Problem Been Solved?' *Journal of Democracy* 19(3): 98–112.
Cockburn, C. 1998. *The Space Between Us: Negotiating Gender and National Identities in Conflict.* London: Zed Books.
Cockburn, C. 2004. 'The Continuum of Violence: A Gender Perspective on War and Peace'. Pp. 24–44 in *Sites of Violence: Gender and Conflict Zones*, edited by Giles, W. and J. Hyndman. London: University of California Press.
Cockburn, C. 2007. *From Where We Stand: War, Women's Activism and Feminist Analysis.* London: Zed Books.
Cockburn, C. 2013. 'A Movement Stalled: Outcomes of Women's Campaign for Equalities and Inclusion in the Northern Ireland Peace Process'. *Interface: a Journal for and about Social Movements* 5(1): 151–182.
Cohn, C. ed. 2013. *Women and Wars.* Cambridge: Polity Press
Connolly, C. 1995. 'Ourselves Alone? Clar na mBan Conference Report'. *Feminist Review* 50: 117–126.
Corcoran, M. 2006. *Out of Order: The Political Imprisonment of Women in Northern Ireland, 1972–1999.* Devon: Willan Publishing.
Coulter, C. 2009. *Bush Wives and Girl Soldiers. Women's Lives Through War and Peace in Sierra Leone.* Ithaca: Cornell University Press.
Coulter, C. 2014. 'Under Which Constitutional Arrangement Would You Still Prefer to be Unemployed? Neoliberalism, the Peace Process, and the Politics of Class in Northern Ireland'. *Studies in Conflict and Terrorism* 37: 763–776.
Davenport, C. 2007. 'State Repression and Political Order'. *Annual Review of Political Science* 10: 1–23.
Davies, S. and J. True. 2015. 'Reframing Conflict-related Sexual and Gender-based Violence: Bringing Gender Analysis Back In'. *Security Dialogue* 46(6): 495–512.

Duffield, M. 2014. *Global Governance and the New Wars. The Merging of Development and Security.* New York: Zed Books.
El-Bushra, J. 2007. 'Feminism, Gender, and Women's Peace Activism'. *Development and Change* 38(1): 131–147.
El-Bushra, J. and C. Mukarubuga. 1995. 'Women, War and Transition'. *Gender and Development* 3(3): 16–22
Enloe, C. 2004. *The Curious Feminist: Searching For Women In A New Age of Empire.* Berkeley, CA: University of California Press.
Farr, V. 2011. 'UNSCR 1325 and Women's Peace Activism in the Occupied Palestinian Territory'. *International Feminist Journal of Politics* 13(4): 539–556.
Frampton, M. 2009. *The Long March: The Political Strategy of Sinn Féin, 1981–2007.* Basingstoke and New York: Palgrave Macmillan.
Galtung, J. 1969. 'Violence, Peace and Peace Research'. *Journal of Peace Research* 6: 167–191.
Gibbings, S. L. 2011. 'No Angry Women at the United Nations: Political Dreams and the Cultural Politics of United Nations Security Resolution 1325'. *International Feminist Journal of Politics* 13(4): 522–538.
Giles, W. and J. Hyndman. eds. 2004. *Sites of Violence: Gender and Conflict Zones.* London: University of California Press.
Gowrinathan, N. 2017. 'The Committed Female Fighter: The Political Identities of Tamil Women in the Liberation Tigers of Tamil Eelam'. *International Feminist Journal of Politics* DOI: 10.1080/14616742.2017.1299369
Handrahan, L. 2004. 'Conflict, Gender, Ethnicity and Post-Conflict Reconstruction'. *Security Dialogue* 35(4): 429–445.
Henshaw, A. 2017. *Why Women Rebel. Understanding Women's Participation in Armed Rebel Groups.* London and New York: Routledge.
Hinds, B. (2011) Women's Resource and Development Agency: 'Women on the Edge Report' Available at: www.wrda.net/Documents/Women%20and%20the%20Economy%20Section%205%20-%20Lone%20Parents.pdf
Hoewer, M. 2013. 'Women, Violence, and Social Change in Northern Ireland and Chiapas: Societies Between Tradition and Transition'. *International Journal of Conflict and Violence* 7(2): 216–231.
Horgan, G. 2006. 'Devolution, Direct Rule and Neo-Liberal Reconstruction in Northern Ireland'. *Critical Social Policy* 26(3): 656–666.
Hughes, J., A. Campbell, M. Hewstone, and E. Cairns. 2007 'Segregation in Northern Ireland: Implications for Community Relations Policy'. *Policy Studies* 28(1): 35–53.
Jansson, M. and M. Eduards. 2016. 'The Politics of Gender in the UN Security Council Resolutions on Women, Peace and Security'. *International Feminist Journal of Politics* (18): 4, DOI: 10.1080/14616742.2016.1189669
Jarman, N. 2004. 'From War to Peace? Changing Patterns of Violence in Northern Ireland, 1990–2003'. *Terrorism and Political Violence* 6(3): 420–438.
Jewkes, R. and N, Abrahams. 2002. 'The Epidemiology of Rape and Sexual Coercion in South Africa: An Overview'. *Social Science & Medicine* 55: 1231–44.
Karam, A. 2001. 'Women in War and Peace-building'. *International Journal of Feminist Politics* 3(1): 2–25.
Kelly, L. 2000. 'Wars Against Women: Sexual Violence, Sexual Politics and the Militarised State'. Pp. 45–64 in *States of Conflict: Gender, Violence and Resistance*, edited by S. Jacobs, R. Jacobson and J. Marchbank. London and New York: Zed Books.

Kelly, F. 2018. 'Clinton Describes Belfast Agreement as "a Work of Genius"'. *The Irish Times* 10 April. Available at: www.irishtimes.com/news/politics/clinton-describes-belfast-agreement-as-a-work-of-genius-1.3457441 (Last accessed 25 September 2018).

Ki-Moon, B. 2012. *Conflict-related Sexual Violence. Report of the Secretary-General. S/2012/33.* New York: United Nations.

Krog, A. 2001. 'Locked into Loss and Silence: Testimonies of Gender and Violence at the South Africa Truth Commission'. Pp. 203–216 in *Victims, Perpetrators or Actors: Gender, Armed Conflict and Political Violence*, edited by C. Moser and F. Clark. New York: Zed Books.

Mac Ginty, R. 2015. 'Hybrid Peace: The Interaction Between Top-Down and Bottom-Up Peace'. Pp. 316–324 in *The Contemporary Conflict Resolution Readers*, edited by E. Woodhouse, H. Miall, O. Ramsbotham, and C. Mitchell. Cambridge: Polity Press.

Mac Ginty, R. and A. Williams. 2009. *Conflict and Development.* London and New York: Routledge.

Maillot, A. 2005. *New Sinn Féin: Irish Republicanism in the Twenty-First Century.* London and New York: Routledge.

McClintock, A. 1993. 'Family Feuds: Gender, Nationalism and the Family'. *Feminist Review* 44 (Summer 1993): 61–80.

McGarry, J. ed. 2001. *Northern Ireland and the Divided World: Post-Agreement Northern Ireland in Comparative Perspective.* Oxford: Oxford University Press.

McKay, S. and C. de la Rey. 2002. 'Peacebuilding as a Gendered Process'. *Journal of Social Issues* 62(1): 144–153.

McLeod, L. 2011. 'Configurations of Post-Conflict: Impacts of Representations of Conflict and Post-Conflict upon the (Political) Translations of Gender Security within UNSCR 1325'. *International Feminist Journal of Politics* 13(4): 594–611.

Meintjes, S., A. Pillay, and M. Turshen. eds. 2001. *The Aftermath: Women in Post-Conflict Transformation.* London and New York: Zed Books.

Mieses, A. 2009. 'Gender Inequality and Corrective Rape of Women Who Have Sex with Women'. *GMHC Treatment Issues* December, 1–3: 5. www.gmhc.org/files/editor/file/ti-1209.pdf.

Mohanty, C. 1988. 'Under Western Eyes: Feminist Scholarship and Colonial Discourses'. *Feminist Review* 30: 61–88.

Molan, P. 2012. Community Relations Council '*Peace Monitoring Report*'. Available at: www.community-relations.org.uk/fs/doc/publications/NIPMR_2012_new_1.pdf

Moser, C. and F. Clark. eds. 2001. *Victims, Perpetrators or Actors? Gender, Armed Conflict and Political Violence.* London: Zed Books.

Nagel, J. 1998. 'Nation'. *Ethnic and Racial Studies* 21(2): 242–269.

Nagel, J. 2018. 'Between Conflict and Peace: An Analysis of the Complex Consequences of the Good Friday Agreement'. *Parliamentary Affairs* 71(2): 395–416.

Naples, N. 1998. *Grassroots Warriors: Activist Mothering, Community Work, and the War on Poverty.* New York: Routledge.

Ni Aolain, F., D. F. Haynes and N. Cahn. 2011. *On The Frontlines: Gender, War and the Post-Conflict Process.* Oxford: Oxford University Press.

O'Hearn, D. 2008. 'How Has Peace Changed the Northern Irish Political Economy?' *Ethnopolitics* 7(1): 101–118.

O'Keefe, T. 2012. 'Sometimes it Would Be Nice to Be a Man: Negotiating Gender Identities after the Good Friday Agreement'. Pp. 83–97 in *Everyday Life After the Irish Conflict*, edited by C. McGratton and E. Meehan. Manchester: Manchester University Press.

O'Keefe, T. 2013. *Feminist Identity Development and Activism in Revolutionary Movements*. London and New York: Palgrave Macmillan.
Ortega, L. 2015. 'Untapped Resources for Peace: A Comparative Study of Women's Organisation of Guerrilla Ex-Combatants in Colombia and El Salvador'. Pp. 232–249 in *Female Combatants in Conflict and Peace*, edited by S. Shekhawat. Basingstoke: Palgrave Macmillan.
Parashar, S. 2014. *Women and Militant Wars: The Politics of Injury*. London and New York: Routledge.
Pettman, J. 1996. *Worlding Women: A Feminist International Politics*. New York and Sydney: Routledge.
Porter, E. 1994. 'Abortion Ethics: Rights and Responsibilities'. *Hypatia* 9(3): 66–87.
Porter, E. 2003. 'Women, Political Decision-making and Peace-building in Conflict Regions'. *Global Change, Peace and Security* 15(3): 245–262.
Porter, E. 2007. *Peacebuilding: Women in International Perspective*. London and New York: Routledge.
Power, M. 2010. 'A Republican Who Wants to Further Women's Rights': Women, Provisional Republicanism, Feminism and Conflict in Northern Ireland'. Pp. 153–170 in *Irish Women at War: The Twentieth Century*, edited by G. McIntosh and D. Urquhart. Dublin and Portland: Irish Academic Press.
Rai, S. and G. Waylen. eds. 2013. *New Frontiers in Feminist Political Economy*. New York: Routledge.
Reardon, B. A. 1993. *Women and Peace: Feminist Visions of Global Security*. New York: State of New York University Press.
Safa, H. I. 1990. 'Women's Social Movements in Latin America'. *Gender and Society* 4(3): 354–369.
Shekhawat, S. ed. 2015. *Female Combatants in Conflict and Peace*. Basingstoke: Palgrave Macmillan.
Shepherd, L. 2008. *Gender, Violence & Security*. London and New York: Zed Books.
Shirlow, P. 2001. 'Fear and Ethnic Division'. *Peace Review* 13: 67–74.
Shirlow, P. 2012. *The End of Ulster Loyalism?* Manchester: Manchester University Press.
Side, K. 2009. 'Women's Civil and Political Citizenship in the Post-Good Friday Agreement Period in Northern Ireland'. *Irish Political Studies* 24(1): 67–87.
Sjoberg, L. 2014. *Gender, War, and Conflict*. Cambridge: Polity.
Sjoberg, L. ed. 2010. *Gender and International Security: Feminist Perspectives*. New York: Routledge.
Spivak, G. 1988. 'Can the Subaltern Speak?' Pp. 271–313 in *Marxism and the Interpretation of Culture*, edited by C. Nelson and L. Grossberg. London: Macmillan.
Thomson, J. and C. Pierson. 2018. 'Can Abortion Rights Be Integrated into the Women, Peace and Security Agenda?' *International Feminist Journal of Politics*, DOI: 10.1080/14616742.2017.1413583
Tickner, A. 1992. *Gender In International Relations: Feminist Perspectives on Achieving Global Security*. New York and Chichester: Columbia University Press.
Tripp, A. M. 2015. *Women and Power in Post-conflict Africa*. New York: Cambridge University Press.
True, J. 2015. 'Winning the Battle but Losing the War on Violence'. *International Feminist Journal of Politics* 17(4): 554–572, DOI: 10.1080/14616742.2015.1046269
Uhde, Z. 2016. 'From Women's Struggles to Distorted Emancipation'. *International Feminist Journal of Politics* 18(3): 390–408, DOI: 10.1080/14616742.2015.1121603

United Nations. 2000. 'Peace Inextricably Linked With Equality Between Women and Men'. 8 March 2000. Available at: www.un.org/press/en/2000/20000308.sc6816.doc.html (Last accessed 25 September 2018).

Vickers, J. 2002. 'Feminists and Nationalism' Pp. 247–272 in *Gender, Race, and Nation: A Global Perspective*, edited by V. Dhruvarajan. Toronto: University of Toronto.

Vickers, J. 2006. 'Bringing Nations in: Some Methodological and Conceptual Issues in Connecting Feminisms with Nationhood and Nationalisms'. *International Journal of Feminist Politics* 8(1): 84–109.

Ward, M. 2006. 'Gender, Citizenship and the Future of the Northern Ireland Peace Process'. *Irish Feminist Studies* 41: 262–283.

Ward, M. 2009. 'Response to Associate Parliamentary Group on Women. Peace and Security Northern Ireland Inquiry: Call for Written Evidence'. Belfast: WRDA. Retrieved 23 June 2017 http://wrda.net/pdf/wrda%20response%20to%201325%20inquiry%20september%202011.pdf

West, L. ed. 1997. *Feminist Nationalism*. London and New York: Routledge.

Whitworth, S. 1994. *Feminism and International Relations*. London: Macmillan Press.

Wibben, A. T. R. 2011. *Feminist Security Studies: A Narrative Approach*. London and New York: Routledge.

Yuval-Davis, N. and Anthias, F. 1989. *Women, Nation, State*. Hampshire: Macmillan.

4 From the front lines of war to the sidelines of peace?

Republican women and the Irish peace process

Introduction

In the aftermath of the 1994 Irish Republican Army (IRA) ceasefire, the principal republican leaders set out the implementation of a new phase of 'unarmed struggle'. The armed struggle failed to bring about an end to partition and so republicans set about grappling with the prospect of working within a state they vowed to dismantle. Central to this political departure was the institutionalisation of the republican struggle, shifting from revolutionary actions and rhetoric in favour of more tempered and mainstream demands regarding universal citizenship, equality, and rights for all. With armed struggle largely abandoned, the post-war battlefield generally resided in the 'hard talk' of formal peace negotiations and the pursuit of electoral advances at the ballot box. This chapter explores the ways in which the institutionalisation of Provisional republicanism during conflict transition impacted upon the political struggles of women within the republican movement. It finds that the shoe-horning of political activism into elite, male dominated peace talks, coupled with the zealous pursuit of electoral politics squeezed many of the political spaces created by women through the conflict years. Despite the prevailing calls within conventional approaches for women's inclusion within both institutional peace talks and the sphere of state-centric politics, the chapter suggests that the institutionalisation of political struggle can prove to be detrimental to the post-war lives of former combatant women.

The chapter begins with an exploration of the changing dynamics within the republican movement during the post-ceasefire period as Sinn Féin 'professionalises' itself and its wider organisation. I then move on to explore women's experiences of the Good Friday Agreement (hereafter the GFA) negotiations, indicating a sidelining of both women and their interests as state power and electoral contests gain primacy. The lack of meaningful input within the negotiations is further compounded by the ambiguous demise of the Sinn Féin Women's Department. This previously vibrant and prolific feminist organisation appears to 'fade away' just at a time when the overall movement firmly accelerates away from its 'revolutionary struggle' towards its post-war overhaul into a constitutional political party. It suggests that the institutional re-positioning of the party required an overhaul of women's previous modes of feminist agitation to fit with its newfound mainstream departure.

'Ceasefire soldiers': post-war republican politics

By the early 1990s Sinn Féin was attempting to recast itself as a 'respectable party of the mainstream'. The sole focus during the peace process was to increase its electoral strength and enter formal peace negotiations (Frampton 2009: 104). During this period electoral imperatives appeared to have supplanted ideological purity for republicans (Tonge 2005: 117). Sinn Féin's electoral success has been remarkable and largely uninterrupted in its ascendancy since 1994 and grew in tandem with its movement into the mainstream and into government where the rhetoric of rights and equality became far more palatable than revolutionary socialism (Bean 2014: 723). In doing so, Sinn Féin essentially repositioned itself as a social democratic voice of the centre left (McGovern 2004: 639). In this sense, republicans became constructive critics of the status quo, pointing out its limitations and suggesting improvement, rather than radicals creating a new space for completing their revolutionary project (Bean 2007: 215). Although always leadership-led, republican women contend that they joined an activist-led movement that was ostensibly concerned with the dismantling of the state through varied means including armed struggle, mass mobilisation, self-sufficient communities, and electoral politics. Scholars of the republican movement are increasingly drawn to social movement theory to explain the emergence and transformations within Provisional republicanism during the years of armed conflict. The birth of the Provisional republican movement was not unique to the global pattern of political and social upheaval in the latter part of the 1960s and indeed the Provisionals share many similarities with those global movements (White 2017). Social movement theory contends that all social movements operate within time-defined cycles or phases, which invariably reach a peak (Porta and Diani 1999; Tarrow 1998). Throughout the cycle of protest, radical leaders of movements will realise that, first, their capabilities to challenge the status quo have peaked, and second, negotiation and moderation offer attractive alternatives to the destruction of their movement by state-led counter-movements (White 2017). While the transition from revolutionary politics to more institutional positions allows for the maintenance of their respective political identity, it does, however, come with the cost of moderating political agendas and demands. Moreover, 'successful' transitions will also bring a movement into more formalised and mainstream political channels. In a succinct summary, 'the IRA went from being a revolutionary movement committed to overthrowing the state to a constitutional party prepared to govern it' (Bean 2007: 135). This section explores the ideological and practical shifts that occurred within the republican movement during conflict transition, from the perspective of women within the movement.

In the aftermath of the 1994 IRA ceasefire, the ranks of Sinn Féin swelled with what interviewees described as a 'new type of person', persons who prior to the ceasefire were absent from the traditional support base of the Provisionals during 'the Troubles'. A term common across interviews is that of 'ceasefire soldiers' or 'ceasefire republicans', which was used to denote these 'new type of persons'. According to Linda:

> ceasefire soldiers were all coming in and who didn't want to know you during the conflict, who would have closed their doors in your face but now it was all respectable to be a republican; [now it is] ok to be in Sinn Féin.

Eileen who joined the IRA in the early 1970s and now works in the community sector recalls a similar change in approach and personnel:

> I could see that they [Sinn Féin leadership] were looking for respectful images and all this [sic] Armani suit brigade. I could see them sidelining people who [now] didn't fit the picture, you had to agree with everything. Things were being taken from the ground and it was now all top-down. Things were centralised and it all had to go through someone else. To me, even at *Ard Fheiseanna*,[1] there used to be actual debates but now it looked like it [policy positions] was decided beforehand. People who were to speak was decided beforehand and I just didn't like what I was seeing. And so you see the community groups I'm on now, I can say what I like, and I can give my viewpoint even though people may not agree with it. Policies and the like [within named group] are from the ground-up.

The quelling of dissent and the imposition of top-down structures bear all the trademark characteristics of the social movement transition towards an institutional political party. The development of Sinn Féin as 'a party ready for government' was problematic; obtaining 'respectability and status' risked diluting, or even destroying, the more radical ethos of the party (Frampton 2009: 143). Most interviewees affirmed this vast sense of change in dynamic in the post-ceasefire period. While the frank testimonies of those now outside of the party, such as Linda and Eileen, are telling yet unsurprising, it is striking to note that most other interviewees still within Sinn Féin recounted similar experiences. Gemma who is now a senior Sinn Féin member recalls:

> We were trying to professionalise ourselves because we knew that Sinn Féin were going to be massive. There was a different atmosphere [after the ceasefire], almost like a sadness but at the same time looking forward but always this sadness. I mean it might seem weird to say but we had wild craic back in the days of the conflict when people were sitting around old buildings with nothing, no heating or no chairs. And when the funds did start coming in, that may have put people off, as it was a wee bit too formalised and some people felt left out but we had to become more professionalised with constituency offices and vote management and how you canvass properly, how you run an election properly and everything was changing and so some people felt left out.

Theresa is a lifelong republican and remains a prominent Sinn Féin member. She also recalls a similar pattern:

> Well, I actually found myself having to pull myself back in from feeling bitter because then you had all these people coming on the scene [after the 1994 ceasefire] and you were thinking 'where did all these ones come from all of a sudden'. So you had all these people saying [sarcastically] *'oh I work in Gerry Adams' office'* and I was saying to them 'where the fuck were yous [*sic*] during the war?', god forgive me because we *could not, could not* get women towards the end of the 1980s; we simply couldn't. They were few and far between.

Despite the obvious trauma of 'the Troubles', there was a strong sense of grassroots and communal solidarity during the years of armed conflict. Gemma's statement reveals a profound tension between a longing for past modes of activism and the need to adopt a more pragmatic approach in order to grapple with the new political realities. The shift towards a more formalised political party brings with it ideological and practical demands. There was widespread belief across interviews that the party needed to retain more of its grassroots fronts to counter those who suggested it is now merely another constitutional political party. Formal politics is often viewed by grassroots activists as a system dominated by wealthy, often white men (and, of course, sometimes women) vying for power for its own sake and for their own personal gain (Naples 1998: 125), which, according to the perspectives of the women interviewed, is the very antithesis of their republican activism. Aoife, a life-long Sinn Féin member describes her experiences:

> Our *cumann*[2] is now business-like and not enough discussion. These days discussion is happening at a different level and maybe more leadership-led. It wasn't leadership-led in the 1980s. Now obviously we elect a leadership, but it feels different for me now; hard to pinpoint. It has been gradual, but it is linked to us going towards constitutional politics.

It suggests the erosion of grassroots space is commensurate with the party's increasing shift towards the mainstream. Interviewees are critically aware that as the party accelerates its move to formalised politics, grassroots spaces and inputs are sequestered. The subsidence of revolutionary actions and rhetoric correlated with the movement's ideological transition towards the political realism of state governance. A pertinent example of this lack of internal debate as described by Aoife arose when the now deceased former IRA member and Sinn Féin Deputy First Minister Martin McGuinness met and shook hands with the British Queen during a visit to Belfast on 27 June 2012. From a republican perspective, the notion of a former IRA commander shaking hands with a British monarch was likely to cause anxiety and anger among many rank and file republicans. Twenty-five interviews occurred during and after this event where most participants expressed dismay, frustration and sometimes anger at the way the handshake was communicated with members by the leadership. The lack of internal party debate and grassroots input to that decision is both potent and unequivocal. Gemma, a senior Sinn Féin member from Belfast sums up the feelings of most at that time:

> The handshake with the queen, we lost a lot of people [republican members and supporters] over that. That was a bitter pill to swallow. I don't think it should have happened. Now I've brought this up at meetings at the time that I wasn't informed that Martin would be shaking the queen's hand, I was *told* [participant's emphasis] that he would be doing that. Like that whole [consultation] process ... the handshake was on, then it was off, it was going to happen, it wasn't going to happen and then two days to go we were *told* that it was going to happen, so we lost a lot of people through that.

It is interesting to note that Gemma's description is almost identical to that of others who recalled attending local Sinn Féin meetings right across Ireland. Rather than debating the issue or having any real input, all described the process as one of 'being informed', rather than debating or impacting the decision that the handshake would go ahead, indicating a top-down 'consultation' process.

JANETTE: At the end of the day you have to toe a party line and follow party lines. Like the queen handshake and all that, you probably could not have changed that outcome, it was inevitable.

The lack of a meaningful debate with its grassroots membership is emblematic of the party's embrace of institutional political organising. This process is not unique to Sinn Féin as most parties require its members, and especially its senior party representatives, to 'toe the party line'.[3] Many interviewees, however, saw this as restrictive, given their previous experiences of grassroots politics within the movement.

AOIFE: There is a big change now, less discussion, less grassroots discussion and my personal analysis of it is that we have become so embroiled in constitutional politics that everything takes second place and perhaps I am not a very constitutional person and I'm in a party that is, so it is a conflict for me. Things are often done because an election is coming, issues should be done because they need to be done.

JANETTE: Well, there were more radical politics around 1984 and 1985 and developing radical politics around that time. And this is my big problem with constitutional, formal politics and I think this is still a valid argument, is that if you have to keep getting elected again and again, then you have to appeal to the least common denominator; appeal to the most inclusive audience. So I think we aren't as radical as we could be because we have to keep getting elected again and again'.

LINDA: That [leadership control] began during the peace process because the peace process was all top-down. You had people deciding the future and drip-feeding everyone else, people within the republican movement were drip-fed. So there is no democratic politics going on within the movement as to what was going to be, you have a few people sitting down and deciding.

Kevin Bean (2007) describes the remoteness of Sinn Féin's politicians and their attempts to restrict debates in the conflict transition period. The erosion of grassroots input may have presented difficulties for rank and file republicans, but unpalatable measures such as engaging with the British monarchy also offered major political benefits for the leadership in terms of presenting its new 'post-armed struggle' outlook. The changes described by interviewees were strategic measures that prepared the ground for the new post-war politics of the Provisionals. The profound sense of change regarding internal dynamics indicates a distinct shift towards a more leadership-led culture. The principal republican leaders sought to advance an unarmed republican struggle through electoral contests, political rhetoric, media sound-bites, and the zealous pursuit of state power. This process of 'professionalisation' ensured that the ranks of the republican movement were swelled with 'ceasefire republicans' coupled with a more institutional, leadership-led approach to politics. These seismic shifts invariably shaped gender relations and the position of women within the movement. In particular, the sidelining of women during the GFA formal negotiations and the ending of the Sinn Féin Women's Department are illustrative of the consequences on women's standing with the movement.

Diminished returns? Reconfiguring gender roles during peace negotiations

Very elite-centred negotiations, despite their presentation as 'inclusive talks' were the method established for tackling the northern Irish conflict (Dixon 2002; McGovern 2004; Power 2011). Like all institutional approaches towards resolving armed conflict, negotiations for what culminated as the GFA followed a top-down framework, choreographed by elites, manipulating most citizens who were excluded from the process (Dixon 2002). From 2008 to March 2012, women acted as signatories in just two of the 61 peace accords reached during this period. Throughout the entire decade of the 1990s, a mere 16 per cent (92 of 585) of peace agreements made specific reference to women and/or gender equality (Bell and Rourke 2010). The issue at stake here transcends matters of visibility or levels of fairness. In Tripp's (2015) thorough examination of post-conflict societies in Africa, regarding women's inclusion within peace negotiations in countries such as Uganda and Liberia, the outcomes were significantly better for women than in those countries where women were excluded. '[W]omen's concerns are still rarely heard, let alone addressed, by policy makers during [formal] peace settlements' (Pankhurst 2003: 155), and the formal negotiation process for the Irish peace accord was no exception.

The signing of the GFA in 1998 was met with a widespread sense of relief, and optimism that 'the Troubles' as they had been prior to the agreement were finally over. On 31 August 1994 and after 25 years of armed struggle, the IRA announced a cessation of military operations; their loyalist counterparts followed on 13 October. While the post-ceasefire years were marred by mistrust and various forms of military violence, formal negotiations between the various political parties began in 1996, with international mediation playing a crucial role. The dearth of women in formal politics and the outright exclusion of a grassroots input ensured that negotiations were a largely all-male affair despite the presence of and attempts made by the Northern Ireland Women's Coalition (hereafter the NIWC) to alter this. Even Sinn Féin, which prided itself for its 'progressive gender stance', had few front-line roles for women during negotiations. Progress was slow and tedious; it took months to establish the ground rules and a vague agenda, before talks on the major substantive issues even began (Cochrane 2013). In marked contrast from previous efforts to resolve the conflict in the 1970s and 1980s, the main architects of this peace process, the British and Irish Governments, went beyond previous approaches of involving just the mainstream, larger political parties. On this occasion they went out of their way to include smaller political parties linked to loyalist paramilitaries, the Progressive Unionist Party (with links to the Ulster Volunteer Force[4] (UVF)) and the Ulster Democratic Party (with links to the Ulster Defence Association (UDA) and Ulster Freedom Fighters[5] (UFF)). By doing so, the two governments inadvertently created the window of opportunity for the participation of the NIWC, comprised of women from NGO's, trade unionism and academics, among others. Although only managing a 1.03 per cent share of the electorate, the endeavours to get smaller loyalist parties involved in the talks ensured that the NIWC had two delegates.

The main talks occurred in the period of October 1997 to March 1998. The word 'talks', however, is highly euphemistic as most of the parties refused to negotiate 'face to face'. After years of stagnation, a deadline of Good Friday was set by the chair, George Mitchell. In the final push, international intervention from Bill Clinton as well as the active presence of both Tony Blair and Bertie Ahern encouraged high expectations that a deal could be done. In addition to the political pressure, generous funding packages from the EU (Tonge 2014) and other international bodies sugar-coated the arduous task of power-sharing by sworn adversaries. For unionists, the main issue of concern was IRA arms and the unionist demand that IRA arms be handed in prior to Sinn Féin's involvement in government. A personal intervention by Tony Blair on the issue of IRA arms appears to have settled unionist uncertainties and having come close to the brink of collapse on many occasions, yet an agreement was reached on Friday 10 April 1998.

While a complex and ambiguous document, the Belfast Agreement or what it is more commonly referred to as the Good Friday Agreement (GFA), can be summed up as containing four key arrangements. First, the constitutional position of Northern Ireland can only be changed with the consent of a majority of its citizens. Second, a united Ireland can only come about through a majority of citizens north and south of the border. Third, all citizens of Northern Ireland have the right to identify themselves as British or Irish, or both. Fourth, the Irish Republic drops its territorial claim over the state of Northern Ireland and defines the Irish nation in terms of people as opposed to territory. The GFA also sets out the new governance structure for the North of Ireland and its relationship with the rest of Ireland and the British Isles. The Northern Ireland assembly, comprising 108 (now reduced to 90) locally elected representatives, is predicated based on providing political power to both nationalist and unionist political representatives. Based on a consociation model, weighted assembly majorities demand that 60 per cent of all Members for the Legislative Assembly[6] (MLA) comprising 40 per cent of both nationalists and unionists, must be in support of proposed legislation. MLAs also elect a First and Deputy First Minister, again balancing power between nationalism and unionism. The remaining ministerial roles are then allocated based on parties' electoral strength, using the d'Hondt formula. The North–South Ministerial Council was established to allow cooperation between the British and Irish Governments, along with the main political parties on issues of mutual benefit to both parts of the island.

Of particular note to feminists and women's groups, Section 75 of the agreement imposes a statutory duty on public authorities to promote equality of opportunity between persons of different religious belief, political opinion, racial group, age, marital, status and sexual orientation, between persons with a disability and without, persons with a dependent and without, and between women and men generally (Side 2009: 70). The agreement, however, was heavy on institutional reform and design but incredibly light on wider political, economic and social relations. Despite Section 75, it had little to say about any future relations between women and men. The GFA was essentially concerned with removing weapons of war and replacing them with weapons of words within an institutional setting. It was an exercise in conflict containment as opposed to conflict resolution. Moreover, it presented no radical transformative potential to positively change the lives of women, or tackle the other forms of insidious inequality and violence which pervades much of northern Irish society.

Given their central part in armed struggle, it was reasonable to assume that republican women were well placed to play a prominent role in peace negotiations. Despite their role as combatants, the political and social capital yielded through the war failed to transfer into seats at the peace talks. Yet, as mentioned above, there remains an unequivocal global pattern of excluding women from peace processes, irrespective of their wartime roles or the professed rhetoric of horizontal comradeship within non-state movements. When asked about their roles within the GFA negotiations period, the word 'leadership' is ubiquitous. Phrases such as total faith in the leadership'; 'blind faith in the leadership'; '100 per cent behind the leadership'; 'they would not let us down'; 'complete trust in the leadership' are common across the many narratives of republican women dealing with the period.

HELEN: There was a great sense of momentum [during the GFA negotiations]. But the main thing that I recall is a lot of confidence in our leadership.

FIONA: People have to show leadership and people like Gerry Adams and Martin McGuinness have shown leadership.

RUTH: I did have great faith in our leadership and Gerry Adams in particular. I would have great faith in his leadership and in his analysis.

MICHELLE: It was time to end the war and when you had leadership like Martin McGuinness then you knew that there was never going to be anything damaging going to happen because Martin had been with us as part of the struggle. But I was always 100 per cent behind the leadership and I knew they'd never let us down. Total faith.

JOANNE: I just knew it would be alright; I just saw it as another step, another step. I did feel all the nervousness that was all around, but I just knew that this was OK, going to be OK. I just trusted the leadership; they were taking a chance so why can't we? But I knew they wouldn't let us down.

BERNIE: Well, we all had apprehensions because you were going into the unknown and, I mean, I didn't agree with everything because it was unknown, and you didn't know how it was going to pan out. But I had and have great faith in the leadership and I knew they wouldn't let us down but I'm not one of these ones that you know, stick a carrot in front of me and I'll go. I have a mind of my own, and my own thoughts so that was difficult too. At the same time, if the movement thought it was necessary to go back to war tomorrow then I would be 100 per cent behind it.

Of the 40 interviewees, not a single person identified as having a direct role or contribution to the formal negotiations. In contrast to the notion in Chapter 2 that 'everyone had a part to play' during 'the Troubles', the peace process resided in the hands of a few, mostly male, republicans. Ultimately, control of the state was at the heart of the negotiations, and 'macho men were at the forefront of those negotiation' (Racioppi and O'Sullivan See 2001: 101). In her analysis of combatant women in Kashmir, Seema Shekhawat finds that despite their high levels of activism and visibility during the conflict, women were all but excluded; women who were once the face of militancy have not been allowed to become the face of peace-making (2015: 100). Equally, in El Salvador and Colombia, the aftermath of armed actions witnessed a regression in the fortunes of female combatants where they were written out of historical narratives and sidelined from political positions (Ortega 2015: 236). From Kashmir to Sierra Leone to the North of Ireland, it appears that while mass mobilisation and popular insurgency are deemed appropriate spaces for nationalist women, the realm of elite, top-down peace talks remains a thoroughly male-dominated and masculine space.

Many interviewees switched from providing a personal experience to providing an observational account of the period in question. While describing their conflict experiences using 'I' or 'we', the discourse changes when the peace negotiations are discussed. During this time, many became spectators in their own story. All research participants had little or no role in the peace negotiations, and instead spoke of their faith in the leadership to lead what were essentially secret negotiations with various parties to the conflict. Notwithstanding that the republican movement has always (and remains) a predominantly male organisation based on a hierarchical structure, the GFA formal peace talks clearly sidelined women. The secret negotiations that embodied the hallmarks of 'the old boys club' (O'Keefe 2013) demanded a reversion to either tokenistic or more 'traditional' roles for women. Linda, a former IRA member from Belfast who now works solely as a community activist stated:

> They (republican women) weren't involved, they were secretaries and that's what they looked like; paper carriers for the men. It was men making all those decisions for all of us. Now the leadership have to lead and sometimes take decisions. But the party became more and more centralised and everything had to go through someone else and they had to give it the all clear.

Even those who remained within the Provisional movement, and who are not inclined to be overly critical, echoed Linda's contention that women's role bordered on the politics of optics, or at best 'traditional' back-room roles. When asked about the lack of women at the front lines of the negotiations, Anne counters such suggestions with an explanation that:

> There were lots of women behind the scenes who were preparing the documents. And there were women on the *Ard Comhairle*[7] there along with everybody else. So you know you had Bairbre De Brun and Dodie[8] and Siobhan O'Hanlon. There were lots of women behind the scenes as well, preparing the way this all shaped up.

Anne's depiction of women's 'behind the scenes' work, indicates that the presence of republican women within the talks process invariably fell into normative gender typecasts. It certainly typified the 'women as backbone' discourse (Chapter 3). Edel recalled anecdotes such as how during negotiations women were told to go use the photocopier in order to prevent their political adversaries in the Democratic Unionist Party (DUP) (who resolutely refused to accept republicans in the peace process) from using it. Former IRA prisoner Rosaleen McCorley vented her frustration at the lack of women's input in the formal peace process during a film documentary organised by the Falls Women's Centre in 1995. She believed that while republican women were visible, they are 'seen but not really heard' (cited in O'Keefe 2013: 144). Similarly, in Colombia, the transition from revolutionary militants to political movement situated women into support roles such as secretaries and administrators (Ortega 2015: 242). Testimonies from combatant women involved in other conflicts around the globe demonstrate that feelings of gender parity in the ranks of the military are displaced by hierarchical roles distinctions in the peace. For many, and despite the hardships and suffering endured, life as a female combatant was better during conflict, not afterwards (Shekhawat and Saxena 2015: 124).

Furthermore, despite the rhetoric of inclusion and numerous manifesto pledges, there exists a striking gender division of labour within North of Ireland's main political parties. Empirical research on the day-to-day operations within North of Ireland's main political parties largely finds women located in 'behind the scenes' work (Matthews 2014). Recent examinations of the DUP, for instance, uncovers similar patterns, with some 'women in branches and associations just making tea' (Braniff and Whiting 2016: 103), and many others undertaking roles such as treasurers, running constituency offices, vote-getting, attending meetings, fundraising and organising events, described internally as the ubiquitous 'backbone roles' (Whiting *et al.* 2014). Like the typical patriarchal household, many political parties appear to exhibit a clear gender division of labour, undoubtedly governed by cultural norms and expectations regarding appropriate masculine and feminine roles. Given the high proportion of women within the bottom ranks of the parties, male dominance in the upper echelons is unquestionably facilitated and enabled by women's unpaid, low-status 'domestic' labour within many of the North of Ireland's political parties. While many may occupy such roles out of choice, there is, however, a striking pattern that exhibits the stock-in-trade characteristics of gender occupational segregation. Regardless, the picture emanating from the republican movement during this important period of transition hardly represents the most nascent conditions in which women's political representation and participation in peace talks is likely to flourish. The concentration of women at the bottom tiers of any political movement undeniably creates, at the very least, a patriarchal culture that only serves to impede women's political progression. While nationalism embedded gender alongside the broader nationalist agenda of equality and ending discrimination, the adversarial masculinity synonymous with competing ethnic blocs finds a privileged position in the style, substance and culture of formal peace negotiations, largely precluding republican women from any meaningful input.

In addition to the absence of a meaningful role in the talks, most interviewees stated that the top-down model used for the GFA effectively excluded many of their demands regarding the tackling of neo-liberal capitalism or the pursuit of social justice, indicating that standard forms of conflict resolution are focused solely on delivering a minimalist 'negative' peace. Many felt that the lack of social issues on the GFA talk's agenda resulted from Unionists and British attempts to prevent Sinn Féin's participation over the arms decommissioning issue. Linda felt that this was done to narrow the space for wider republican demands at the talks:

> Bringing issues of social justice to the talks table would have been perceived as a weakness; a stick to beat republicans with so the focus had to be on the constitutional issues or the Brits would have walked all over us.

Edel feels that this type of 'jockeying for position' by the various parties resulted in top-down, high-wire peace negotiations in which both women's participation and issues of social justice were simply marginalised. Nicola, a republican activist who currently works solely in the community sector recalls:

> I thought the peace agenda was very narrow to start with, but it just became narrower and narrower. It was not interested in hearing women's voices and just look at the reaction to the NIWC, the contempt shown by men within the unionist parties was really disappointing and I just thought 'there is that again'. Unionism has equal contempt for women and republicans, specifically republican women; bucket loads of contempt. So I felt the agenda being narrowed all the time and that initial hope and expectation just evaporated as the talks went on. This is what I termed earlier as the narrowing of the ground for women within the movement.

The 'narrowing of the ground' for women saw peace defined and anchored in a very state-centric outlook, with little or no radical potential. Karen, a former IRA volunteer who is now a Sinn Féin and community activist, echoes the sentiments of Nicola in believing that it was the state-centric nature of process itself which precluded any issues deemed outside standard conflict resolution:

> It was probably not possible to negotiate more than was done at each particular time and while I can see it would be a good thing to gain a lot more in terms of your negotiations like education and the like, it was probably more important if you can get the main things, get sufficient things agreed to move on because it was about moving it on and I think that's what makes it a bit tricky. There's a certain window of opportunity where you have to make progress or else things slide back.

Republican women seem profoundly aware of the limitations in standard approaches towards armed conflict. There is an acceptance that this form of 'conflict resolution' is capable of delivering only a negative peace, the de-escalation of military violence. The narrow agenda, and the prevailing threats of Sinn Féin's exclusion, effectively precluded any issues of social justice being on the agenda, according to interviewees. The view that it was only possible to address the 'main issues' indicates a hierarchical, exclusionary approach which sees state-centred issues deemed as the primary objectives, rendering all others subordinate. The stock-in-trade characteristics of standard institutional approaches to resolving armed conflict are marked by an unreceptive terrain for alternative, broader conceptualisations of peace.

Furthermore, interviewees also articulated a distinct sense of physical alienation from the process itself. Many stressed that armed conflict literally came in through their front doors, blurring traditional gender lines and creating spaces for women's active involvement. The proximity of the conflict, particularly in the urban centres and highly militarised regions along the border, ensured that republicans and nationalists lived and breathed the conflict daily. The political dynamic and physical location, however, shifted away from those working-class epicentres and relocated in the corridors of Stormont or Hillsborough Castle. There is a palpable sense of detachment among interviewees. Very few were involved within the talks at Stormont. It was felt that the conflict was fought on peoples' front doors, but the peace was very much devised behind closed doors.

SANDRA: The peace process came and it all sort of moved to Stormont. The political environment moved them away from the street up into Stormont. So you felt a detachment and certainly as a woman I feel detached from that sort of politics. And I think that's one of the things that has happened since the peace process ... a feeling of detachment.

The secretive and top-down approach was the antithesis of the grassroots, mass mobilisation of 'the Troubles' experienced by many of the interviewees. The absence of street politics, or perhaps more accurately, the lack of attention given by the leadership in the 1990s to street politics, indicates the focus of republican attention had shifted towards the higher levels of state power.

JANETTE: The benefits of grassroots democracy, and I think the problem is it shouldn't be high wire negotiations *unless* they are held accountable by the community. And I think that is why I would never want to be involved only in formal politics because of that lack of [grassroots] accountability.

Siobhan, a former IRA volunteer in Derry who now works as a Sinn Féin and community activist, recalls:

I think that whole period leading up to and after the GFA alienated and isolated a lot of people and it didn't have to happen that way. One part of the movement should have been negotiating while the other part should have been doing something with their grassroots people.

According to Kevin Bean, the republican movement 'moved from the politics of the streets into the anterooms of power; the days of revolutionary mobilisation in anything other than a commemorative or rhetorical sense were long over' (2007: 151). There is a sense that the political process, which had previously been a mixture of ad hoc demonstrations in reaction to local events, mass demonstrations and rallies and grassroots activism, was now formalised and highly technocratic.

LINDA: So when you look at how republican politics was through the early 1980s up until the early 1990s, it was all mass mobilisation, a sense of community solidarity. People who were not even what you would call republican were out marching with us against lots of different issues. After the war ended, and indeed in the years leading up to that, things really died down and got much slower, politically. So by the time of the ceasefire, there was virtually nothing in terms of street activism and community politics.

Orla, joined the IRA in Belfast in the late 1970s and is a former prisoner. She now works solely as a community activist and broadly supports the republican movement today but believes that the peace process was marked by a sense of disconnection between the leadership and grassroots activists:

> At a grassroots level, people on the ground are just not being kept in the loop. People are not being informed enough of what's happening. So there were meetings being held [at the time of the GFA] but it was more a case of 'this is what's happening at the talks' as opposed to 'what do yous think' and gauging peoples' opinions. So it was sort of 'this is happening and this happening, so you're either with us or you're not', that type of thing. Sort of then, I was starting to question myself; 'is this really what you want?'

Even those who remain within the party and close to the leadership acknowledge that Sinn Féin operated along strictly vertical lines of control during the peace process, where a 'very powerful and dominant leadership' led the way on issues of 'fundamental' importance' (cited in Frampton 2009: 117). This view was also shared by others within the party such as Eoin O'Broin who concurs that the party was probably 'a little more centralised' than it needed to be during the period of the peace process (cited in Frampton 2009: 117). It is this emerging 'leadership-led' culture that saw Eileen, and others, sever her ties with the Provisional republican movement:

> Then (after the GFA) you had all this so-called consultation; it wasn't a consultation, it was a *fait accompli*. It was signed, sealed, and dusted and I knew they were going to accept it but all they wanted was time to convince people. I saw a terrible change in the leadership's attitude; if you questioned what they were doing, you were pushed out.

Even among those reticent to be critical, many interviewees recall that communication with the grassroots was 'not as good as it should have been' during this period, with many indicating that such secrecy breeds suspicion among activists. The dearth of meaningful participation within the peace talks is therefore compounded by the complete absence of grassroots input or the mass mobilisation which characterised republican politics in the 1980s. A key attraction of mass mobilisation resides in the non-hierarchical and autonomous nature of grassroots organising, where 'rather than follow the dictates of union bosses, party leaders or church officials, women seek more autonomous forms of organisation where their own voice could be heard' (Foweraker 1995: 55).

The mass mobilisation as envisaged by republicans failed to materialise and so 'the picture of political demobilisation that emerged in the 1990s and 2000s was in marked contrast to this [1980s] vibrant activism' (Bean 2007: 151). This is certainly evident among many of the research participants. The use of mass mobilisation and grassroots input are vital components in politicising and attracting women to nationalist movements due to its bottom-up, grassroots dynamic, which stands in contrast to mainstream political action; grassroots organising is an essential component in politically mobilising nationalist women (Aretxaga 1997; Molyneux 1985). In other words, the absence of the mass mobilisation dynamic narrowed the spaces for republican women who were part of a movement which was increasingly relying on electoral strength and the adversarial 'hard bargaining' behind closed doors at Stormont to pursue its objectives. Despite their vital roles during armed struggle (Chapter 2), the immediate post-ceasefire period, particularly the GFA negotiations, sees women distinctly sidelined from any direct role in peace talks. Some of those within this research cite this juncture as the decisive moment in which they chose to leave the Provisional republican movement. While also critically aware of the perils regarding a change in direction and culture, others, however, chose to agitate from within, through the establishment of semi-autonomous women's groups. One of those was a group called *Clár na mBan*.

'Put a feminist stamp on it': Clár na mBan

By the early 1990s, it was clear that certain groups of republican women were profoundly aware of the vast pitfalls if the North's burgeoning peace process followed the standard, top-down format. Once again, republican women were organising autonomously to agitate around their needs and interests. *Clár na mBan* grew out of this ambivalent period of hope and fear among republican women. Most women within the movement were aware of the historical trends regarding the marginalisation of women and gender equality in the aftermath of revolutionary armed conflict.[9] As the question of state power gained prominence within the republican agenda in the mid-1990s, *Clár na mBan* articulated the belief that both the struggle for national self-determination and gender equality could not be mutually exclusive (Hackett 1995). As such, *Clár na mBan* were effectively holding the republican movement to account by ensuring that the feminist agenda did not disappear, reminding the leadership of their promises regarding feminism.

Clár na mBan began with a series of informal meetings of women in 1993 prompted by concern at the marginalisation of women's voices in the debate (Hackett 1995: 112). They criticised the absence of an independent women's voice within the Sinn Féin party (O'Keefe 2013; Sales 1997). Following the revelations of contacts between Hume and Adams, and particularly in the aftermath of the Downing Street Declaration in December 1993, *Clár na mBan* came together to discuss ways in which women's participation, demands, and needs would be represented within any future peace talks. This culminated in a conference in March 1994 entitled 'Women's Agenda for Peace'. It brought together republican women from across Ireland with the explicit aim of ensuring the meaningful inclusion of women's voices within any negotiated settlement. The main criticism from the conference focused on the secretive nature of the contacts and the very narrow political agenda, which was limited to discussing violence in a particular way (Connolly 1995; Sales 1997: 197).

Nicola was an activist in *Clár na mBan*:

> I remember after the ceasefire, myself and other people who were in the republican movement were all getting involved in the like of 'Disband the RUC' campaigns, and then you were just thinking what would replace that? You were realising what would be there for women in the peace? Like all these issues and questions are flying around and so this group emerged from that, *Clár na mBan* which came out of a conference. What could we do with this situation to put a feminist stamp on it; put a social justice stamp on it ... shaking the whole thing up; putting *everything* on the agenda for change.

Clár na mBan attracted criticism from those who saw any diversion from the national question as unhelpful. More ominously, there was a perception that challenges from women within the movement were 'often seen as disloyal, to be breaking ranks which need to be solid in order to be strong' (Hackett 1995: 113). At the conference held in March 1994, a statement was read from the female IRA prisoners at Maghaberry articulating their views for the future, stating that 'if the rights of women are to be supported, they must be supported fully and not be addressed in wishy-washy legislation' (cited in Connolly 1995: 124). Contributions to the conference were full of hope and cautious optimism while consistently balanced by a strong awareness of historical trends regarding the sidelining of women.

In discussions with interviewees, it was mentioned that another women's group, *Sheela na Gig*, had also formed at the same time. The group established itself in the mid and upper Falls road area in 1995. They were primarily motivated by a lack of communication from the leadership and by their need to have more women inputting into the peace process. Ruth, a former IRA member, Sinn Féin political representative and community activist was a founding member of the group:

> Well there was a sense of not knowing exactly what's going on here because you have to remember here, that after the ceasefire we were told little or nothing about what was going on. So we had no real idea about where this thing was going. So there was a group called Sheela na Gig set up and they were a group of women who weren't sure whether Sinn Féin was going the right way or whatever and that group was formed by republican women and what they did was murals, local pamphlets that were fired out again and again.

The inference from the data is that small circles of republicans at a leadership level were largely deciding the trajectory of the republican movement. While Ruth maintained that the group was short-lived and comprised a relatively small number of members, she maintains that it was the 'quality' of the membership which indicated its political weight. Ruth named many prominent republicans, and illustrates that prominent women were prepared to organise themselves to pursue their demands within the movement. *Clár na mBan* and *Sheela na Gig* are in themselves evidence that republican women organised autonomously to pursue their interests and ensure their contributions were heard.

When asked about the disbandment of *Sheela na Gig*, Ruth elaborates that the leadership opened a bit more in response to their formation and actions and in doing so explained in more detail where they saw the peace process going. After this, *Sheela na Gig* participants were 'persuaded' that the leadership was taking the right path, and so quickly disbanded with most members remaining within the fold of the Provisional republican movement. Republican women were galvanised into action by a compounding fear that women's interests would not be represented at the talks table and a firm belief that formal peace negotiations and new peace accords 'in and of itself does not create the conditions for gender equality' (Holt 2003; Richter-Devroe 2012; Sharoni 1998: 1089).

With the dismantling of the North of Ireland state now firmly displaced by a largely reformist agenda, the new political realism within Sinn Féin demanded a more pragmatic approach which saw the party display all the staples of a formal, mainstream party. The reassertion of patriarchal cultures and expectations, perhaps best illustrated by attempts to allocate women tokenistic or 'backroom' roles during the GFA negotiations, occurs at a time when the party was moving towards a more mainstream, constitutional standpoint. Women and their objectives were effectively sidelined, despite their resistance, when state power was at stake. If the specific conditions of armed conflict mobilised republican women, then it is unsurprising that such seismic changes during conflict transition severely impacted upon the mobility of their political struggles. Perhaps the most potent illustration of this shift within Provisional republicanism, and the declining fortunes of republican women, is the ambiguous demise of the Sinn Féin Women's Department.

A gendered casualty of peace: the Sinn Féin women's department

From the late 1970s republican women began organising within the republican movement to assert their own political agenda and interests. A prominent outlet was the establishment of the Sinn Féin Women's Department in 1979. This section critically explores the establishment, activism and eventual demise of this bastion of republican feminism, arguing that its decline substantiates the argument that the republican movement moved towards a more institutional position, producing a less radical stance on feminist and women's issues. While the discourse and iconography within nationalist ideologies can position women's semi-autonomous organisations as nothing more than 'glorified tea clubs' (Geisler 2004: 89), nevertheless it is important to examine the ways in which women can use such spaces for the advancement of their particular needs and interests.

The foundation of the Women's Department represented a collective effort by republican women to ensure that they had a voice and political spaces within the republican movement. Former head of the Women's Department Mairead Keane explains that

> women came together through their involvement in the nationalist struggle … to discuss the issues that were affecting them not only as women but as women political activists, and there was a need to have an organised political voice within the party. This culminated in the discussion about departments and the need to have a separate department in which women could come together and meet as women, as women only, to discuss, to debate, and to push forward the issues important to us. There was a need for a group that would serve as a support for women within the party.
>
> (Lyons and Keane 1992: 265)

Anne was involved in the establishment of the Women's Department and recalls:

> There were very strong women like Maire Moore and like that and Rita O'Hare of course, so I was involved in the whole development of women's first policy document that was put in front of the *Ard Comhairle*, which was fully endorsed. Then we broadened it out to male comrades because this had to be sold to the male membership before it went to an *Ard Fheis* so those were very intense and eye opening experiences as well and of course you had some of the traditional, macho men within the party resisting but then when you talked them round after more discussion then they mellowed a little and saw the merits because our objective was to get this passed in the *Ard Fheis* so I'm proud to say I was part of that.

Echoing Anne, Janette who was also heavily involved is the establishment of the Department, says:

> The Sinn Féin *Ard Fheis* and *Ard Comhairle* recognised the need for a women's voice and that this was the time to set up a Women's Department, so women could develop and come to the fore. Now, the reason this is happening is because some women were linking up with Women Against Imperialism. They were involved in setting up the Rape Crisis Centre in Belfast and so you had all these really strong republican women.

This indicates that the roots of the Women's Department resided solely with the agency of republican women themselves with little input from the male-led leadership. It is indicative of a vibrant and powerful feminist voice within the republican movement, particularly their links to wider women's groups and organisation within working-class republican communities. Some have posited a rather cynical appraisal of the republican movement's newfound gender ideological awakening during this time, arguing that women and feminism were used as 'window dressing' (Power 2010). Such a perspective, however, neglects the fact that sustaining the Women's Department as a potent and radical political force within republicanism stemmed from republican women themselves, not the leadership. Moreover, the activism and energies of the Women's Department achieved some remarkable feats within what was (and remains) a male-dominated movement containing many conservative forces among its eclectic membership.

Within the largely conservative and male-dominated sphere of formal Irish politics in the early 1980s, the creation of the Women's Department was an important development, particularly given the issues they pursued. The development of a 'women's section' was not unique to Sinn Féin; other parties such as the Ulster Unionist Party did have a women's section as such, although their main role was that of an auxiliary or 'vote getter'. The Sinn Féin Women's Department, however, advocated around issues that at the time were deemed highly controversial topics such as divorce, access to contraception, domestic violence, and equality for LGBT, among others (Maillot 2005; O'Keefe 2003; Power 2010).

FIONA: Well, the Women's Department was a separate department within Sinn Féin. It was organised solely by women and there were quite a few events and campaigns that we run. The right to march to the city centre [for International Women's Day], highlighting issues that were particularly important to women that maybe at one stage would have got swallowed up by the party. But you had women's conferences and we had that every year in all different places and all well attended, and it gave women that wee bit of space to organise on their own and organise around their own issues. It worked very well but obviously it's more mainstreamed into the party now.

EDEL: What was interesting in Sinn Féin at that time was the Women's Department and that gave us an outlet for that [feminism]. Women like Mairead Keane, Jenifer McCann and Una Gillespie and that definitely gave a sense that while the party was completely imperfect when it came to those issues especially issues around choice, there was, however, a core radical feminist analysis that was valued and we could agitate even within the party and that and try to find a voice for a republican feminist analysis in broader society and because there was a feminist analysis of what was occurring to women in jail.

LINDA: Well, there were a lot of women in the [Women's] Department from Dublin and that and a lot in there with feminist views and that is what attracted me to the Women's Department and even now I'm still into the thing of standing up for women and I love to work with women in the job of helping women.

This suggests that an overt feminist outlook informed much of the activism in and around the Women's Department, with many stressing the presence of strong feminist voices coupled with the political space as key strengths of the Department. From a feminist perspective, it is also an important development, because the department identified two main sites of political struggle: formal politics and grassroots activism (O'Keefe 2003). Republican women were not merely concerned with increasing their visibility or quantity within the ranks of the party or as political representatives. Similarly, Palestinian women have long organised in parallel structures within popular committees, refugee, camps and local NGOs as branches of the PLO (Aharoni 2016: 7). In El Salvador, combatant women in the Marxist FMLN organised semi-autonomous women's organisations to denounce violence against women, highlight the differences between male and female experiences of the war (Ortega 2015: 234). While many combatant women in El Salvador were not initially motivated by feminist or gender concerns, the revolutionary platform and agenda of Farabundo Martí National Liberation Front (FMLN) provided the ideological and practical space for women to engage in feminist political thought and activism (Ortega 2015). In a similar fashion, republican women were also challenging patriarchal structures and cultures of domination 'by advocating on practical, day-to-day issues of fundamental importance to many women, issues that mirror those of the broader women's movement'. (O'Keefe 2013: 135). In addition to agitating for change within Sinn Féin and formal party politics, the Department also sought opportunities to address directly the issues impacting upon the lives of working-class women in nationalist and republican communities. The establishment of women's community centres and services in working-class communities in the cities of Derry and Belfast is littered throughout the interview data as a prominent achievement. In particular, the links between the Women's Department and the establishment of Women's Centres, particularly in Derry and the Falls Women's Centre in Belfast are most prevalent.

JANETTE: I didn't see myself as a feminist until 1979 because we established the Women's Department in 1980 but I had never read anything about feminism. By 1979, that had changed, and I was reading about feminism and things like that. I had some socialist feminist friends and I suppose I was just naïve about [women] being discriminated against. But once I began thinking about the social and economic impact on women. And so we [republican women] set up the first Women's Centre here in Derry, particularly around issues of domestic violence.

ANNE: I was heavily involved with the Department and the connections we had working with women in the community as well. We got the Falls Women's Centre up and running in an old derelict building which was the old Sinn Féin centre at the bottom of Clonard Street. An old building, three storey building, a dump but we all got together, and we fixed it up. Some money came from the movement, but we set it up and it was for women who were suffering domestic violence, women who needed advice, women's issues, you know, around at that time and also the focal point for advocacy with protests on the streets and reclaiming our streets, like women who were afraid to go out, perhaps women who were raped. After that we started a campaign to get statutory funding for a proper Women's Centre which now sits on the Falls at Beechmount.[10] But it was only a handful of us really. But that was just real determination you know? We [republican women] saw the need in the area and said, 'what will we do about it' and we just did it.

Kelly, who previously worked as a manager of the Falls Women's Centre, states that it was the direct input of republicans, particularly the Women's Department, which established the centre. Equally, Karen states that 'a lot of the women's community organisations grew out of the republican struggle too, like the Falls Women's Centre'. There is a relatively long-standing history of community activism in nationalist/republican communities (Bean 2011; Cassidy 2005). From the late 1970s onwards, there was a marked rise in the number of Women's Centres established, which provided space and services to tackle a myriad of issues directly outside of those related to armed conflict. While state violence was unsurprisingly a pressing concern within these centres, many also dealt with issues of poverty, gender-based violence and education, among many others. In other words, republican women were agitating around issues such as sexual and domestic violence, poverty, women's education, at a time when such issues were considered outside of male-led, mainstream party politics in Ireland. There is an overwhelming sense of satisfaction echoed across most interviews when discussing the endeavours and achievements of the Women's Department. Their political agenda and activism is indicative of a vibrant level of feminist consciousness among many republican women, despite the confines and limitations of a male-dominated political party.

In addition to the links and activism for women within working-class republican communities, the Women's Department also had an impact on the formal politics of Sinn Féin. Within the party's 'equality agenda', gender equality was defined as a fundamental principle within Sinn Féin's republicanism (Maillot 2005: 107). Sinn Féin is keen to be viewed as taking the necessary steps to become a more gender-balanced party and consistently returns the largest number of women to the North of Ireland Assembly (Maillot 2005; Side 2009: 75). A key contribution of the Women's Department was the women's policy document, the first of its kind of any of the political parties on the island, in which was included appeals for public childcare and childcare to be shared by both parents (O'Keefe 2013: 135). Sinn Féin became the first political party in Ireland to provide childcare at its annual *Ard Fheis* (party conference); a subsequent motion at the 1986 *Ard Fheis* ensured that the party would pay childcare costs when such facilities are unavailable at party meetings or functions. While today Sinn Féin is widely hailed for its relatively progressive stance on women (Buckley 2013; Galligan 2013), recent controversies regarding allegations made by women and men of sexual abuse at the hands of male republicans has certainly impacted the validity of this stance

Sinn Féin has displayed a sustained commitment to gender equality (Galligan 2013: 429). 'Positive action' (Lovenduski 2005) has been a key strength in Sinn Féin's post-war strategy and most research participants welcomed party actions around changes to start and end times for meetings, protests and commemorations as well as the provision of crèche and childcare facilities at all major party meetings and functions. They also advocate strongly around LGBT rights, domestic violence and access to contraception in party policy. According to party policy, Sinn Féin advocates 'the use of all possible mechanisms for advancing gender equality including: equality and other legislation; funding for women's groups; affirmative action; gender-proofing; gender mainstreaming' (Sinn Féin 2004: 1). The party's policies in these areas are motivated by the 'vital need for equal participation for women in politics'. Sinn Féin has made good its promise around affirmative action and in 2003 the party adopted a 50:50 gender representation for its *Ard Comhairle*. Gender proofing and mainstreaming were also integrated as standard practice within party policy. In the South of Ireland general election manifestoes of 2007 and 2011 the party advocated a 40 per cent share of cabinet positions to women, a review of the working hours of Leinster House and the creation of a more family-friendly environment.

When it comes to the issue of electoral candidate selection, the zealous pace of Sinn Féin's participatory rights for women decelerates considerably. The Sex Discrimination (Election Candidates) Act, 2002, under the GFA allows political parties the option of undertaking positive discrimination in the selection of female candidates for electoral contests but so far, not a single party in the North of Ireland has utilised this measure. Despite pledges of affirmative action, Sinn Féin uses informal targets around female candidate selection in attempting to increase female candidates (Buckley 2013; McGing 2013), although the party is also credited 'with offering women winnable seats' (Galligan 2013: 421). While other endeavours around divisive matters such as abortion proved far more arduous and troubling, the Women's Department agitated around topics often taboo in a largely conservative, Catholic Ireland. In particular, the demands of the Women's Department were all the more significant given that divorce, reproductive rights and contraception were illegal in the South of Ireland at the time (O'Keefe 2013: 136).

Of course, these successes need to be qualified in the context of a feminist struggle within a formal political party. The actions and spaces utilised by the Women's Department are not archetypal feminist ways of organising. Many feminists organise either through non-hierarchical autonomous groups and collective actions, or through participation within social movements (Naples 2013; Safa 1990). Progressive social movements seek to build the collective power of the excluded, marginalised or oppressed constituents so that they can access human rights and challenge dominant ideologies and power relations (Batliwala and Brown 2006). The notion of women organising within a formal political party therefore appears to be the antithesis of any type of feminist organising other than liberal. Formal political parties are imbued with relations of power, hierarchical control and organise for the attainment of state control, and so are hardly the likely sites that will foster a progressive feminist agenda (Young 2000).

Given the largely conservative nature of most mainstream political parties in Ireland (Galligan and Wilford 1999; Sales 1997), feminist organising within a male-dominated movement whose primary concern was the national question is an atypical environment in which to pursue a feminist struggle. Undoubtedly, strict limitations were placed on the scope of republican feminist activism, where they faced formidable internal battles with those of a more conservative standpoint, particularly around the issue of abortion (Frampton 2009). Given its male domination, and the prevalence of a strong commitment to Catholicism, the battle by some republican women for a pro-choice position calls into question the validity of a party that claims to be both socialist and progressive on the issue of women's equality. Most interviewees are profoundly aware of these limitations. Despite the claims to equality within the republican ranks both by interviewees and rhetorically from the leadership, the fact remains that the national cause takes precedence always, ensuring the gender or feminism was never the primary objective. Gemma, a self-described republican feminist, sums up this position:

> In so many ways things have improved but in others it hasn't in the ways that I'd like it to. But in terms of Sinn Féin, they are still the most progressive and radical in terms of gender and now it's not perfect and wonderful but if you look at the other parties, Sinn Féin are a hell of a lot more forward.

There is overwhelming support among interviewees for Sinn Féin's current position on gender equality and women's rights. Despite this however, acknowledgements regarding the imperfections and tensions between party policy and what women themselves want are scattered throughout the interview data, indicating that many are cogent of the enforced boundaries imposed on women's struggles within a male-led political party. In sum, while the many endeavours of the Women's Department undoubtedly produced meaningful and discernible results, measuring feminist activism within male-dominated formal party politics is hardly the most radical gauge. Despite its successes and its prominence in the lives of republican women in this research, the subsequent demise of the department is characterised by confusion and ambiguity.

'Just faded away?' A most ambiguous ending

The demise of the Women's Department in the mid-1990s, and the emergence of the Equality Department in its place, is perhaps the most compelling illustration of the regression experienced by republican women during the conflict transition years. Having endured, and even politically thrived during some of the worst years of armed conflict, I suggest here that the ambiguous collapse of the Women's Department is directly related to the ideological shift to institutional politics within the post-ceasefire period. The feminist politics of the Women's Department and the overall movement's shift towards institutional politics constructed two incompatible strategies; the former, an echo of their revolutionary past, the latter, the future constitutional direction of the movement. When asked about the ending of the Women's Department, not a single participant could pinpoint exactly the date or the reasons for its demise. There was no great fanfare, no statement from the party hierarchy announcing the ending of the department, no vast restructuring of the party apparatus; according to most interviewees, the Women's Department just 'fell away'.

According to Anne, the Department had succeeded in bringing republican women to the fore:

> Women are now discussing politics in every sphere of the organisation, so their views will be fed into the *Ard Comhairle* and their views will be fed into the *Ard Fheiseanna*. The Women's Department was needed at that particular time, but policy overall now is determined by *cumann*, from the grassroots so that's where you start to impact on women's lives with difference policies and different projects. If there's a [women's] need then the party centrally takes those needs and women are at the centre of all of that and centre of the party.

Bernie echoes the sentiments of Anne arguing that the Department was a product of its time and is no longer needed in the current environment:

> Well, by the time armed struggle ended we had already secured equality within the movement; women were equal. And I believe Sinn Féin are actively promoting women, because, I mean, the many women candidates that stood there in the last elections, thankfully, the majority were all successful. There are more women now than there ever was.

Both Bernie and Anne's thoughts typify the voice of those who believe that the achievement of equality in the party structures rendered the work of the Women's Department completed (Sales 1997: 175). There are several problems with such a sentiment. First, ostensibly the objectives of the Women's Department were far broader than simply including women as formal equals in party politics. Second, we know that women were – and still are – struggling for equality and recognition within the republican movement, despite their rhetorical assurances to the contrary. Third, it contradicts the vision of women's equality as the eradication of patriarchy, as explored in Chapter 3. The notion that 'equality' has been achieved within the party suggests that some republican women interpreted the Women's Department as a vehicle for change solely within the republican movement, and not outside of it.

Most others however, cited the shift towards institutional politics and the primacy afforded to the demands of the 'peace process' as the downfall of the Department.

> KELLY: I don't know, it just appeared to fade into the background [during the peace process] and it just needs looking at again and I know it has. I think we [republican women] did regress for a while, I think women were put

back in the background again. The peace process was on now so let them ones [male republicans] make the decisions. But when we opened the women's garden [2007 in Roddy McCorley Club, Belfast] that was the first time we said 'where's the women in all of this' and 'let's get this back again'. When Siobhan[11] died [2006] and it was just about asking 'where are the women' who just disappeared and then they [the leadership] did the garden and nothing much since and I think the politics too is changed as well. So some people fell away by the way side and didn't stay with the republican movement and went to other organisations.

Kelly, like many other interviewees, invariably conflates the 'peace process' and a 'new type of politics', suggesting that the vast ideological transformation within the republican movement was the catalyst for the demise of the Women's Department. Many other interviewees echo her thoughts on the primacy of peace:

ELAINE: I was actually talking to someone recently about this and we were discussing the women in the party in the 1980s and looking at the things that were written back then and we were asking 'where are those women today?' And I think something happened after the GFA, or maybe even just after the ceasefires but it looks like the women involved at that time [1980s] were far more radical and militant in their views. So what happened was that they left or were just exited from activism and then took with them all of these progressive views on feminist issues.

GEMMA: I don't know ... there was this party development where a lot of structures were put in together and I think we had a new head of gender equality and this was a salaried position, so it fell away. So there was a Women's Department until the mid-1990s but then you had the ceasefires, the GFA, and everyone was so involved in those events [peace process] so that is why the focus was lost a wee bit and then after that each *cúigí*[12] had to have their own gender equality representative.

There is a distinct lack of clarity when recounting this period, where the materialisation of the peace process and electoral politics appears to displace other political outlets within the republican movement. Outside of the formal interviews, I made numerous formal and informal inquiries to the Sinn Féin party (which I detail in full a little later in this section), which failed to yield a clear and unequivocal answer to the question of what happened to the Women's Department. Nevertheless, consistent throughout many of the replies to my inquiries is that the period of the mid-1990s was consumed with the capricious peace process and formal negotiations. With control of state power at stake, many of the other political struggles were cast aside until the 'bigger question' of institutional power was resolved. To pursue the formal peace process, all republican energies, including those of the Women's Department, were channelled into formal peace negotiations and electoral gains, mirroring similar trends in other revolutionary struggles.

Once again, the similarities between republican women and those in other regions of the globe are striking. In Kashmir, all-women groups were formed to promote and justify women's participation in the separatist movement, with Dukhtaran-e-Millat (DM) being the largest (Shekhawat 2015: 105). They fell short, however, in advocating for women's rights and the right of women's participation in peace talks. Seema Shekhawat concurs that the absence of a genuine and organised voice to advocate for women's rights, significantly diminished the chances of women's inclusion in the peace process. In Nicaragua, the Sandinista National Liberation Front (FSLN) women's organisation Association of Women Confronting the National Problem (AMPRONAC) advocated radical stances on many issues, rooted in women's experiences and the assumption that women have gender-specific experiences and issues (Chinchilla 1990: 374). In the aftermath of the 1979 victory AMPRONAC was restructured and retitled the Luisa Amanda Espinoza Association of Nicaraguan Women (AMNLAE). Its primary objective as specified by the FSLN would be to mobilise its energy behind campaigns of national reconstruction (Chinchilla 1990: 376). Counter-revolution, military threat, and economic scarcity however, was taking its toll on the Sandinista experiment. AMNLAE reduced its public identification with feminism and its priority now was 'the defence of the revolution' (Molyneux 1985: 238). Just as in Nicaragua and elsewhere, the transition away from armed conflict in the North of Ireland witnessed a re-ordering of priorities that saw women's struggles subordinated for more pressing matters of concern, perfectly encapsulating what Cynthia Enloe describes as the 'not now, later' (2014: 120) moment.

When asked about what happened to the Women's Department, Fiona, a prominent member of the Department replies:

> I don't know, I really don't know. I think what happened was at the time you had like Maire Moore, Mairead Keane and myself and people there that were pivotal, people who organised it and then some of them women went into different roles within the party and then there was a view that it would be more mainstreamed. The peace process was probably a big part of that [disbandment] and we were going into that type of politics there and the drive was for the peace process and a lot of the leadership people were driving that type of agenda.

Like Kelly's thoughts outlined earlier, Fiona's report touches on two hugely important issues; first, that the focus of the entire movement centred upon the ever fragile and often failing peace process and second, that the movement itself was experiencing a transition towards a different 'type' of politics. The transition period witnesses a vast ideological departure within Sinn Féin that is marked by leadership-driven policy changes and a radical shift from purported revolutionary standpoints (Tonge 2006). And 'as the party becomes increasingly preoccupied with electoral success, the interests of women fade from prominence' (O'Keefe 2013: 138). Fiona's account, like most of the interviews, reveals an awareness that the movement was shifting towards a more institutional path and so, the radical, grassroots activism was something that required tempering and refinement to fit in with the new institutional departure. Elaine, a senior Sinn Féin member and community activist, outlines her explanation for the winding down of the Women's Department:

> In a conflict situation, you're not involved in any institutions and you can get up and say what the hell you like because there is nothing to lose. You can talk about war or abortion and be involved in it because you're in a war situation, but once you're in [political] institutions then it is very different and then you're fighting elections and very conscious around who says what, and I am sure that had a big part to play.

As electoral contests gained primacy, public perceptions and popularity limited previously radical positions. Elaine's explanation divulges that electoral politics required an ideological reformation within the republican movement. Undoubtedly, the transition years witnessed a leadership-driven discipline within the movement (Bean 2007; Tonge 2006) where the party moved from 'purported revolutionary republican vanguardism towards becoming a competitive actor in the political marketplace. 'New' Sinn Féin 'seeks respect for its electoral mandate, co-operates with other parties and constructs its agenda primarily based upon equality and rights rather than issues of sovereignty and territory' (Tonge 2006: 136). While acknowledging that both the IRA and Sinn Féin always existed as hierarchical structures (and mainly male-led leadership), many research participants recall witnessing a hardening of party lines during this period, which contrasted with the spaces previously available to discourse and debate within the movement during armed struggle.

Though Maria Power (2010) suggests that the Women's Department was defunct by the late 1980s, there is much archival material documenting publications by the department throughout the 1990s and even as recently as 2000.[13] Through extensive searches on-line but more importantly at the vast political literature collection at Belfast's Linen Hall Library, the final publication from the Women's Department that I could find dates to the year 2000 with *Women In An Ireland Of Equals*. After this, there is an abundance of party literature and policy documents on women's rights, yet they appear not as Women's Department publications but under different headings, again highlighting the ambiguity over the demise of the department. For example, in 2002, a document also entitled *Women in an Ireland of Equals* is published by the Sinn Féin Women's Committee, while in 2007 the Sinn Féin Women's Manifesto is a Sinn Féin only publication. The lack of an actual date or event marking the end (or at best, the reformulation) of the department muddies the waters on its exact demise, but it is distinctly apparent that by the mid-1990s the Women's Department was defunct and the new Equality Department emerged.[14]

During this research I made both formal and informal inquiries (through phone conversations, email and face-to-face informal conversation) to people in various positions in Sinn Féin. The replies I received were mixed, and at times opaque. Informally (through phone conversation), I was told that the Women's Department formally ended in the late 1990s, when Lucilita Bhreatnach, who was prominent within the Department changed role within the party. Another source informed me that it 'never officially ended' because of the existence of a 'women's group' within the party today but then went on to reiterate that it is no longer an official 'department'. Another source told me that the Women's Department was still technically in existence after the formation of the Equality Department in 2002 and was subsequently re-named 'Gender Equality'. Another prominent Sinn Féin member told me through email that

> there is a lot of confusion regarding the dates. It's quite possible the Women's Department formally ceased in the late 1990s, or just ceased functioning as a department at that time, and there were maybe one or two people who issued documents under the name afterwards.

In 2006, a conference in Belfast called 'Entitled Voices – Women in International Struggle' was organised by the Sinn Féin Equality Department.[15] A key speaker at this event was Eibhlín Glenholmes, a senior republican who was listed as Sinn Féin's National coordinator for Gender Equality at the time. In an interview published in the party newspaper *An Phoblacht/Republican News* in March 2006, she states that

> Sinn Féin's Party Development Department has been charged with creating and developing programs and mechanisms by which we will truly become representative of society. Within that department I have responsibility to ensure gender equality. I will use whatever tools are necessary to ensure that women are not just seen but are also heard.
>
> (An Phoblacht 2006)

I contacted Eibhlín[16] by email and in her reply, she states that

> The department was known as 'The Women's Department' under Lucilita but when I came into post as Co-ordinator in late August 2005 (after the 28th of July *Oglaigh na HEireann* statement[17]) the Department became known as the Gender Equality Department. Along with the Recruitment Department and the Education Department the three departments formed the Party Development Department. In February 2006 I was elected to the *Ard Chomhairle*. The really interesting stuff [within this department] was the training of young women into leadership roles. They committed to three days intensive training every two to three months for a year. The programme had a 100 per cent retention rate – I actually had *more* women at the end than I started off with. I remained in that post until June 2011.

Of course, an alternative reading of the data could postulate that the real story here is that now the crisis of armed action has passed, the reserve army of women were supplementary to requirements. Carol Coulter (1993) and Margaret Ward (1989) have both documented the historical pattern of women's marginalisation by Irish republicanism and nationalism in the aftermath of independence struggles of the past. Both concur that women have never been accepted as equals by men within such movements. There is undoubtedly more than a grain of truth to such assertions, yet it is entirely premised on the ways men situate women as opposed to examining where women situate themselves in the aftermath of armed conflict. Unquestionably, women were marginalised during the period in question, yet that is but a partial telling of the story. There is no suggestion at all that Sinn Féin is excluding women. On the contrary, there is a chorus of feminist praise for the party's consistent progressive record on women (Buckley 2013; Galligan 2013; Sales 1997). After the resignation of Martin McGuinness in January 1917, the republican leadership endorsed and appointed Michelle O'Neill as its party leader in the North of Ireland. In the last Assembly elections in the North in March 2017, Sinn Féin returned 11 female MLAs out of its 27 MLAs, once again retaining its position as the party with the highest percentage of women among its elected representatives. In other words, the 'reserve army' thesis does not stand in the face of Sinn Féin's relatively progressive record on promoting women. What I argue here is that it is feminism, not women, which is the reserve army, now supplementary to post-war requirements.

Therefore, it is important to link the shift towards institutional methods with the diminishing feminist politics associated with the Women's Department. According to Eibhlin Glenholmes, Co-ordinator for Gender Equality, the body which replaced the Women's Department actively trained women in areas of 'leadership' in order that they progress through the ranks of the party, yielding many benefits for the party's increase in female candidates. The demise of the Women's Department therefore should not be read as an outright exclusion of women within the movement as such, but is more indicative of the new ways in which the party re-conceptualised women's equality as women's participatory rights within formal politics.

The end of the Women's Department, however, does largely represent the end of republican feminism within Provisional republicanism. The ideological departure from revolutionary agitating towards a more mainstream position invariably shaped the spaces available to republican feminists. During the peace process, republicans adopted the language and ideas more closely bound to mainstream politics (Ryan 1997); 'the softer language of transition and gradualism has replaced the maximalist imperatives of a revolutionary party' (Bean 2007: 141). In keeping with this new form of politics, the emergence of the 'Equality Agenda' during the peace process significantly blunted the cutting edge of republican feminism without cutting off republican women.[18] By adopting relatively mainstream mechanisms such as quotas and utilising a discourse of citizenship and rights to pursue gender equality, the republican movement effectively included republican feminists while excluding feminism.[19] In other words, it illustrates the perilous downfalls for women's radical political organising within institutional-orientated political movements, which invariably produces a strategy synonymous with liberal feminism.

Across most interviews there is an acceptance that the previously strong feminist standpoints and agitation by republican women was the product of the specific context of armed struggle. The party's pursuit of electoral gains in the transition demanded that women's feminist positions, like the armed struggle itself, would be firmly associated with past tactics. While individual women may gain through mainstream mechanisms of quotas and increased visibility, evidence here indicates that state-centric politics remains inhospitable for anything other than liberal approaches to feminist politics. The dilution of overt republican feminism within the emerging conflict transition landscape was profoundly felt by those within the Women's Department. Aoife states that;

> I got involved in *Clár na mBan* because for me the Women's Department were not doing enough for me anymore and I wanted something far more radical, more room for debate.

The merging of the Women's Department with other political issues within what would be called the catch-all 'Equality Department' meant that what was once a relatively radical tool for republican feminism was replaced with the gender-neutral terminology of 'citizenship', 'equality' and 'rights', therefore removing the gender specifics of women's struggle. Janette, a life-long republican who is now a Sinn Féin member and community activist expresses that sense of loss:

> It [women's struggle] did get lost and I think it did become the Equality Department and I think there is definitely a loss there, that is a loss, just like I think if you have a women's specific party or whatever bringing up women's issues on their own then I think it far more pertinent and more focused than bringing up general equality issues.

Fiona, a former IRA prisoner who is currently a Sinn Féin representative, was a prominent activist within the Women's Department and believes that the subsuming of women's struggle within an overall equality agenda has closed spaces previously available to republican women.

FIONA: Well the Women's Department were highlighting issues that were particularly important to *women* [with emphasis] that otherwise would have got swallowed up by the party. So you had women's conferences every year in all different places and all well attended, and it gave women that wee bit of space to organise on their own and organise around their own issues and it worked very well but that space is now gone obviously as it's more mainstreamed into the party now.

GEMMA: When it became the Equality Department it became less militant because it's [women's struggles] not to the forefront then, it is always way down low on the list and we were constantly reminding people of things such as last week we had a conference and there was no childcare so a few of us got together to try and put gender back to the top of the agenda again because we seem to be forgetting about it again.

Gemma's testimony is typical in her acknowledgement that republican politics has shifted away from radical or what Gemma terms 'militant' politics towards a more mainstream position, obviously causing difficulties for those who preferred grassroots advocacy in pursuit of women's struggle. Findings suggest that feminist spaces opened by and for women's political activism during the conflict years were slowly squeezed by a sense of retrenchment during the peace process, which I contend, correlate to Sinn Féin's shift towards a more institutional position. The entire energy and focus of the republican movement in the years of 1994 to 1998 and beyond was the peace process and electoral politics. All other spheres of political activism around gender, class, and minority equality were put on hold as the pursuit of state power became central.

Within the formal peace process, republican politics would now manifest solely in party policy, legislation and, of course, political rhetoric. In this new era, 'equality and rights' replaced the strategies of revolutionary agitation and so, women's struggle for emancipation would be sequestered and emerge in the post-ceasefire period as something far more tempered and modest. Previous advocacy around reproductive rights or strip searching by state forces were watered down and substituted by mainstream actions such as legislative affirmation around gender equality of opportunity and the selective use of positive discrimination by use of gender quotas. What emerged in its place, the Equality Department, bore little or no resemblance to the radical politics and feminist struggles that went before in the Women's Department.

While women's struggle was deemed an essential part of the revolutionary strategy during the conflict by women themselves, armed conflict itself appears to have been a specific pre-condition for the housing of such a strong feminist voice within the movement's ideological canon. Implicit within the post-war re-ordering is a view that feminism is somehow associated with revolutionary, subversive politics. To reflect the new state-centric political positioning, feminism was deemed unsuitable and replaced with a more fitting 'Equality Agenda'. The emerging political landscape within the new 'peaceful' dispensation had little time or space for a radical struggle. Women's struggle within the republican movement was diluted, de-radicalised, and sanitised within the new post-ceasefire landscape; it was repackaged, rebranded, and subsumed within the ambiguously titled 'Equality Department'. The shape and methods employed in pursuing women's interests within the republican movement required some enforced bespoke tailoring to fit the new straitjacket of formal peace process politics.

At the time of field research (2012–2013), 14 interviewees stated that there were significant efforts already underway to resurrect the Women's Department. It remains to be seen if such efforts come to fruition. Many of those interviewees are currently involved in such endeavours, something strongly supported by the vast majority of research participants. Edel felt that a new Women's Department is essential if the party is to move on the abortion issue:

EDEL: Without a Women's Department that articulates and advocates for that, how will it [pro-choice position] ever happen? Sinn Féin as a party and republicanism in general can only benefit from people who have strong feminist views, especially on issues of women's choice and not worrying about looking out of step. It's healthy to have diverse voices within a movement, voices that others within the party don't necessarily agree with. But republicans can say 'look we're a diverse party with different voices within it'.

GEMMA: Things are far from perfect for women. Gender equality is my main interest in the party and I currently sit on a group with other women with a view to forming a new Women's Department.

Just as was the case with the original Women's Department in the late 1970s, the contemporary efforts stem from a frustration at the lack of women's voice within republican politics, a voice that articulates and agitates on a broader spectrum beyond women's institutional participation.

Notwithstanding the sense of loss among interviewees about the demise of the Women's Department, it is important to also state that most of them supported Sinn Féin's current approaches to promoting women and gender equality within the party. There is a discernible frustration however, that such measures do not wholly encompass the type of women's equality as envisioned by many republican women. It reaffirms that while the institutional staples such as rhetorical affirmations, positive discrimination, gender quotas, legislative and constitutional guarantees regarding women's equality are positives, they are clearly insufficient to meet their specific demands and needs of working-class republican women. As the peace process 'beds down' some 20 years on from the 1994 ceasefires, some republican women are now asking the question 'where are the women?' The ambiguous ending of the Women's Department, I concur, is indicative of the limitations of pursuing a feminist struggle solely within formal party politics.

Conclusion

Conventional narratives of war and peace tend to depict a straightforward division of roles between female 'victims' and male 'protagonists'. Gendered assumptions regarding the linkages of femininity with peacefulness and vulnerability perhaps find their clearest expression in women's exclusion from formal peace negotiations. Given their perceived 'anomalous' role as combatants, one might therefore expect to find female combatants taking their rightful place at the negotiating table alongside their male comrades. Despite the wealth of scholarly research displacing the gender tropes of war, and, notwithstanding the passing of SCR 1325 affirming the importance of women's participation in conflict resolution, women, regardless of their wartime roles, are generally excluded from formal peace processes. While both male and female combatants may contend that the crisis of war diminishes the saliency of gender, the post-war reordering of men and women's roles however, are profoundly gendered. Regardless of women's various roles in armed conflict, the experiences of combatant women remind us of the centrality of gender in processes of conflict transition and the way it is utilised to undermine women's agency and participation.

The central argument developed in this chapter has been focused on the consequences for women during the transition of a male-led movement from revolutionary agitation to a mainstream, political party vying for state power. The conflict transition period witnessed not only a relinquishing of armed struggle but also a departure from strong feminist standpoints on many issues. Through the years of armed conflict, republican women pursued a broad-based struggle against multiple sources of oppression, most notably through the activities of the Women's Department. Republican feminists were remarkably successful at steering the overall republican movement towards recognising women's multiple sources of oppression. Moreover, the spaces created within the movement, such as the Women's Department, achieved some major successes when one examines the relatively progressive positions Sinn Féin has on women's equality. Perhaps their most enduring and important success was their vital role in the establishment of Women's Centres, such as the Falls Women's Centre, in working-class communities right across the North of Ireland.

Much of the prevailing literature on women, peace and equality in the North of Ireland frequently cite state structures and formal political parties as sites of potential transformation for women and feminist post-war struggles (Anderlini 2007; Cowell-Meyers 2003; Deiana 2013; Fearon 1999; Fearon and McWilliams 2000; Galligan 2013; Hammond-Callaghan 2011; Hinds 2011; Hoewer 2013; Murtagh 2008; Porter 1998, 2000; Side 2009). While women's engagement and participation within formal, state-centric institutions is an important part of conflict transition, the experiences of republican women stand as a formidable caution. The limitations of women's role in formal peace negotiations and their specific organising within Sinn Féin signifies the period in question as one of regression for republican women. However, just as was the case with their commemorative struggles in Chapter 2, there is far more to the story of republican women and conflict transition than simply loss and exclusion. While this chapter reveals some of the deleterious outcomes for republican women during this period, this does not suggest that they are solely victims of male-led nationalism or bereft of agency. On the contrary, as the North of Ireland continues its transition away from armed conflict, the following chapter examines the multiple ways and spaces in which they organise for peace and equality today.

Notes

1 Gaelic (Irish language) for annual meeting or conference for Sinn Féin.
2 *Cumann* is the Gaelic (Irish language) word for branch, association or local unit.
3 A 'whip' is a party official whose primary role is to ensure party discipline in areas of voting on legislation and policy. The whip system is a trademark characteristic of the UK and Republic of Ireland parliaments.

4 The Ulster Volunteer Force (UVF) is a loyalist paramilitary group. It emerged in 1966 and is named after the original UVF of the early twentieth century. The group undertook an armed campaign of almost 30 years during 'the Troubles' with a declared intent of defending the state from Irish Republicanism. Most of its victims, however, were uninvolved Catholics. It declared a ceasefire in 1994 and officially ended its campaign in 2007, although some of its members have continued to engage in violence and criminal activities.

5 The Ulster Defence Association (UDA) is the largest loyalist paramilitary organisation. Formed in September 1971 out of a coalition of loosely organised vigilante groups, it undertook an armed campaign lasting almost 30 years. Incredibly, it was a legal organisation for most of the conflict, despite its involvement in hundreds of killings. To mask its role in killings, it formed the Ulster Freedom Fighters (UFF) to avoid proscription of the UDA. The British Government outlawed the UFF in November 1973, but the UDA itself was not proscribed as a terrorist group until August 1992. Both the UDA/UFF were responsible for more than 400 deaths. While the organisations were involved in killing a small number of involved republicans, the overwhelming majority of its victims were Irish Catholic civilians, killed at random, in what the group called retaliation for IRA actions or attacks on Protestants.

6 Stands for Member of the Legislative Assembly; an elected representative to the Northern Ireland Assembly.

7 Gaelic (Irish language) for executive of Sinn Féin.

8 Dodie McGuinness was a life-long republican who left the Sinn Féin in 2007 after she was made 'redundant' from a party position. She took a case of gender discrimination against the party who paid £15,000 without an admission of liability, once again highlighting the complexities and contradictions of a party widely hailed for its relatively progressive stance on gender equality and promoting women.

9 Women have historically played a comparatively prominent role in various Irish nationalist struggles over the centuries and in particular during the 'revolutionary period' of 1916–1923. Despite playing a relatively central role in the national struggle and the rhetorical promises of a more gender-equal post-Independence society, women's position after 1923 remained largely unchanged. Given the power of the Catholic Church in Ireland, some would argue that their position, in fact, deteriorated in the aftermath of British withdrawal from the South. See Carol Coulter (1993) *The Hidden Tradition: Feminism, Women and Nationalism in Ireland.* Cork: Cork University Press.

10 The Falls Women's Centre remains a prominent space and service provider for women in West Belfast. It is now located opposite the corner of Beechmount Avenue and the Falls Road, in the mid-Falls area. According to its mission statement

> the Falls Women's Centre was the first of its kind in the area and has continually worked to raise awareness within the community and with statutory agencies on issues that affect women's lives. Falls Women's Centre is a women-only center. It is staffed and managed entirely by women and is an important support for women and their families. It was established to improve the quality of life for women and their families living in areas of extreme deprivation and most affected by the conflict.

For more, see www.fallswomenscentre.org/

11 Siobhan O'Hanlon was a prominent republican who died of cancer in 2006. At her graveside oration, Gerry Adams described Siobhan as 'brave and courageous' in her life as an IRA activist, political prisoner and Sinn Féin activist.

12 Sinn Féin is organised hierarchically into *cumainn* (branches), *comhairle ceantair* (district executives), *cúigí* (regional executives).

13 Many interviewees were of the view that the Department effectively ended in the mid-1990s.

14 It appears that by 2006, the Women's Department is undoubtedly subsumed into the Equality Department, with the party listing Eibhlin Glenholmes as 'National Co-Ordinator for Gender Equality', a position dealing with gender as opposed to an overall department.
15 Full conference report available at www.anphoblacht.com/contents/14924
16 This email extract is published with kind permission from Eibhlín.
17 IRA statement announcing its disbandment.
18 Notwithstanding the fact that some of those women prominent in the establishment of the Women's Department appear to have relocated their activism to other spheres outside of the Sinn Féin party.
19 I tip my academic hat to Anthony McIntyre (2008) for this sequence of words. In describing the death of republicanism after the GFA, McIntyre argues that the GFA effectively 'included republicans while excluding republicanism'.

Bibliography

Aharoni, S. B. 2016. 'Who Needs the Women and Peace Hypothesis? Rethinking Modes of Inquiry on Gender and Conflict in Israel/Palestine'. *International Feminist Journal of Politics*, DOI: 10.1080/14616742.2016.1237457

An Phoblacht. 2006. 'Belfast Women's Conference: Raising the Profile of Women in Sinn Féin'. Available at: www.anphoblacht.com/contents/14924 (Last accessed 25 September 2018).

Anderlini, S. N. 2007. *Women Building Peace: What They Do, Why It Matters*. Boulder and London: Lynne Rienner Publishers.

Aretxaga, B. 1997. *Shattering Silence: Women, Nationalism and Political Subjectivity in Northern Ireland*. New Jersey: Princeton Press.

Batliwala, S and D. Brown. eds. 2006. *Transnational Civil Society: An Introduction*. Boulder, CO: Kumarian Press.

Bean, K. 2007. *The New Politics of Sinn Féin*. Liverpool: Liverpool University Press.

Bean, K. 2011. 'Civil Society, the State and Conflict Transformation in the Nationalist Community'. Pp. 154–171 in *Building Peace in Northern Ireland*, edited by M. Power. Liverpool: Liverpool University Press.

Bean K. 2014. 'Endings and Beginnings? Republicanism Since 1994'. *Studies in Conflict & Terrorism* 37(9): 720–732.

Bell, C. and C. O'Rourke. 2010. 'Peace Agreements or Pieces of Paper? The Impact of UNSC Resolution 1325 on Peace Processes and Their Agreements'. *International and Comparative Law Quarterly* 59(4): 941–980.

Braniff, M. and S. A. Whiting. 2016. 'There's Just No Point Having a Token Woman': Gender and Representation in the Democratic Unionist Party in Post-agreement Northern Ireland'. *Parliamentary Affairs* 69(1): 93–114.

Buckley, F. 2013. 'Women and Politics in Ireland: The Road to Sex Quotas'. *Irish Political Studies* 28(3): 341–397.

Cassidy, K. 2005. 'Organic Intellectuals and the Committed Community: Irish Republicanism and Sinn Féin in the North'. *Irish Political Studies* 20(3): 341–356.

Chinchilla, N. S. 1990. 'Revolutionary Popular Feminism in Nicaragua: Articulating Class, Gender, and National Sovereignty'. *Gender and Security* 4: 370–397.

Cochrane, F. 2013. *Northern Ireland: The Reluctant Peace*. New Haven and London: Yale University Press.

Connolly, C. 1995. 'Ourselves Alone? Clar na mBan Conference Report'. *Feminist Review* 50: 117.

Coulter, C. 1993. *The Hidden Tradition: Feminism, Women and Nationalism in Ireland*. Cork: Cork University Press.

Cowell-Meyers, K. 2003. 'Women in Northern Ireland Politics: Gender and the Politics of Peace-building in the New Legislative Assembly'. *Irish Political Studies* 18(1): 72–96.

Deiana, M.-A. 2013. 'Women's Citizenship in Northern Ireland after the 1998 Agreement'. *Irish Political Studies* 28(3): 399–412.

Dixon, P. 2002. *Northern Ireland. The Politics of War and Peace*. Basingstoke: Palgrave Macmillan.

Enloe, C. 2014. *Bananas, Beaches and Bases: Making Feminist Sense of International Politics*, 3rd edn. Berkeley, CA: University of California Press.

Fearon, K. 1999. *Women's Work: The Story of the Northern Ireland Women's Coalition*. Belfast: Blackstaff Press.

Fearon, K. and M. McWilliams. 2000. 'Swimming Against the Mainstream: The Northern Ireland Women's Coalition'. Pp. 117–138 in *Gender, Democracy and Inclusion in Northern Ireland*, edited by C. Roulston and C. Davis. London: Palgrave.

Foweraker, J. 1995. *Theorising Social Movements*. London and Boulder: Pluto Press.

Frampton, M. 2009. *The Long March: The Political Strategy of Sinn Féin, 1981–2007*. Basingstoke and New York: Palgrave Macmillan.

Galligan, Y. 2013. 'Gender and Politics in Northern Ireland: The Representation Gap Revisited'. *Irish Political Studies* 28(3): 413–433.

Galligan, Y and R. Wilford. 1999. 'Women's Political Representation in Ireland'. Pp. 130–148 in *Contesting Politics: Women in Ireland, North and South*, edited by Y. Galligan, E. Ward, and R. Wilford. Boulder, CO: Westview Press.

Geisler, G. 2004. *Women and the Remaking of Politics in Southern Africa: Negotiating Autonomy, Incorporation and Representation*. Uppsala: Nordic Africa Institute.

Hackett, C. 1995. 'The Republican Feminist Agenda'. *Feminist Review* 50: 111–116.

Hammond-Callaghan, M. 2011. 'Peace Women', Gender and Peacebuilding in Northern Ireland: From Reconciliation and Political Inclusion to Human Rights and Human Security'. Pp. 93–110 in *Building Peace in Northern Ireland*, edited by M. Power. Liverpool: Liverpool University Press.

Hinds, B. 2011. 'Women's Political Participation'. Pp. 98–116 in *Everyday Life After the Irish Conflict*, edited by C. McGratton and E. Meehan. Manchester: Manchester University Press.

Hoewer, M. 2013. 'UN Resolution 1325 in Ireland: Limitations and Opportunities of the International Framework on Women, Peace and Security'. *Irish Political Studies* 28(3): 450–468.

Holt, M. 2003. 'Palestinian Women, Violence, and the Peace Process'. *Development in Practice* 13(2/3): 223–238.

Lovenduski, J. 2005. *Feminising Politics*. Cambridge: Polity.

Lyons, L. E. and M. Keane. 1992. 'At the End of the Day: An Interview with Mairead Keane, National Head of Sinn Féin Women's Department'. *Feminism and Postmodernism* 19(2): 260–286.

Maillot, A. 2005. *New Sinn Féin: Irish Republicanism in the Twenty-First Century*. London and New York: Routledge.

Matthews, N. 2014. 'Gendered Candidate Selection and the Representation of Women in Northern Ireland'. *Parliamentary Affairs* 67(3): 617–646.

McGing, C. 2013. 'The Single Transferable Vote and Women's Representation in Ireland'. *Irish Political Studies* 28(3): 322–340.

McGovern, M. 2004. 'The Old Days are Over: Irish Republicanism, the Peace Process and the Equality Agenda'. *Terrorism and Political Violence* 16(3): 622–645.

McIntyre, A. 2008. *Good Friday: The Death of Irish Republicanism*. New York: Ausubo Press.

Molyneux, M. 1985. 'Mobilization without Emancipation? Women's Interests, the State, and Revolution in Nicaragua'. *Feminist Studies* 11(2): 227–254.

Murtagh, C. 2008. 'A Transient Transition: The Cultural and Institutional Obstacles Impeding the Northern Ireland Women's Coalition in its Progression from Informal to Formal Politics'. *Irish Political Studies* 23(1): 21–40.

Nagel, J. 1998. 'Nation'. *Ethnic and Racial Studies* 21(2): 242–269.

Naples, N. 1998. *Grassroots Warriors: Activist Mothering, Community Work, and the War on Poverty*. New York: Routledge.

Naples, N. 2013. 'Sustaining Democracy: Localization, Globalization, and Feminist Praxis'. *Sociological Forum* 28(4): 657–681.

O'Keefe, T. 2013. *Feminist Identity Development and Activism in Revolutionary Movements*. London and New York: Palgrave Macmillan.

Ortega, L. 2015. 'Untapped Resources for Peace: A Comparative Study of Women's Organisation of Guerrilla Ex-Combatants in Colombia and El Salvador'. Pp. 232–249 in *Female Combatants in Conflict and Peace*, edited by S. Shekhawat. Basingstoke: Palgrave Macmillan.

Pankhurst, D. 2003. 'The "Sex War" and Other Wars: Towards a Feminist Approach to Peace Building'. *Development in Practice* 13(2/3): 154–177.

Porta, D and M. Diani. 1999. *Social Movements: An Introduction*. Oxford: Blackwell.

Porter, E. 1998. 'Identity, Location, Plurality: Women, Nationalism and Northern Ireland'. Pp. 36–61 in *Women, Ethnicity and Nationalism: The Politics of Transition*, edited by R. Wilford and R. L. Miller. London and New York: Routledge.

Porter, E. 2000. 'The Challenge of Dialogue across Difference'. Pp. 141–162 in *Gender, Democracy and Inclusion in Northern Ireland*, edited by C. Roulston and C. Davis. London: Palgrave.

Power, M. 2010. 'A Republican Who Wants to Further Women's Rights': Women, Provisional Republicanism, Feminism and Conflict in Northern Ireland'. Pp. 153–170 in *Irish Women at War: The Twentieth Century*, edited by G. McIntosh and D. Urquhart. Dublin and Portland: Irish Academic Press.

Power, M. ed. 2011. *Building Peace in Northern Ireland*. Liverpool: Liverpool University Press.

Racioppi, L. and K. O'Sullivan See. 2001. 'This We Will Maintain: Gender, Ethnonationalism and the Politics of Unionism Northern Ireland'. *Nations and Nationalism* 7(1): 93–112.

Richter-Devroe, S. 2012. 'Defending Their Land, Protecting Their Men'. *International Feminist Journal of Politics* 14(2): 181–201.

Ryan, M. 1997. 'From the Centre to the Margins: The Slow Death of Irish Republicanism'. Pp. 72–84 in *Peace or War? Understanding the Peace Process in Northern Ireland*, edited by C. Gilligan and J. Tonge. Aldershot: Ashgate.

Safa, H. I. 1990. 'Women's Social Movements in Latin America'. *Gender and Society* 4(3): 354–369.

Sales, R. 1997. *Women Divided: Gender, Religion and Politics in Northern Ireland*. London and New York: Routledge.

Sharoni, S. 1998. 'Gendering Conflict and Peace in Israel/Palestine and the North of Ireland'. *Millennium Journal of International Studies* 27(4): 1061–1089.

Shekhawat, S. 2015. 'Visible in Conflict, Invisible in Peace: Positioning Women in the Militancy in Kashmir'. Pp. 100–116 in *Female Combatants in Conflict and Peace*, edited by S. Shekhawat. Basingstoke: Palgrave Macmillan.

Shekhawat, S. and Saxena, C. 2015. 'Victims or Victimisers? Naxal Women, Violence and the Reinvention of Patriarchy'. Pp. 117–131 in *Female Combatants in Conflict and Peace*, edited by S. Shekhawat. Basingstoke: Palgrave Macmillan.

Side, K. 2009. 'Women's Civil and Political Citizenship in the Post-Good Friday Agreement Period in Northern Ireland'. *Irish Political Studies* 24(1): 67–87.

Sinn Féin. 2004. *Engine For Change – Women in an Ireland of Equals*. Dublin: Sinn Féin.

Tarrow, S. 1998. *Power in Movement: Social Movements. Collective Actions, and Politics.* Cambridge: Cambridge University Press.

Tonge, J. 2005. *The New Northern Irish Politics?* Basingstoke: Palgrave Macmillan.

Tonge, J. 2006. 'Sinn Féin and 'New Republicanism' in Belfast'. *Space and Polity* 10(2): 135–147.

Tonge, J. 2014. *Comparative Peace Processes*. Cambridge: Polity Press.

Tripp, A. M. 2015. *Women and Power in Post-conflict Africa.* New York: Cambridge University Press.

Ward, M. 1989. *Unmanageable Revolutionaries: Women and Irish Nationalism.* London: Pluto Press.

White, R. W. 2017. *Out of the Ashes: An Oral History of the Provisional Republican Movement.* Dublin: Merrion Press.

Whiting, S., Tonge, J., Braniff, M., Hennessey, T., and McAuley, J., 2014. *The Democratic Unionist Party: From Protest to Power.* Oxford University Press.

Young, I. M. 2000. *Inclusion and Democracy*. Oxford: Oxford University Press.

5 Beyond regression

Change and continuity in women's post-war activism

Introduction

Gender equality has gained a central place on the global political agenda over the last 30 years where parity of political participation is framed as central to the realisation of 'good governance' (Squires 2007). While the broad women's movement of second-wave feminism was defined by its commitment to eschew electoral politics in favour of autonomous organising, a feminist reorientation towards state-centric politics in recent times has renewed interest in both gender and women's participation within parliamentary politics. Issues of formal political representation are a key focus of research on gender and politics, with a number of identified dimensions including formal, descriptive, substantive, and symbolic representation (Celis *et al.* 2008). Furthermore, the idea of gender equality, and, specifically, commitments to women's full and equal participation in formal politics is now a staple of international approaches to conflict resolution. The passing of UN SCR1325[1] in October 2000 is indicative of the importance of gender equality to the conventional agenda for resolving armed conflict, and has rightly energised many feminist and women's groups who have long-campaigned for women's inclusion in all aspects of conflict transition. While a renewed feminist interest in gender and parliamentary politics is evident, others, however, have sought to caution against the idea that representation and the representation of women's interests is the sole activity and preserve of electoral politics. Michael Saward (2006) argues that representations can be made by a variety of actors, including NGOs and informal interest groups. Judith Squires (2008), among others, also argues for extending the spheres of representation practices under consideration to include not only parliamentary but also extra-parliamentary arenas such as civil society groups and feminist NGOs. While an increase of women in electoral political and national assemblies is a tantalising and important avenue of feminist exploration, parliaments are only one possible arena among many, including social movements, political parties, NGOs, among others, which can and often are equally as effective in representing women (Celis *et al.* 2008). While the feminist turn back towards parliamentary participation is an important development, particularly in the realm of conflict transition, it is important to also incorporate and be attentive to a broader range of actors, organisations, and mechanisms, which typically fall outside the boundaries of formal, electoral politics.

In addition to the arduous task of ending decades of violent conflict and securing power-sharing among the main political parties, the Good Friday Agreement (hereafter the GFA) also marked itself out as significant for its inclusion and commitment to 'the right of women to full and equal participation in political life'. Moreover, the wider peace process was unique due to the relatively high levels of visibility and participation of women (Deiana 2013). The GFA went beyond political institutional design and sought to address issues of political, civil, and citizenship rights. From a gender perspective, the agreement recognises the 'right of women to full and equal participation', as well as the right of [all] individuals to 'pursue democratically national and political aspirations'. Section 75 of The Northern Ireland Act 1998 imposes a statutory duty on public authorities to promote equality of opportunity between persons of different religious belief, political opinion, racial group, age, marital status, and sexual orientation, between persons with a disability and without, persons with a dependent and without, and 'between women and men generally' (Side 2009: 70). Despite the unequivocal commitments in the peace accord, the record of women elected as political representatives in the region between 1998 and 2016 is profoundly bleak. Low levels of female political representation are, of course, not unique to the North of Ireland, with vast swathes of research revealing male political dominance as a dogged global pattern (Dahlerup and Freidenvall 2005). The signing and ratification of the GFA in 1998 however, was lauded by many, though by no means all, as a catalyst for a new type of post-war politics in the North of Ireland. Specifically, there existed a widely held contention that the peace accord held the potential for diversity and equality in political life with respect to gender (Braniff and Whiting 2016; Cowell-Meyers 2003; Hayes and McAllister 2012). While some women have made significant progress in areas of paid employment, public bodies, and senior civil service, their opportunities for public governance and political representation has stagnated (Galligan 2013: 418). Despite the commitments enshrined in the 1998 Agreement, the North of Ireland consistently lags the UK's other regional assemblies, where devolution in Scotland and Wales has yielded significant dividends for levels of female representation (Matthews 2014).

In 1998 the prospect of a new chamber comprising 108 Assembly members presented a sizable and promising field of opportunity for women to cultivate political advances. Furthermore, the use of a PR electoral system has proved to be favourable in increasing levels of female representation (Dahlerup and Freidenval 2005; Randall 1987). Despite the inimical masculine culture of northern Irish politics, auspicious omens such as the introduction of a PR electoral system, the presence of the Northern Ireland Women's Coalition (NIWC), and the unambiguous commitment to women's full political participation in the text of the Agreement, all gave grounds that the newly formed political structures were, at the very least, relatively receptive to a new era of female representation. Despite some recent modest increases, women's formal participation over the course of the last two decades is marked by vast levels of under-representation, where the gendered characteristics of northern Irish formal politics since 1998 have proven quite resilient and reticent to change. Regardless of the spotlight on gender and women's right political participation during the GFA negotiations, the first 1998 Assembly dolefully indicated 'business as usual', with women comprising 16 per cent of the overall candidates and a paltry 13 per cent of those elected to the new chamber. Due to an increase of female candidates among Sinn Féin and the Alliance Party (10 and 11 per cent respectively), the 2003 Assembly elections produced a modest increase from 14 female Members of Legislative Assembly (hereafter MLA) in 1998 to 18. Indicative of the lacklustre approach among the main political parties, the 2003 and 2007 Assembly elections revealed overt stagnation in the political fortunes of women, with 18 female political representatives elected. Appraisals of Northern Ireland's female representation would be entirely sombre were it not for the modest yet significant upturn in the 2016 Assembly contest. While the number of female MLAs rose to 20 in 2011, a total of 30 female Members were elected to the Assembly in May 2016, representing a 50 per cent increase on 2011. The recent Assembly elections in March 2017 once again reaffirmed the relatively progressive trend with women comprising 27 of the now reduced figure of 90 seats, again representing a respectable 30 per cent. The 2016 and 2017 figures stand out as the largest number of female MLAs elected since 1998 but are also important gains given that they effectively 'stopped the rot' in the dismally low levels of female MLAs up to that point.

Given this, it is important to examine where republican women position *their* post-war activism today. Sinn Féin marks itself out from others through several direct strategies. The party reserves 50 per cent of its *Ard Comhairle* (National Executive) seats for women. Furthermore, the party hierarchy has the power to overturn local candidate selections if their overall gender candidacy falls short of its 'unofficial' 30 per cent target for female election candidates (Matthews 2014). The unofficial quota of 30 per cent has a measurable impact, particularly in its Assembly representation, thus positioning the party as one of the most progressive in terms of female representation. Despite the dismal record of women as elected representatives, republican women have made significant progress within constitutional politics when compared with other political parties, and Sinn Féin is accredited with a strong record of promoting women (Galligan 2013; Sales 1997). Furthermore, many of their elected female representatives in the North of Ireland are former IRA prisoners. Notwithstanding their relative 'successes' in entering formal politics in relatively significant numbers and presence, many have also retained their grassroots, community activism, indicating the importance placed on both sites of political activism. Despite avenues and opportunities to the upper echelons of executive power, the post-war politics of republican women comprises a hybrid, or dual struggle, encompassing both formal and informal activism. Therefore, this chapter provides important insights into the ways republican women organised for peace and equality during conflict transition. The chapter finds a shared ambivalence towards institutional politics and its restricted transformative potential among these republican women. Although they do deem it an important sphere for women, formal, parliamentary politics alone is appraised as having insufficient potential to deliver the type of change envisioned by interviewees. Moreover, this chapter finds that while women's inclusion within electoral politics is rhetorically incorporated within the mainstream peace and security agenda, the experiences of republican women in the 'new post-conflict politics' in the North of Ireland reveals another site of post-war gender struggle. While gender equality is now exalted by the mainstream as an essential litmus test for a genuinely transformed society, formal politics in the aftermath of war in the North of Ireland remains profoundly gendered in terms of barriers, norms, and cultures. Given this, it is community engagement that is seen to provide the transformative space to address the specific issues that impact their lives and the lives of those within working-class, republican communities. Despite their perceived 'unconventional role' as combatants, their gendered experiences of post-war politics represent a continuum of conflict and struggle. This chapter argues for the need to step back from primarily examining women's post-war activism solely through the prism of formal institutional politics and instead, pay closer attention to the entirety of ways in which all women organise for peace and equality in post-war scenarios.

'It's important, but it's not enough': institutional politics and conflict transition

Efforts to increase women's presence in formal structures have accelerated considerably since the passing of SCR 1325 in 2000. In recent years, demands for women's formal inclusion has been seen by many women's organisations across the globe as a promising avenue of post-war feminist struggle. Furthermore, the idea of gender equality has been adopted as a fundamental principle and goal by most political parties and international organisations. The pursuit of gender equality in the formal political sphere has increasingly taken three distinct forms: the increased participation of women in national assemblies; the improved incorporation of women's policy concerns; and the introduction of a gender equality perspective into all policy-making areas. The strategies used in pursuit of these objectives typically involve the use of gender quotas in various political roles, and the use of gender mainstreaming in policy processes and outcomes (Squires 2007: 23).

Proponents see women's formal participation in decision-making on peace and security as both an outcome of, and a vehicle for, women's empowerment (Anderlini 2007; Arostegui 2013; Erzurum and Eren 2014; Hoewer 2013). Gender equality therefore typically relates to equal rights, responsibilities, and opportunities of women, men, girls, and boys (Bouta at al. 2005: 5; Mazurana *et al.* 2005: 13). Others, however, are more sceptical of the state-centric focus, given the abundance of feminist scholarship illustrating the limited capabilities of the state to deliver. Its function as a 'protection racket', safeguarding the interests of the already powerful are well documented (Pateman 1988, 2012; Okin 1989). Top-down approaches to conflict transition democracy, which invariably focuses on institutional democracy and the re-establishment of political rights and citizenship, are also cited as providing limited results (Waylen 1994: 352). Others suggest that 'elections and electoral systems have little real impact on inviting women and minorities as stakeholders in the power structures of a transitioning state' (Ni Aolain et. al 2011: 234), and so 'the institutionalisation of electoral democracy is by no means a sufficient guarantee that the emerging political structures will reflect popular interests' (Luciak 1999: 44). Furthermore, the adding of women to existing structures risks the co-opting of women's struggle, running the risk of diluting feminist goals and objectives (Waylen 1994: 340), where the prescribed actions of quotas or gender mainstreaming 'is less ambitious, or at least less radical' (Ni Aolain *et al.* 2011: 12), leading some to appraise such approaches as insufficient to tackle the underlying causes of women's subordination (Dolgopol 2007).

While conventional and mainstream approaches to conflict transition increasingly looks towards top-down, institutional inclusion as a mechanism for securing women's equality and a genuine peace, such an approach neglects the feminist contention that a sustainable peace is one that is built from the grassroots up (Cordero 2001; Karam 2001). In so doing, women who agitate across a myriad of political spaces using power from below may be neglected. The disproportionate focus afforded to women's institutional inclusion within dominant approaches distorts the reality of women's post-war politically orientated activities and spaces.

This section explores the experiences of republican women within constitutional politics and finds that, while deemed important, institutional politics alone are seen to be insufficient to deliver the type of political and social change envisioned by republican women.

Despite the claims by some that Sinn Féin is merely another mainstream constitutional party in the political market place (Evans and Tonge 2013), it is a party that emerged primarily from street agitation and the mass mobilisation of the nationalist and republican community in the early 1980s (Bean 2007). As it accelerated its embrace of constitutional electoral politics in the post-ceasefire period, the party 'was keen to retain its radical edge, to continue to be seen as a militant, activist-led party' (Maillot 2005: 54). During the 1980s, it fused street agitation, community activism, and electoral contestation in a cauldron of activism that provided the republican movement with many political outlets and fronts. Given this, it is unsurprising to find that the overwhelming majority of interviewees today are full-time activists in both formal and informal politics. Thirty-one research participants are currently both Sinn Féin members and active in one or more community or grassroots organisations. Of these, 15 are elected representatives at various levels, from local councillor up to senior levels of government. Ruth joined the IRA in Belfast in the early 1970s and is now a Sinn Féin member, a former elected councillor and a community activist. Her extract typifies the type of eclectic activism interviewees are engaged in today:

> I'm a Sinn Féin activist and a community activist in the mid-Falls area and I'm also the Sinn Féin representative for the mid-Falls, for constituency

> matters. I work full time and I'm a mother of three children. I'm also the chairperson of a local area forum which is made up of residents groups, youth groups, women's groups and through the forum we would deal a lot on street issues and the door-to-door issues and I see that as a very important part of being a Sinn Féin representative. That you are there doing the work and you're there for and with the people. I'm a great believer that if you talk the talk, then you walk the walk. So if you're spouting republican or socialist ideologies then you have to put them into practice on the ground.

When asked about their current roles, interviewees described a multi-sited terrain of political and social struggle across a myriad of issues and concerns. Within Sinn Féin, some are constituency office workers, grassroots activists, paid party employees, political advisors, elected town and city councillors, right up to senior levels of the party's elected representatives. Within the informal sector, their roles primarily involve community centres, Women's Centres, tenants and resident associations, republican ex-prisoner centres, NGOs, among others. Community centres form the bulk of their informal activism and play a hugely important role in the lives of citizens in working-class republican and nationalist communities. Many of these community centres are in the Bogside/Brandywell in Derry and areas such as Turf Lodge, Short Strand and Ardoyne in Belfast. Given their high level of services and supports, the importance of these centres within working-class republican communities cannot be overstated. Orla is a full-time employee at one such centre, and she described the typical services and supports provided:

> I'm a community worker here in [named area] and have been working here since I got out of jail in [1990s] and my role is supposed to be in finance, but you end up doing anything and everything in the centre. So we look after elderly people and look after children and I love it; I love the work. We have everything here; a crèche, an after school club, a senior citizens group, residents' groups, women's groups, men's groups … you know, everything. Like a one stop-shop for this whole community. There's counselling services available, and some of those would be for ones affected by the conflict, some for other issues such as alcohol and substance abuse. We help people in financial trouble or people with problems in their benefits. Everything really … so this centre is very much at the heart of this community.

Even though Sinn Féin are widely credited with providing women with relatively higher levels of access to formal politics (Buckley 2013; Galligan 2013; Sales 1997), it was important that the research explored the reasons for the high levels of 'dual roles' involving both formal and informal activism. Why not locate their entire activism in formal politics? What are the reasons behind their continued community organising? Which spaces are deemed politically effective and potentially transformative for women's post-war struggle? The structural barriers to women's meaningful participation in formal politics are well-documented (see

Lovenduski and Norris 1993, 1996; Matthews 2014; Okin 1989; Sales 1997). While this body of scholarly literature is incredibly important to enhancing our understanding of formal politics as gendered institutions and systems, often it seems that the responsibility for overcoming these exclusions resides with women themselves, as well as with political parties and policy makers. There is an implicit belief that existing androcentric norms, structures and institutions can and will be suitably rectified by quotas, gender mainstreaming, thus paving the way for women's quantitative increase as political representatives (Squires 2007). Often overlooked, however, are the voices and experiences of women themselves. I began by asking former and current elected representatives of their experiences of formal politics.

Patricia, who joined the IRA in the early 1970s and who is now an elected city councillor, recalls:

> Well, when I sat as a councillor for the first time I was quite surprised at the hostility and the heckling from the males when I first spoke and bad manners and an effort to put women in their place; to make it so uncomfortable for me to speak, that I wouldn't do it again. Now I don't shy away from anything, but I was quite uptight about it, I was blushing.

Patricia's description is echoed by those who are current or former elected representatives and indicates high levels of hostility towards republican women *as* women. There is a striking awareness that such tactics of male heckling and verbal abuse are mechanisms in which men attempt to exert control over women within the formal realm. Many spoke of the masculine and adversarial nature of formal politics as stifling and unproductive. Bronagh, a former member of the IRA, was previously an elected councillor and articulates a similar sentiment:

> I really respect our politicians, especially our women because I think it takes a certain type of person to do that, to go into these places and all the shouting and bureaucracy … I hated every moment of it.

Most felt that levels of resentment and verbal abuse was directed towards them because they were republican *women*. Many interpreted the vitriolic attacks and behaviour as deliberate tactics to ensure that the realm of formal politics remained inhospitable to republican women. As outlined in Chapter 1, gender as a structural power relation not only shapes individual identities, it also shapes and is shaped by institutions. It is well established that gender relations are institutionalised, and embedded political institutions that constrain and shape social interactions (Mackay *et al.* 2010). In other words, formal, electoral politics is imbued with gender in that they are constructed and function in ways that draw upon specific notions of masculinity and femininity, where their rules, procedures and practices prescribe (as well as proscribe) 'acceptable' masculine and feminine forms of behaviour, rules and values for men and women within such institutions (Chappell 2006). While conventional approaches view the state as a key site for the betterment of women, the narrow definition of politics as formal and institutional ensures that formal politics becomes a largely male activity (Waylen 1994: 333) and therefore the culture and norms of politics become masculinised. State-centric political institutions – by their cultures, norms and practices – are not gender-neutral. Formal politics is often viewed by grassroots activists as a system dominated by wealthy, often white men (and, of course, sometimes women) vying for power for its own sake and for their own personal gain (Naples 1998: 125), and therefore is inimical to the development of feminist politics within the formal sphere. Elite power-sharing within the structures of governance in the North of Ireland enshrines fissures of political difference firmly along ethno-national lines. It follows that adversarial masculinity synonymous with competing ethnic blocs finds a privileged position in the style, substance, and culture of parliamentary politics. The prevalence of belligerent, adversarial ethno-national politics and a conservative gender order reinforces the notion that the qualities required and revered within formal politics are quintessentially masculine in character. The positing of the state as embodying a masculine form is explored in the work of Connell who argues that 'public politics on almost any definition is men's politics' (1995: 204). Connell outlines that the few women who do manage to break into this male-led realm do so on men's terms, in accordance with masculine cultures and norms. Given the widespread adversarial nature of the North's deeply polarised formal political structures, many interviewees found institutional realms as male-saturated and 'unproductive'. Ruth, who joined the IRA in Belfast in the mid-1970s and is now an elected representative described her frustration:

> And I think the reason that sort of thing [male disruptive behaviour] goes on is because politics is dominated by men and men are very childish both in private and public. Like, you'll see this DUP man standing up in the chamber and making a valid point and then when he finishes four or five other men from his party will all get up and concur with him. Now that to me is just childish; time wasting where most women would not be at that sort of behaviour, probably because they've to get home to the kids or whatever.

Procedures, practices and policies within formal politics are dominated by masculinity, where the behaviour and skills most valued to qualify for party or elective office are those associated with stereotypical masculinity such as forceful assertiveness, adversarial debating styles, competitiveness (Verge 2015). Verge refers to this as the 'gendered rituals' with repeated interjections by male participants who reference each other, and repeating points already made. Consequently, meetings take longer, and these performative rituals ensure that men conversationally saturate proceedings (Verge 2015: 757). It is well documented that the gendered division of labour inhibits women's ability to participate in formal political activism while allowing men to pursue and engage in full time activities outside the domestic home (Okin 1989). While many interviewees viewed the culture and business of formal politics as 'masculine' or 'very manly', the issue of childcare is equally prevalent across many interviews. Brenda, an elected Sinn Féin representative, believed that:

> Women could contribute a lot more, but they had to put the kids first where men don't need to think about that, they have a woman there to do that for them. So they're let off the hook, free to go on and get involved. I have three kids and it's a real balancing act where my male colleagues don't have to consider any of that, no doctors, no schools. So women have their full time political work *and* they have their full-time work as mothers.

The barriers to women's participation in the North of Ireland are attributed to several factors including, the propensity of gender stereotypes, male monopoly of power, gender division of domestic labour, education, training, and occupational status, among others (Porter 2003; Galligan and Wilford 1999). Society in the North of Ireland retains a clear sexual division of labour in the domestic realm, a marked segregation of gender in paid occupational roles, and a prevailing conservative outlook regarding gender roles and sexuality. In this context, it is consistently and almost exclusively women who need to consider the burden of 'work–life balance'. Women's assigned role as primary care-giver along with a multiplicity of other unpaid domestic tasks, invariably deprives women of the appetite and/or the opportunity to enter formal, paid employment. Moreover, the gender division of domestic labour ensures that men and women do not enter the public realm on an equal footing. Twenty-six of the 40 interviewees are also mothers, and stated that the birth of a child resulted in a retreat from full-time activism, either as a militant during 'the Troubles' or from full-time political activism in the post-war period, only to slowly return once children grew older and more independent. Most interviewees felt that formal political structures are designed to accommodate a particular gender order which advantages men.

> JOANNE: I was a local councillor for years but I'm not anymore; up until last year. So I was elected in the late 1990s and I resigned from the council last year just due to time. I have the children and a full-time job and didn't have the time for all the constituency work and council work and I felt it was getting to me. Something had to give, and the children had to come first, and I couldn't give up my job because it was our only income. I just felt I wasn't being fair to the party or the constituents because they weren't getting the time they deserved. It was much easier when I was single and had no kids.

According to all interviewees, the unsociable working hours does not suit those with children or dependents, with many concluding that formal politics 'is not very family-friendly'. Most participants stated that parenting is not an insurmountable obstacle to political participation, yet it is usually women who must deal with the conflicting demands of the two roles. Despite Sinn Féin's comparatively high number of female elected representatives, it appears that republican women are very much aware of structural and institutional barriers to women's participation in formal politics (Alison 2009: 203).

Notwithstanding these 'unproductive' experiences, others provided a more positive appraisal of their formal political experiences. Anne is a former city councillor:

ANNE: So going into [Belfast] City Hall is just another arena of struggle. It didn't intimidate me at all and I loved it, I loved council. I never really regretted going into council even though my kids were small, and I missed out on an awful lot with them. So overall, I did love council. I wasn't keen on some of the committees, so I got myself shifted onto ones where I wanted to be in, where I was making a difference because I was the party person on equality. That was my brief and I was there advocating that money and policy needs to be targeted towards those who need it most based on the deprivation indices. So you target the money towards those people and those areas that need it most and improving peoples' lives based on those indices.

GRAINNE: Well I'm a councillor here in [named town] for Sinn Féin and have been now for over 20 years and I'm busy in that role and we work in among the community. It's a very busy role and my work as a councillor, the main part of it is, which is what I enjoy most, is working for other people and improving their lives, that is for me the most rewarding part of my role. And I'm very proud to be a Sinn Féin councillor.

Echoing Anne and Grainne, Ruth, also a former elected representative, stated that

I enjoyed being a councillor and I was sorry to lose my seat, but it showed me that all you had to do was lift the phone and you'd get something done. So now I can see the difference of not being a councillor and I try to tell people to use their councillor.

In terms of how effective their electoral roles were, all broadly replied that as a political representative, the title or position adds 'political clout' to their activism. Being a formal political representative as described by Ruth has the effect of cutting through some of the bureaucracy; headed note paper or titles such as councillors or MLA[2] provided elected Sinn Féin members with 'political teeth' and commands the attention of civil servants. In addition, many believed that women's roles within Sinn Féin was meaningful and that the party's role in government is changing the ways in which state-centric politics is currently conducted. While this research reflects the perspective and experiences of the republican women, their reporting of republicanism challenging the conduct and state-centric nature of politics is worth contextualising. Though respecting the views of interviewees, it is important to note that many opponents of the Provisional republican movement have attacked the party over its role in government in the North, with the party implicated in the administration of austerity through its role in the Executive (Cox 2012; O'Keefe 2013; Patterson 2012). Representatives, members and supporters of the party vehemently reject this, pointing to the fact that the consociation arrangement severely precludes its ability to resist austerity, and, furthermore, argue that the presence of Sinn Féin in government mitigated the severity of austerity cuts. Helen is currently a senior Sinn Féin elected representative but also maintains her work within her local community centre, and again, reflects the views of most interviewees that republicans are delivering change regarding issues of social justice:

> Sinn Féin has made the difference, a small bit of difference as we try and move not just our society forward but also practices and policies in place that will deliver social change. We're hoping that we have the ingredients to create a just society especially for our most vulnerable people. And Sinn Féin is delivering that.

Fiona is an ex-prisoner who previously worked as a community activist in Belfast. Like Helen, she is also a senior Sinn Féin elected representative.

> Certainly, politics is changing, certainly, and more women into politics and Sinn Féin need to send women into all male-dominated places. We did it very well like in government ministries because most ministries are male, as are most political parties and that is starting to break down and Sinn Féin is at the forefront of that.

Most interviewees believed that Sinn Féin is making a difference, albeit a small one, in the realm of formal politics, particularly with regards to the deconstruction of masculine cultures:

BRONAGH: I'm not even sure if there is a crèche in the Dáil or at Stormont.[3] But I know there's a gym and two bars! It has been a male institute for so long and that needs to change. And it is changing and the male culture within politics is changing, slowly, and Sinn Féin is certainly at the forefront of that change in terms of republican women.

RUTH: You only have to look at Belfast City Council today, which was previously dominated by men, and look at the changes there. When I first was a councillor [1980s], I mean, some of them [male politicians], their knuckles were still scraping the ground.

KELLY: I think women do need be there at that level as politicians ... em ... because it is still seen as a very male-dominated thing and I think we should encourage as many people into it as possible, to make sure women are involved at that level and making decisions. And I know that does work and it makes [*sic*] sure that women's issues are on the agenda and are considered but I don't know whether it would work for all political roles.

Kelly, Ruth and Bronagh's thoughts are typical of those in the majority of interviews. Many cited republican women's role within Sinn Féin as vital to the dismantling of masculine cultures and male domination right across various arenas of institutional politics, from Belfast City Hall to Stormont.[4] Many also argued for women's inclusion at all levels of formal politics, and the importance of having women at all levels of decision-making. In the final sentence of Kelly's extract however, there is also a distinct note of caution that institutional politics alone would not 'work for all political roles'. While cited as important, interviewees are also critically aware of the limitations in pursuing politics solely through institutional approaches. The data and discussion advanced thus far suggests optimism that women's role within Sinn Féin and formal political structures is making a difference despite the ubiquitous male dominance and sexist norms and cultures. Politically, the growing visibility and numbers of republican women participating in constitutional politics was cultivated by a combination of their wartime experiences as political activists as well as deliberate policy initiatives within the party which provided relatively favourable conditions. Despite the masculine culture and slow pace, most interviewees reported the importance of women's presence and participation in electoral politics. The question of why so many remained active in grassroots, community organising however, reveals a deep-seated awareness of the limitations of formal, electoral politics.

'We want results': grassroots and community organising

While there is evidence of a feminist turn back towards parliamentary politics (Squires 2012), constitutional party politics remains saturated in masculine dominance, which underpins its institutional structures, practices and norms, as well as constraining the expression and articulation of marginalised perspectives (Mackay *et al.* 2010). Furthermore, despite some discernible improvements, political institutions are profoundly gendered (Kenny 2014). The feminist maxim that 'the personal is political' sought to redefine the very fundamentals upon which male-led, institutional politics is premised. For many women and feminists, the formal arena of politics was just another part of the patriarchal order, and one that was so masculine that it was best avoided altogether (Roulston 2000: 26). Given this, many women have historically turned to grassroots activism and community politics to have some influence over the policies that affect their families, communities and themselves (McCoy 2000: 7). Progressive social movements seek to build the collective power of the excluded, marginalised or oppressed constituents so that they can access human rights and challenge dominant ideologies and power relations (Batliwala and Brown 2006). The notion of women organising within a formal political party therefore appears to be the antithesis of any type of feminist organising other than liberal or perhaps, socialist. Formal political parties are imbued with relations of power, hierarchical control and organise for the attainment of state control, and so are hardly the likely sites that will foster a progressive feminist agenda (Young 2000). There is a strong history of women organising outside of formal political structures in the North of Ireland (Fearon and McWilliams 2000; McCoy 2000; Miller *et al.* 1996; Sales 1997). For the most part, this activism is not concerned with aping or paralleling the formal structures, but rather is seen as an alternative form of politics, which addresses issues that are all too often neglected or excluded by state-centric politics.

The data presented here in this section suggests that the institutional inclusion and participation of women is an important but also an inadequate measure through which to address their specific political needs and concerns. In particular, the sluggish pace of formal politics is a key source of dissatisfaction when contrasted with the high velocity of community organising. Kelly, who joined Sinn Féin in the early 1980s and is still a member, also manages a community centre in Belfast. Her thoughts epitomise many of the attitudes towards the pace of party politics:

> Formal politics is too slow for women and that's why the sector of community activism holds so much in attracting women towards it. I just know from experience [as an elected representative] that it is so slow moving. We drive issues here from this [named] Centre and say 'here's a big issue for us' and arrange a meeting with our MLAs and then they take it up to a political level at Stormont. But, once it goes in there [Stormont], it seems to get lost and takes forever to get a decision about it.

Kelly is broadly representative of most interviewees, and, interestingly, her views are also shared, even by those at senior levels of elected representation. Fiona, a former IRA member, previously worked solely in the community sector and is now a senior elected representative for Sinn Féin:

> It is very slow up here [Stormont], because I could have been dealing with four or five families in a week who had drug problems when I was in the community [sector] and get access to services for them and moving that on. Up here is just so slow it's like watching paint dry, where when you're used to working on the ground you're seeing your work and things getting done.

Fiona's extract is typical of most others; on the one hand, formal politics is slow and frustrating, while on the other, she describes her community activist role as a space where she can address specific issues that affect the lives of citizens within republican communities. According to these women, community organising provides the political potential to make a discernible difference within working-class, republican communities. Emily, who joined the IRA in the early 1970s concurs, arguing that 'constitutional politics is very unsatisfactory for anyone like me who comes from a background of activism from the 1960s and 1970s and that is very difficult. It is very unexciting for women'. Karen is a Sinn Féin activist, a member of a residents' group and works in a Women's Centre in West Belfast. Echoing Fiona's and Emily's thoughts, Karen reflects:

> Here [community activism] you can make sure people get a house or whatever and get an instant result where politics is very slow. You see if you try

and get a decision about anything [in formal politics], it just puts my fucking head away, you know. It is too slow for women and that's why they go into community politics and empower themselves to do it.

Right throughout 'the Troubles', republican women's community activism acted in tandem with their formal politics within Sinn Féin. Exploring the post-war experiences of republican women through the prism of formal politics only is therefore a partial gauge. Often, the women in this research are active in more than one community organisation. In addition to the multiplicity of their roles, their politically orientated activism is also eclectic and wide-ranging dealing with issues such as drugs and alcohol addiction, housing, gender-based violence, education, abortion or Women's Centres. Others are involved in ex-prisoner centres such as *Tar Anall* in Belfast or *Tar Abhaile* in Derry, as well as grass-roots organisations directly relating to 'the Troubles', particularly around the issue of state violence. It is the pace, structures and plurality of their community activism however, which holds much sway for many interviewees. While women's grassroots and community organising is nothing new or unique to this research, we need to bear in mind that women's *type* of community organising is culturally embedded and established in diverse ways according to their differing needs and concerns. The informal and enabling space allows interviewees to address the issues that affect their lives and the lives of the people within clearly defined working-class communities.

In addition, many interviewees revealed a shared value of participatory activism and cite a direct link between grassroots organising and discernible results from such actions. Ruth, a former IRA volunteer who is now a Sinn Féin member and community activist, was once also an elected representative. She explains the importance of participatory activism to republican women:

Well, community activism is more dynamic, and you can just get on with whatever needs doing. I spoke at the parliament last year and you'd need a medal to put up with the half of it so for me, I much prefer the community politics because you can make a difference and you can see the difference whether it's an anti-graffiti campaign or building a community garden.

Ruth's statement regarding the quicker and visible changes made at a community level typifies the distinct value placed on the discernibility and effectiveness of their activism. Community activism, or what Elizabeth Porter (2000) terms the 'situated politics of everyday life', are opportunities for women to engage in issues that directly affect them and their communities. In particular, many interviewees are directly involved in various Women's Centres in working-class, republican communities dealing with issues such as domestic and sexual violence, child-care facilities and education, among others. Women's Centres in the North of Ireland 'provide a space for more radical groups and individuals for whom the concerns and practices of the formal political parties holds no attraction' (Sales 1997: 188). According to interviewees, Women's Centres provide them with the mechanisms to address issues that formal politics is either unwilling or incapable of dealing with. While they are not unique to republican women, Women's Centres in republican communities are largely focused on issues directly related to working-class, nationalist and republican women.

When examining the narratives in the data presented here, republican women are fully cognisant that issues of domestic violence, poverty, childcare, drug addiction, among others, will not be tackled in the political spheres of Stormont or Leinster House. The apparent inertia of formal politics in the North of Ireland is widely cited as the main reason for the lack of peace dividend among wider society, where the new consociation architecture of formal politics is having limited impacts on the daily lives of citizens (Cochrane 2013; McGrattan and Meehan 2012; Kennedy *et al.* 2016). As the latest endeavours by political elites to deal with problematic issues such as welfare reform, flags and emblems, dealing with the past, run aground,[5] the ineffectiveness of institutional politics in the North of Ireland would undoubtedly test the patience of even its greatest advocates. The collapse of the devolved power-sharing Executive in the region in January 2017 only serves to compound levels of despondency towards formal politics.

At the heart of many interviews, is the contention that issues of importance and concern to republican women require direct, participatory political action. The thematic issues addressed by interviewees in their community roles are consistently those that impact upon the everyday lives of people within working-class, republican communities. In other words, this demonstrates that women's ways of peace-building are contextual, profoundly shaped by historical forces and cultural processes. Research data corroborates the argument that women build peace in ways that have meaning in their own cultural setting (Richter-Devroe 2012). The inability of institutional politics to deliver meaningful change at that level undoubtedly motivates much of their grassroots organising, despite their relatively high levels of formal political activism. Transversal feminist approaches often hold out that women-only spaces offer the potential for women in deeply polarised societies to work across the divide on issues of mutual benefit. While mainstream Women's Centres are cited for providing linkages between differentially positioned women, interviewees here are involved in Women's Centres, which are embedded in the socialist, feminist and republican politics of their defined communities. Of the 40 research participants, only one identified as being previously involved in any sort of transversal or cross-community activism. The notion that 'women' are a coherent group with a set of shared needs and interests has been the subject of much feminist theoretical interrogation resulting in a broad rejection of essentialism, with a focus more on the heterogeneity of women's identities and experiences (Kantola and Dahl 2005). The extra-parliamentary activism of republican women does not claim to represent or benefit all women. On the contrary, their community activism tends to deal primarily, though not exclusively, with issues that directly affect the lives of working-class, republican women within specifically defines communities. In other words, the women in this research are overwhelmingly concerned with issues and concerns within clearly defined working-class, republican communities.

While traditional political science and mainstream IR defines power in straightforward terms of 'power over', domination, or as a forms of control, Hartsock (1983) contends that women typically stress power as capacity, potential, and the ability to act as a collective. The ideals of solidarity and reciprocity resonate with themes of feminist ethics and politics, which stress mutuality, interdependence, and shared values (Frazer and Lacey 1993: 123). Grassroots and civil society forms of politics conceive democracy as a response to suffering, involved resistance to elite governance, and transforms citizens political capabilities (Squires 2007: 171). Interviewees claimed that their republican activism, whether armed struggle, electoral politics, community organising, or other, is informed by the pursuit of social justice and a 'positive peace' on behalf of a defined community. Linda, who joined the IRA in Belfast in the early 1970s expresses that prevalent ethic among research participants of politics as participatory and self-empowering:

> My politics has always been and still is about helping people. You see women do things from a very practical point of view and see what's needed and say, 'yes I can get involved there and make a difference', so women want to do things that are practical. Some people say, 'where did women go after the conflict?' A lot of women just looked around and said 'right what's the next thing for us to do', so women went off into community groups, or helping their families. They don't dwell on the conflict; they move on and are practical and move towards what needs to be done next.

When asked why some republican women did not pursue those objectives solely through formal politics, Linda replied:

> Because they see that that is not the best way to get things done.

Linda is now active in community activism only, severing her ties with Sinn Féin and formal politics. Her views are wholly reflective of all seven research participants who are in community activism only. While the overall republican movement has shifted from 'party of protest to the party of government' (Frampton 2009), the mistrust of the state remains palpable among interviewees. The historical complexities of the relationship between republicans and the state ensures that despite Sinn Féin's participation, the state is widely viewed with ambivalence, and is largely incapable of delivering on the needs and interests of working class republican communities. Gemma, who describes her conflict role as a 'republican activist' and now works in Sinn Féin and the community sector, demonstrates the links made by many research participants between women's grassroots activism and state politics:

> I like the idea of 'the personal is political'. We had the British Government who gave us nothing and certainly gave women nothing. So we had to go

out and get it ourselves, so we saw the poverty, deprivation and so we got educated and began agitating and setting up community centres, residents associations, co-ops and you were politicised, although at the time you didn't realise it because you were just doing what was needed and those needs sadly are still there today.

The idea of equality, services and rights are primary concepts within Provisional republican ideology and is rooted in the historical psyche of nationalist exclusion and discrimination at the hands of the unionist state. Much of the community sector's motivation is the perceived inadequacies of the state, inextricably linked to the historical 'discrimination or deprivation at the hands of the state or the unionist community' (Cassidy 2005: 349). Despite the vast overhaul of the state and Sinn Féin's fervent participation within its political institutions, the scars of previous wrongdoings at the hands of the state are still tangible within working-class nationalist communities. Janette, who joined Sinn Féin in the early 1970s, succinctly captured this ethos:

> The fact that I am here in mental health is like republicans seeing something that is a really bad situation and going and doing something about it. I help disenfranchised people, get guide dogs for blind citizens, help people with disabilities and all those things are where you make a difference where you can. The community sector in this city, which is providing vital services for the people of this community, are all run by republicans and ex-prisoners and that is not an accident. We were just so used to accepting that the state was not there to help and so it was up to us to provide those services.

The ideological characteristic of this approach is the analytical distinction between a reliance on the state or the grassroots approach in a politics defined as participatory and self-empowering. Despite Sinn Féin's zealous participation within state institutions, the state itself is often framed in adversarial terms by many research participants. In addition, some interviewees identified formal institutions themselves as deeply problematic. Linda, a former IRA volunteer in the 1970s typifies the feeling of those interviewees now outside of formal politics:

> I always felt that this [formal] political system is corrupting and that once you get into that system then you're working that system. How can you protest against yourself? How can Sinn Féin mobilise their people against austerity measures when they're sitting up there [in Stormont] delivering it?

Much of the criticism levelled at the party from those who have now severed their links with Provisional republicanism stemmed not from dogmatic republicanism regarding their acceptance of 'partitionist structures', but was, in fact, rooted in class politics. Like Linda, Eileen joined the IRA in Belfast in the early 1970s and today works solely in the community sector:

> Nothing changes in this political system regardless of elections; all the civil servants are still there, the policies are still there. So once you're in a capitalist political system you deliver capitalist policies and in order to deliver that, you're going to have people who are very poor and people who are very rich and that's what we're stuck with. How can they [Sinn Féin] call themselves republicans and then inflict them [*sic*] cuts on working class people? It's not in me to do that to people; politics is supposed to be about helping people.

Eilish, is a former IRA volunteer in Belfast and like Eileen and Linda, is now active solely in grassroots organisations outside of Sinn Féin:

> In [formal] politics, the status quo is the status quo and overall, it really doesn't change. Maybe I don't have the patience for it and all the nonsense that goes with it. Here (in community and voluntary sector) I can agitate, I can help people and most importantly I give people the opportunities to change their own lives which I couldn't do if I was sitting up in Stormont.

For Linda, Eileen and Eilish, electoral contests involving the interchange of power between various political parties are largely superficial exercises. Their main point of contention was that institutional politics presents a political *cul-de-sac* for those advocating a more radical form of politics. The failure of constitutional politics to deliver meaningful change, and moreover, its perceived culpability as a source of post-war structural violence, has led to profound disappointment and disillusionment for some. Linda and Eileen have severed their links with Sinn Féin and formal politics, preferring to concentrate their energies solely on community activism.

In their thorough analysis of women and formal politics in a number of Melanesian countries, Ceridwen Spark and Jack Corbett (2016) find that 'the goal of civic and political activity is not to enter parliament but rather to create positive change in the lives of their families and communities, a role that is nevertheless inherently political' (Spark and Corbett 2016: 9). Becoming an elected representative may be empowering for the individual, and of course of benefit to the political party and portions of the electorate, but the overwhelming sentiment is that formal, top-down politics is unlikely to bring about progressive political changes likely to improve the lives of those most marginalised in a post-war scenario. While most interviewees advocate the importance of increasing women's participation in male-dominated formal politics, very few cite this as the optimum space for pursuing their vision of peace and equality. The republican women interviewed here hold a clear belief that while institutional structures are important they are also limited in their transformative capacity to deliver the type of post-war society they envision. Janette joined Sinn Féin in the early 1970s and today is still a party member and full-time community activist. I asked Janette her thoughts on why so many republican women are active in community organising given their high levels of involvement in formal politics:

Why are there so many women in the community sector? Because women want to make changes (laughs). Women, like to be on the ground, making changes, make a quick strike, bounce back into their own lives, and then make another quick strike; *we want results* [with emphasis]. And I think in formal politics you don't get a lot of it [results].

When international organisations and leading political figures talk of the need to include women within formal, top-down peace processes, they are overlooking the vast body of powerful work that women do in the pursuit of peace and equality outside of the formal realm. Assessing women's post-war peace activism through an institutional prism not only fails to reflect women's peace-building in its entirety, but it limits approaches to a single tier of political activism. In contrast, interviewees are not reliant on formal, political structures alone to pursue their post-war agenda. Often, they are agents of change who establish their own spaces, sometimes women-only spaces, where they can address their specific interests and concerns. It is the transformative potential and political mobility within community organising which creates opportunities for interviewees to address the shortfalls and inefficiencies of institutional politics.

The analysis of republican women offered here, is broadly in-line with existing global research highlighting the gendered and relatively ineffective realm of formal, parliamentary politics. For most, their civil society activism provides an important political space which accompanies their roles in formal, constitutional politics, despite the well-documented barriers. Obtaining some seats at parliament or at the formal negotiating table is an important tier of women's post-war organising. Examining the lives of republican women not only bring their lives into view, but by doing so it also yields a more accurate picture of women's post-war activism in its entirety. Despite relatively high levels of access to institutional politics through Sinn Féin, the overwhelming majority of women in this research, including senior elected representatives, remain committed and full-time community activists. Despite the opportunities and constraints, and the limitations of women's organising within formal party politics, it is perhaps unsurprising to see women organising on issues outside of formal structures in areas such as drugs, housing, education, abortion, and gender-based violence.

According to Elizabeth Porter, 'unless we see the [formal] inclusion of political spaces such as women's community activism, much of women's political activity goes theoretically unrecognised and practically undervalued' (1998: 50). At the heart of many feminist contentions regarding women's formal political inclusion, is that without doing so, women's eclectic activism remains unrecognised and undervalued. When we examine interviewees' grassroots peace-building and post-war struggle here, however, we find a vibrant and active sphere of political struggle that is highly valued *and* recognised by both its participants and the communities that benefit from their services. These community activists are neither marginalised nor victims (Jordan 2003). A study on the Women's Sector in Northern Ireland, commissioned by the Community Foundation in 2001, estimated that there were some 1071 'traditional' Women's organisations active across the North, and 423 'activist' women's groups/centres, with most of the latter (some 90 per cent) being community-based women's groups (Kilmurray 2013). The ability of this sector however, to influence those who wield power in the formal realm remains relatively low, where formal and informal politics remain governed by rigid boundaries. Much of the increased possibilities for informal politics has come because of state reconfiguration, consisting broadly of a process of 'downloading and off-loading' (Squires 2008). The downloading comes in the form of creating devolved regional assemblies with various powers. The off-loading refers to processes whereby certain state powers are transferred to civil society organisations, using them as partners in policy-making and implementation. This shift in state powers is accredited with providing new roles and powers to feminist NGOs and civil society organisations. The downside is the lines separating formal and informal politics have blurred. Taking on new roles and responsibilities has also led to a technical turn, with many NGOs adopting a more professionalised approach (Squires 2008). Furthermore, the effectiveness of women's community and civil society activism as a valuable counterbalance to the state is significantly tempered by issues of funding. In exchange for steady support from the Department of Social Development, Belfast community centres have to a large extent become service providers. According to Cynthia Cockburn (2013), centre managers must devote a great deal of their time to paperwork if they are to satisfy the authorities and secure resources, and the time and stress involved in this has increased with the downturn in the economy and cuts to public sector spending. The centres must increasingly compete with each other, and thus cooperation has greatly diminished. In a situation where civil society relies heavily on state fiscal sustenance, it is inevitable that many women's groups are reticent to be overtly critical towards the state; therefore, the reliance on funding tends to temper the levels of critical and oppositional stances towards the state and its agencies.

While the women's informal sector continues to work at the coalface of social and economic disadvantage, the prospects of maintaining previously high levels of such community organising is significantly challenged by the dearth of funding available, particularly since the on-going crisis in global capitalism began in 2008. In 2008, the Northern Ireland Women's European Platform (NIWEP) urged the government to develop a specific stream of funding for women's civil society organisations, particularly in relation to key areas such as training and education. The current agenda of economic austerity however, is having a negative impact on the government's response to this call, and thus undermines women's community organising (Deiana 2013). Recent research among many in the women's community activism reveal doleful appraisals of the current dispensation, with many believing that the women's sector has become too 'professionalised' and 'NGO-ised', with a loss of a discernible political dynamic (Cockburn 2013). As EU peace funding to the North of Ireland continues to dry up, women's future community sector organising will be more dependent on state funding through the Department of Social Protection. Under the 2015 Fresh Start Agreement (at A3.9) there is a commitment for the 'development of a program to increase the participation and influence of women in community development'. At the same time, the continuing austerity agenda represents once again, the inherent contradictions between the rhetoric and the reality of women's political organising in the 'new' and 'post-conflict' North of Ireland.

Conclusion

Under the auspices of a transition from armed conflict to the peace process, constitutional politics had increasingly become the primary conduit and concern of republican politics, though by no means exclusively so. The ramifications of the shift towards institutional formal politics caused a tilt away from a broad, grassroots movement towards a more leadership-led style, not atypical of most formal political parties. For some, entering the arena of state-centric, electoral politics was inevitable and welcome; for others, it heralded a seismic shift away from dynamic grassroots organising to standard electoralism with little space for the activism, rhetoric, and mobilisation synonymous with the years of armed conflict. Notwithstanding, this chapter finds all 40 interviewees are full-time political activists today. In addition, most them are in both formal and informal political roles. Feminist scholars and activists who stress the importance of state-centric institutions as a central site for political struggle, focus on the use of gender quotas, women's inclusion within formal institutions or processes, constitutional guarantees of equality, equal pay in employment, among others. However, if formal political institutions are thoroughly gendered, Louise Chappell (2006) poses the obvious but important question: what is the point of encouraging social actors, especially feminists to engage with them? Although state-centric politics and their various institutions often appear rigid and incapable of change, as socially constructed institutions they contain an inherent dynamism which creates the potential for activists to re-inscribe their gendered foundations (Chappell 2006: 231). As already noted, former combatant republican women in this volume are cognisant of both the potential and constraints within constitutional politics. While advocating for the importance of women's presence and participation, their entry into formal politics represents another post-war tier of gender struggle. The narratives contained in this chapter point to gendered barriers, practices, norms and cultures.

Furthermore, while most are content with the progress republicans are making within electoral politics, its rigid nature and slow pace is also cited as a persistent source of dissatisfaction. The argument and analysis offered in this chapter serves as a formidable caveat to conventional approaches which advocate that the inclusion of women within the site of institutional politics as the most nascent sphere of women's post-war struggles. A more nuanced exploration of differentially positioned women such as this reveals the ways in which women politically organise according to their own specific interests and concerns. The formal/informal dichotomy evident throughout this chapter is derived from two different concepts of democracy, one being liberal, representative democracy, and the other a more deliberative and direct form. While the former refers to representative, institutionalised and often elite-driven forms of politics, the latter is typically characterised by direct, deliberative developmental practices (Pateman 2012). While there is undoubtedly a recent reinvigoration of feminist interest in gender and constitutional politics, many feminists continue to advocate the model of participatory democracy within grassroots and civil society as an alternative to the elitist, and expert-bureaucratic model of formal politics. Judith Squires, among others, argues that formal politics must be open to inputs from an informal, vibrant public sphere, where deliberations from within civil society can be transmitted to the formal arena of political decision-making. Mechanisms such as citizen assemblies, consensus conferences, citizen initiatives and referendums, deliberative opinion polls have proven to provide the capacity to shape policy in ways that are informed by a wide variety of viewpoints and experiences (Squires 2007: 174). The post-war politics of republican women are emblematic of the strengths and drawback within both approaches.

Elections and formal political representation is not the most radical or revolutionary avenue of political change. In a post-war society based on equality, surely women's right to formal political representation constitutes the most moderate and unoffending objective. Despite being enshrined in the text of GFA, the promise and political potential of 'women's right to full political participation' have given way to doleful realisation that formal politics is viewed by many political parties, as largely a male preserve. From a feminist perspective, the post-Troubles political landscape is largely, business as usual. While the GFA did undoubtedly provide the potential for a new era of gender politics, 20 years on, northern Irish society exhibits all the trademark and insidious characteristics of a patriarchal society that has yet to undergo a genuine transformation in gender relations.

Notes

1 Adopted in October 2000, SCR 1325 reaffirms the important role of women in the prevention and resolution of conflicts, peace negotiations, peace-building, peacekeeping, humanitarian response, and in post-conflict reconstruction, and stresses the importance of their equal participation and full involvement in all efforts for the maintenance and promotion of peace and security. Resolution 1325 urges all actors to increase the participation of women and incorporate gender perspectives in all United Nations peace and security efforts. Full text of the resolution available at www.un.org/womenwatch/osagi/wps/
2 Stands for Member of the Legislative Assembly; an elected representative to the Northern Ireland Assembly.
3 Stormont is the parliament buildings for the government of Northern Ireland and Leinster House is the parliament of the Republic of Ireland in Dublin referred to in Irish language as the Dáil.
4 While this is the standpoint of these republican women, I think it is important to bear in mind that the republican movement remains overwhelmingly male-led and stands accused of masculine dominance and patriarchal practices. In recent times, the republican movement has been accused of covering up allegations of rape and sexual abuse by members of the IRA. Perhaps the most high-profile case is that of Maria Cahill.

Maria hails from a strong republican family in Belfast. In October 2014 she waived anonymity as a complainant in a sexual abuse trial to highlight the fact that members of the IRA held an 'internal investigation' into her complaints of sexual abuse at the hands of an IRA member in the 1990s. The criminal trial of those accused of involvement in the 'internal investigation' collapsed with all acquitted. There are other instances too, but I think the notion of Sinn Féin acting as a catalyst for challenging masculinity needs to be clarified and contextualised, particularly for those who disagree with the perspectives and experiences of interviewees in this book.

5 Highly sensitive or contentious issues relating to 'the Troubles' have been largely placed on the political back-burner since the restoration of power-sharing in 2007. Despite the efforts of US diplomats Meghan O'Sullivan and Richard Haass in 2013, all major political parties failed to reach agreement on these matters. In 2014, vast disagreement between the political parties over welfare reform in the North again brought matters to a head. Despite reaching an agreement (Stormont House Agreement) in December 2014, the text and substance of the agreement remains a highly guarded secret. More ominously, Sinn Féin pulled out of the Agreement in March 2015, kick-starting yet another round of crisis talks, involving the main political parties and the British and Irish Governments. While the latest effort, the Fresh Start Agreement has largely dealt with ideological and political schisms over budgets and welfare reform, the legacy of dealing with the armed conflict remains unresolved.

Bibliography

Aharoni, S. B. 2016. 'Who Needs the Women and Peace Hypothesis? Rethinking Modes of Inquiry on Gender and Conflict in Israel/Palestine'. *International Feminist Journal of Politics*, DOI: 10.1080/14616742.2016.1237457

Alison, M. 2004. 'Women as Agents of Political Violence: Gendering Security'. *Security Dialogue* 35(4): 447–463.

Alison, M. 2009. *Women and Political Violence: Female Combatants in Ethno-national Conflict.* New York: Routledge.

Anderlini, S. N. 2007. *Women Building Peace: What They Do, Why It Matters.* Boulder and London: Lynne Rienner Publishers.

Arostegui, J. 2013. 'Gender, Conflict, and Peace-building: How Conflict Can Catalyse Positive Change for Women'. *Gender and Development* 21(3): 533–549.

Batliwala, S and D. Brown. eds. 2006. *Transnational Civil Society: An Introduction.* Boulder, CO: Kumarian Press.

Bean, K. 2007. *The New Politics of Sinn Féin.* Liverpool: Liverpool University Press.

Bouta, T., G. Frerks and I. Bannon. 2005. *Gender, Conflict and Development.* Washington DC: The World Bank.

Braniff, M. and S. A. Whiting. 2016. 'There's Just No Point Having a Token Woman': Gender and Representation in the Democratic Unionist Party in Post-agreement Northern Ireland'. *Parliamentary Affairs* 69(1): 93–114.

Buckley, F. 2013. 'Women and Politics in Ireland: The Road to Sex Quotas'. *Irish Political Studies* 28(3): 341–397.

Cassidy, K. 2005. 'Organic Intellectuals and the Committed Community: Irish Republicanism and Sinn Féin in the North'. *Irish Political Studies* 20(3): 341–356.

Celis, K., S. Childs, J. Kantola, and M. L. Krook. 2008. Rethinking Women's Substantive Representation, *Representation* 44(2): 99–110.

Chappell, L. 2006. 'Comparing Political Institutions: Revealing the Gendered Logic of Appropriateness'. *Politics & Gender* 2(2): 223–235.

Cochrane, F. 2013. *Northern Ireland: The Reluctant Peace.* New Haven and London: Yale University Press.

Cockburn, C. 2013. 'A Movement Stalled: Outcomes of Women's Campaign for Equalities and Inclusion in the Northern Ireland Peace Process'. *Interface: a Journal for and about Social Movements* 5(1): 151–182.

Connell, R. 1995. *Masculinities.* Berkeley, CA: University of California Press.

Corcoran, M. 2006. *Out of Order: The Political Imprisonment of Women in Northern Ireland, 1972–1999.* Devon: Willan Publishing.

Cordero, I. 2001. 'Social Organisations: From Victims to Actors in Peace Building'. Pp. 151–164 in *Victims, Perpetrators or Actors: Gender, Armed Conflict and Political Violence,* edited by C. Moser and F. Clark. New York: Zed Books.

Cowell-Meyers, K. 2003. 'Women in Northern Ireland Politics: Gender and the Politics of Peace-building in the New Legislative Assembly'. *Irish Political Studies* 18(1): 72–96.

Cox, L. 2012. 'Challenging Austerity in Ireland: Community and Movement Responses'. *Concept* 3(2): 1–6.

Dahlerup, D. and L. Freidenvall. 2005. 'Quotas as a 'Fast Track' to Equal Representation for Women'. *International Feminist Journal of Politics* 7(1): 26–48.

Davenport, C. 2007. 'State Repression and Political Order'. *Annual Review of Political Science* 10: 1–23.

Deiana, M.-A. 2013. 'Women's Citizenship in Northern Ireland after the 1998 Agreement'. *Irish Political Studies* 28(3): 399–412.

Dolgopol, U. 2007. 'Women and Peace Building'. *Australian Feminist Studies* 21(50): 257–273.

Erzurum, K and B. Eren. 2014. 'Women in Peacebuilding: A Criticism of Gendered Solutions in Postconflict Situations'. *Journal of Applied Security Research* 9(2): 236–256.

Evans, J. and J. Tonge. 2013. 'From Abstentionism to Enthusiasm: Sinn Féin, Nationalist Electors and Support for Devolved Power-sharing in Northern Ireland'. *Irish Political Studies* 28(1): 39–57.

Fearon, K. and M. McWilliams. 2000. 'Swimming Against the Mainstream: the Northern Ireland Women's Coalition'. Pp. 117–138 in *Gender, Democracy and Inclusion in Northern Ireland,* edited by C. Roulston and C. Davis. London: Palgrave.

Frampton, M. 2009. *The Long March: The Political Strategy of Sinn Féin, 1981–2007.* Basingstoke and New York: Palgrave Macmillan.

Frazer, E. and N. Lacey. 1993. *The Politics of Community: a Feminist Critique of the Liberal-Communitarian Debate.* Cambridge: Harvester Wheatsheaf.

Galligan, Y. 2013. 'Gender and Politics in Northern Ireland: The Representation Gap Revisited'. *Irish Political Studies* 28(3): 413–433.

Galligan, Y and R. Wilford. 1999. 'Women's Political Representation in Ireland'. Pp. 130–148 in *Contesting Politics: Women in Ireland, North and South,* edited by Y. Galligan, E. Ward, and R. Wilford. Boulder, CO: Westview Press.

Gowrinathan, N. 2017. 'The Committed Female Fighter: The Political Identities of Tamil Women in the Liberation Tigers of Tamil Eelam'. *International Feminist Journal of Politics,* DOI: 10.1080/14616742.2017.1299369

Hackett, C. 1995. 'The Republican Feminist Agenda'. *Feminist Review* 50: 111–116.

Hartsock, N. 1983. *Money, Sex, and Power: Towards a Feminist Historical Materialism.* Boston, MA: Northeastern University Press.

Hayes, B. C. and McAllister, I. 2013. 'Gender and Consociational Powersharing in Northern Ireland'. *International Political Science Review* 34(2): 123–139.

Hoewer, M. 2013. 'UN Resolution 1325 in Ireland: Limitations and Opportunities of the International Framework on Women, Peace and Security'. *Irish Political Studies* 28(3): 450–468.

Jordan, A. 2003. 'Women and Conflict Transformation: Influences, Roles and Experiences'. *Development in Practice* 13(2/3): 239–251.

Kantola, J. and H. M. Dahl. 2005. 'Gender and the State'. *International Feminist Journal of Politics* 7(1): 9–70.

Karam, A. 2001. 'Women in War and Peace-building'. *International Journal of Feminist Politics* 3(1): 2–25.

Kennedy, R., C. Pierson and J. Thomson. 2016. 'Challenging Identity Hierarchies: Gender and Consociational Power-sharing'. *The British Journal of Politics and International Relations* 1–16, DOI: 10.1177/1369148116647334

Kenny, M. 2014. 'A Feminist Institutionalist Approach'. *Politics & Gender* 10(4): 679–684.

Kilmurray, A. 2013. 'UN Resolution 1325: The Experience within Local Communities'. *Working Papers in British–Irish Studies.* Institute for British-Irish Studies, University College Dublin.

Lovenduski, J. and P. Norris. 1993. *Gender and Party Politics.* London: Sage.

Lovenduski, J and P. Norris. eds. 1996. *Women In Politics.* Oxford: Oxford Publishing.

Luciak, I. A. 1999. 'Gender Equality in the Salvadoran Transition'. *Latin American Perspectives* 26: 43–67.

Mackay, F., Kenny, M. and Chappell, L. 2010. 'New Institutionalism Through a Gender Lens: Towards a Feminist Institutionalism?' *International Political Science Review* 31(5): 573–58.

Maillot, A. 2005. *New Sinn Féin: Irish Republicanism in the Twenty-first Century.* London and New York: Routledge.

Matthews, N. 2014. 'Gendered Candidate Selection and the Representation of Women in Northern Ireland'. *Parliamentary Affairs* 67(3): 617–646.

Mazurana, D. and A. Raven-Roberts. eds. 2005. *Gender, Conflict and Peacekeeping.* Lanham, MD: Rowman and Littlefield Publishers.

McCoy, G. 2000. 'Women, Community and Politics in Northern Ireland'. Pp. 3–23 in *Gender, Democracy and Inclusion in Northern Ireland,* edited by C. Roulston and C. Davis. London: Palgrave.

McGratton, C and E. Meehan. eds. 2012. *Everyday Life After the Irish Conflict.* Manchester: Manchester University Press.

Meintjes, S., A. Pillay and M. Turshen. eds. 2001. *The Aftermath: Women in Post-Conflict Transformation.* London and New York: Zed Books.

Miller, R. L., R. Wilford, and F. Donoghue. 1996. *Women and Political Participation in Northern Ireland.* Aldershot: Avebury.

Nagel, J. 1998. 'Nation'. *Ethnic and Racial Studies* 21(2): 242–269.

Naples, N. 1998. *Grassroots Warriors: Activist Mothering, Community Work, and the War on Poverty.* New York: Routledge.

Ni Aolain, F., D. F. Haynes and N. Cahn. 2011. *On The Frontlines: Gender, War and the Post-Conflict Process.* Oxford: Oxford University Press.

O'Keefe, T. 2013. *Feminist Identity Development and Activism in Revolutionary Movements.* London and New York: Palgrave Macmillan.

Okin, S. M. 1989. *Justice, Gender and the Family.* New York: Basic Books.

Pankhurst, D. 2003. 'The 'Sex War' and Other Wars: Towards a Feminist Approach to Peace Building'. *Development in Practice* 13(2/3): 154–177.

Pateman, C. 1988. *The Sexual Contract*. Cambridge: Polity Press.

Pateman, C. 2012. Participatory Democracy Revisited. *Perspectives On Politics* 10(1): 7–19.

Patterson, H. 2012. 'Unionism after Good Friday and St Andrews'. *The Political Quarterly* 83(2): 247–255.

Porter, E. 1998. 'Identity, Location, Plurality: Women, Nationalism and Northern Ireland'. Pp. 36–61 in *Women, Ethnicity and Nationalism: The Politics of Transition*, edited by R. Wilford and R. L. Miller. London and New York: Routledge.

Porter, E. 2000. 'The Challenge of Dialogue across Difference'. Pp. 141–162 in *Gender, Democracy and Inclusion in Northern Ireland*, edited by C. Roulston and C. Davis. London: Palgrave.

Porter, E. 2003. 'Women, Political Decision-making and Peace-building in Conflict Regions'. *Global Change, Peace and Security* 15(3): 245–262.

Randall, V. 1987. *Women and Politics*. New York: Macmillan Education.

Richter-Devroe, S. 2012. 'Defending Their Land, Protecting Their Men'. *International Feminist Journal of Politics* 14(2): 181–201.

Roulston, C. 2000. 'Democracy and the Challenge of Gender: New Visions, New Processes'. Pp. 24–26 in *Gender, Democracy and Inclusion in Northern Ireland*, edited by C. Roulston and C. Davis. London: Palgrave.

Safa, H. I. 1990. 'Women's Social Movements in Latin America'. *Gender and Society* 4(3): 354–369.

Sales, R. 1997. *Women Divided: Gender, Religion and Politics in Northern Ireland*. London and New York: Routledge.

Saward, M. 2006. 'The Representative Claim'. *Contemporary Political Theory* 5: 297–318.

Side, K. 2009. 'Women's Civil and Political Citizenship in the Post-Good Friday Agreement Period in Northern Ireland'. *Irish Political Studies* 24(1): 67–87.

Spark, C. and J Corbett. 2016. 'Emerging Women Leaders' Views on Political Participation in Melanesia'. *International Feminist Journal of Politics*, DOI: 10.1080/14616742.2016.1189680

Squires, J. 2007. *The New Politics of Gender Equality*. Basingstoke and New York: Palgrave Macmillan.

Squires, J. 2008. 'The Constitutive Representation of Gender: Extra-Parliamentary Re-Presentations of Gender Relations'. *Representation* 44(2): 187–204.

Squires, J. 2012. 'Feminism and Democracy'. Pp. 466–477 in *Political Sociology*, edited by E. Amenta, K. Nash, and A. Scott. Chichester, Sussex: Blackwell Publishing.

Verge, T. 2015. 'The Gender Regime of Political Parties: Feedback Effects between "Supply" and "Demand"'. *Politics & Gender* 11(4): 754–759.

Ward, M. 2006. 'Gender, Citizenship and the Future of the Northern Ireland Peace Process'. *Irish Feminist Studies* 41: 262–283.

Waylen, G. 1994. 'Women and Democratization: Conceptualizing Gender Relations in Transition Politics'. *World Politics* 46(3): 327–354.

Young, I. M. 2000. *Inclusion and Democracy*. Oxford: Oxford University Press.

6 Conclusion

Introduction

My purpose in writing this book was twofold: to examine the often-overlooked stories of combatant women within a non-state nationalist movement in transition; and, uncover the ways in which gender, which being the multiple workings of masculinity and femininity, shapes their conflict transition experiences. The theoretical framework for this research primarily resided in the gendered continuum of violence since it makes clear the linkages and continuities between political, economic, and social violence before, during and after war. Ending armed actions and the signing of major peace accords does not signify the presence of peace or the end of violence. Using the pluralised standpoints of republican women and drawing on the feminist theory of a continuum of violence, this book finds that the dichotomous separation of war and peace within conventional approaches represents a gendered fiction. Despite undertaking wartime roles that were empowering, agentic, and subversive, this book has shown that the 'post-conflict moment' as experienced by female combatants represents not peace and security, but a continuity of gender discrimination, violence, injustice, and insecurity. The purpose of undertaking exploratory research into their post-war lives is not motivated solely by producing a counter-narrative to prevailing approaches, but also endeavours to problematise the practices, ideas, and discourses that undergird male-dominated 'one-size-fits-all' approaches to conflict transition. The experiences contained in this book challenge the discursive deployment of terms such as post-conflict, peace, and security, and moreover, shed light on many forms of violence and insecurities concealed by a limited and partial form of peace-making which addresses certain forms of violence while normalising others.

In addition, conventional narratives of war and peace tend to project an oversimplified vision of male soldiers, fighters, and protectors, with women largely relegated to the sidelines of the battlefield as peacemakers, bridge-builders or victims. The capacity of feminist scholars to challenge established approaches to war and conflict transition is predicated on the diverse and eclectic output of theoretical and empirical studies, which displace both the universalising tendencies and narratives, and the gender stereotypes they are predicated on. In-line with that feminist challenge, this book plays its role by shedding light on republican combatant women. While existing accounts of war and peace tend to present singular narratives of non-state nationalist military movements, a feminist interrogation such as this opens important schisms that provide insights into the gendered realities of war and peace. Despite the long-standing endeavours of feminist scholars to highlight the centrality of gender to the constitutive purposes of ethno-nationalism, war, and peace, gender stereotypes retain significant weight within conventional approaches to war and peace. Given the stories and experiences contained in this book, it is demonstrably evident that women not only defy the gender archetypes as active combatants, but are also a vital part of military structures, particularly in those deemed non-state, liberation struggles, despite the propensity of gender tropes that seek to marginalise such realities. The acknowledgement of women as fighters does not represent a panacea to the marginalisation of women within patriarchal societies. However, once we begin to deconstruct the gendered myths by uncovering women's silence and absence, then the prevailing narrative of war and peace no longer appears as simplistic or solid as it once was. The experiences and narratives of combatant women not only provide a more accurate account of the ways in which non-state militaries function, but also uncover the practices and processes that legitimise the marginalisation of combatant women in the aftermath of armed conflict. Each of the preceding chapters in this book covered several diverse issues, but were thematically linked by a motivation to problematise the realm of 'post-conflict' from the perspectives of female combatants.

Women's struggle after armed struggle

While the Good Friday Agreement (hereafter the GFA) continues to draw plaudits from a range of global actors and institutions, the lived reality for republican women counter those who propagate the current dispensation in the North of Ireland as representing peace. The continuum of violence indicated by republican women in Chapter 3 is unquestionably gendered, but it is also delineated through other sources of insecurity including the partition of Ireland, the vagaries of global capitalism, and gender-based violence. Dominant approaches to peace are sustained by their fictitious universality and predicated on the clear separation between the 'exceptional' violence of war and the trivialisation of other violence as the 'everyday'. Asking combatant women about their post-war visions of a just society therefore advances a series of needs, interests and concerns normally omitted by traditional approaches to peace and security. Despite persistent resistance to acknowledge their post-war lives, such understandings can only enhance the endeavours, academic and otherwise, for a peace by addressing a wider range of violence and insecurities.

One of the strengths of this book is its use of first-hand testimonies of women to undermine the notion that the terrain of war is solely male-saturated. Building on the work of others, I contend that women's roles and contributions to military movements are not anomalous individuals or events; women's roles and labour

– from unpaid domestic labour, prostitutes, active combatants – are essential to the production and reproduction of all militaries (Basham and Catignani 2018; Enloe 2014; MacKenzie 2012). Despite the mounting evidence, the gendered reification of violent men and peaceful women persists and finds clear expression in the almost universal marginalisation of women's combatant roles and their wartime contributions. The post-war commemorative battles waged by republican women in Chapter 2 are constituted by the cultural violence inflicted by male-dominated remembrance, thus demonstrating how language and symbolism are utilised as a means of attaining male power, while diminishing the reality and value of women's wartime contributions. The attempts to sequester the 'combatant role' as masculine and male-only, signifies the salience of gender in understanding processes of power and domination in post-war scenarios. The post-war commemorative struggles of republican women transcend issues of historical accuracy; their exclusion from memorial work is a process of re-masculinising both the public realm of commemoration and the overall narrative of republican armed struggle. Moreover, the attempted erasure of women's contributions within various acts of remembrance represents a source of conceptual and cultural violence with major consequences. For male soldiers, their masculinity and manliness is both affirmed; for female combatants, their position is invariably viewed as an anomaly; a fleeting moment until the crisis has passed. Rather than entering the post-war phase with their wartime roles and contributions consolidated and acknowledged, Chapter 2 signified post-war commemoration as a new tier of struggle for the recognition of women's roles and contributions to armed resistance. Notwithstanding, the chapter was also attentive to the ways in which combatant women's attempts to record and commemorate their wartime experiences brings to light their agency and the centrality of their wartime roles. After a decade or so of negligence within republican commemorative formats, the chapter noted the relatively successful resurgence of women's practices of commemoration from 2007 onwards.

With that in mind, Cynthia Cockburn (2004) reminds us that militaries are, of course, not feminine cultures, and moreover, that the presence and participation of women within their ranks does not alter the character, culture, and hierarchy, regardless of their level of sacrifice. Male-dominated nationalist movements are not (overly) concerned with women's emancipation, despite the revolutionary rhetoric they espouse. During the post-ceasefire period, the ideological standing of the republican movement switched dramatically towards an institutional positioning with a zealous focus on electoral politics. The top-down, male-dominated, exclusionary, and often secretive formal GFA negotiations heralded a significant sidelining of republican women, despite the efforts of many. A common reason postulated for women's exclusion from formal peace talks is that they 'were not waging the war' (Anderlini 2007: 4). Some have suggested that prevailing gender stereotypes frames dominant visions of a post-war society. In other words, if wars are primarily waged and fought by men, then it surely follows that it is their needs, interests, and experiences that will dictate the post-war reconstruction. Yet, despite the central role of republican female combatants and the rhetoric of gender equality within Provisional republicanism, it is evident that republican women were absent from any direct role in formal negotiations. Ultimately, control of the state was at the heart of the negotiations, and 'macho men' were at the forefront of those negotiations' (Racioppi and O'Sullivan See 2001: 101). As Provisional republicanism 'professionalised' itself in preparation for its post-war institutional struggle, a marked contrast emerged in the ways in which women's equality was conceptualised and pursued. In particular, as the radical agitation and organising of the Women's Department was furtively wound down, what emerged in its place embraces visions and strategies that are largely indistinguishable from any other mainstream political party. As Sinn Féin moved towards an institutional position, prolific feminist political outlets such as the Women's Department were rebranded in favour of a more mainstream approach, one that was in vogue with the new institutional look. To this end, Chapter 4 highlighted the pitfalls of institutionalising feminist political struggles.

Despite the evidence of loss and regression replete throughout this book, it is the response of republican women to various forms of violence, both within and outside of the republican movement, that also warrants attention. While the post-war site is undoubtedly riddled with ambiguities regarding their position within the republican movement, nevertheless, their continued vibrant activism is indicative of the agency carefully nurtured during the war years and carried into the peace process. Chapter 5 found that the post-war activism of republican women resided not solely in institutional politics, but across a broad-based political struggle of grassroots activism, semi-autonomous organising, electoral politics and community work. From their perspectives and experiences, women's formal political participation provided an important but ultimately a restrictive terrain of political struggle with limited transformative potential. Republican women have not abandoned their grassroots activism, despite relatively high levels of access to formal politics through Sinn Féin. Today, they are continuing a political struggle that mirrors their wartime political activism, that being, grassroots, republican, and often socialist and feminist struggle across both formal and informal spheres. The continuity of civil society activism among republican women not only challenges dominant understandings of what counts as 'political', it signifies the issues and barriers to the development of a truly peaceful, equal and secure post-war society. Peace activism in this sense refers not simply to the pursuit of politically oriented issues in the aftermath of a peace accord, but rather seeks to identify and challenge the structural practices and discourses that provide the enabling conditions for such forms of post-war violence to flourish. Recognising and acknowledging this eclectic work offers the potential to transform the dominant peace agenda. Moreover, their presence and participation during and after the armed conflict has led to advancements for women, feminism, and gender equality within the wider republican movement, which despite its many instances of controversy, is widely accepted as a more progressive movement on women's struggles than many of its counterparts and opponents. Undoubtedly, Sinn Féin's relatively progressive stance on gender equality and the promotion of women stems directly from the agency and fortitude of republican women, from the years of armed conflict right through to contemporary times.

As to the question of gender and nationalism in the post-war period, this book uncovered some significant findings. Feminist critics of nationalism as a patriarchal structure often cite post-war regression as robust evidence of the consequences for women's participation within such movements. Women pursuing a feminist agenda alongside their nationalist struggle are consistently told by their male counter-parts to park their gender concerns for the more pressing issues of state formation. On the face of it, a conventional reading of the stories of republican women and conflict transition appears to corroborate those who point to the overwhelming losses for participating women within nationalist movements as emblematic of the pitfalls for nationalist women. While the deleterious effects of conflict transition on former combatant women is important, it is, however, only one of several important threads within the overall narrative. In its stated pursuit of state formation and state power, many post-war nationalist movements invariably shed their revolutionary strategies and rhetoric, and gradually embrace parliamentary democracy and electoral politics. Numerous attempts to explain the seemingly persistent global pattern of post-war regression by combatant women typically do so through the prism of where male-led nationalist movements position women after armed struggle. While this primarily Western-based literature makes an important contribution, it nevertheless fails to adequately theorise the reality that many combatant women are politically active and mobilised in the aftermath of war. There are several key factors to consider if we are to fully understand why many combatant women do not return to pre-conflict roles. First, there are theoretical links between the post-war continuum of violence and nationalism's inability to recognise, let alone challenge many of these sources of insecurity seriously. Second, is the shift within revolutionary groups from grassroots movements and collective action to institutionalised, top-down formal bodies concerned with constitutional politics and electoral contests. While the ending of armed struggle and creation of nation-state structures and institutions may mark the end of national struggle, the existence of various sources of violence in the aftermath of the peace accord constitutes a continuum of conflict, thus providing instances of injustice and oppression like those that initially mobilised their wartime activism. Furthermore, many of the contemporary issues tackled by republican women – poverty, austerity, abortion, housing – were already incorporated as part of their ideological outlook and political agenda during the wartime years, particularly from 1979 onwards. While nationalism may be the primary force driving their interest and activism, non-state nationalism typically functions as a springboard that expands the political spectrum, interests and pursuits of its members into many other spheres. While the end products of nationalism – governance, sovereignty, self-determination – are, of course, important, the ending of national armed struggle should not be interpreted as the automatic end-point for nationalist women's struggle. In this sense, their post-war activism is a continuity of consciousness and practice, which is reacting to the post-war continuity of violence and conflict, despite the signing of a peace accord.

The women in this study, as in others (Alison 2009; O'Keefe 2013), were mobilised and heavily politicised by their participation within a non-state nationalist movement. In addition, the formation of the Women's Department mid-way during 'the Troubles' suggests that women were carving out feminist spaces successfully within the republican movement, despite some formidable barriers. Consistent throughout Chapters 4 and 5 is the contention that it is the institutionalisation of the Provisional republican struggle that presents multiple barriers and high levels of regression for women's political struggle in the post-war period. While the 'revolutionary' phase of the national struggle fostered high levels of women's activism, it is, in fact, the current institutional post-war phase of the republican struggle that is proving more problematic. Many, if not all the issues identified within the pages of this book, stem from a movement that is shedding radical politics and switching to an electoral and institutionalised position. The common problematic denominator across the findings therefore is not nationalism as such, but the institutionalisation of political struggle. The vibrant post-war activism of republican women indicates that empowerment and political mobility gained through the armed nationalist struggle is directly carried over into the post-war period. The thematic issues of state violence and confronting injustice that mobilised many republican women during armed conflict are the same issues that inform and motivate their high levels of contemporary activism.

It is important to state that the Provisional republican movement during 'the Troubles' did not represent some type of feminist utopia. On the contrary, existing research indicates its gendered and often patriarchal approaches to women (O'Keefe 2013). This book makes clear that republican women today are struggling to have their experiences, contributions, and needs recognised within the broader republican agenda. That struggle is not unique to the post-war period and is, in fact, a continuity of a struggle for equality within the movement since its very inception. It therefore underscores the need to be attentive to the ways in which women respond to all forms of domination and marginalisation, as opposed to assuming the male nationalist voice that often dismisses women's struggles in the aftermath of armed actions is the final word on the matter. Undoubtedly, republican women faced marginalisation and regression both within and outside the republican movement during the post-war period. The significance of this book is that it moves beyond both the demobilisation and demilitarisation moment and the disproportionate focus on regression, and instead, endeavours to document the ways combatant women themselves organised in the face of such challenges to resist it.

Notwithstanding the ambiguous experiences of republican women, the conclusions here should not be read as an outright exclusion of women by the republican movement. On the contrary, Sinn Féin is lauded for its exemplary track record in consistently returning the highest percentage of female elected representatives (Buckley 2013; Galligan 2013). Women's institutional participation, however, is hardly the most radical gauge to measure the struggle against patriarchy and other forms of oppression. To reiterate, Sinn Féin do include women in relatively significant numbers but they do so in ways that suit the political trajectory of the party. Today, women's equality and inclusion in Sinn Féin is redefined and measured by an established discourse regarding the need for increasing women's political participation and visibility. By shedding the radical politics of yester-year, Sinn Féin includes women today in a way that is virtually indistinguishable from any other mainstream political party. In other words, while women are included, the overt republican brand of feminist politics appear consigned by the movement to its revolutionary past.

While Sinn Féin's current position on women is not atypical of any other mainstream party, by paying close attention to combatant women in a holistic way, we gain a better measure of the ways in which *they* pursue peace and equality, both within and outside of the republican movement. Sinn Féin's re-branding of women's struggle, like other movements in pursuit of state power, should not be interpreted as an accurate representation of republican women. Given this, there is far more to the story of republican women and conflict transition than simply their positions in Sinn Féin. On the contrary, they remain committed activists in various organisations in their pursuit of republicanism, women's equality and a genuine peace. While formal party politics is an important front in that battle, it is, nevertheless, one of many. Community activism also provides many other fronts in their post-war struggle. From eradicating domestic violence to ensuring reproductive rights, from anti-drugs campaigning to collective resistance to neo-liberal austerity – these are the struggles of republican women in pursuit of their vision of peace and equality. I concur that focusing solely on institutional politics produces a partial and ultimately an inaccurate picture of women's post-war struggles. It once again illustrates the benefits of remaining attuned to the narratives and actions of women themselves, not top-down structures, to yield a more accurate vision of conflict transition experiences.

This book, I hope, has demonstrated the benefits of looking beyond the stereotypes, and by doing so, has indicated the urgency for similar research on the post-war lives of combatant women in other regions blighted by armed conflict. In particular, there is a need to expand explorations of female combatants beyond the DDR moment and capture their entire transitionary experiences. Despite a small yet burgeoning body of research on female fighters and conflict transition, few studies such as these exist, and therefore the collection of women's war and post-war stories – all sorts of stories – represents a pressing gap in knowledge and data (Sjoberg 2014: 157). To sustain the feminist challenge, research across a diversity of women's lives remains indispensable, thus providing the feminist tools required to deconstruct the gendered layers inherent within dominant narratives of war and peace. In particular, the pattern mapped out in Chapters 4 and 5 paradoxically suggests that periods of military engagement decreases (not erases) levels of masculine dominance, only to reassert itself in the aftermath of war. Such reasoning indicates that potentially, nationalist women experience greater levels of agency *during* war, not afterwards. The

North of Ireland, like many other transitioning regions, is host to an eclectic mix of contemporary 'spoiler groups', both republican and loyalists, who reject the current dispensation and remain actively committed to the continued use of political violence. Research on women's motivations and the role of gender within such groups is unquestionably warranted. As Chapters 4 and 5 outlined, some participants in this research have severed their links with the Provisional republican movement for its embrace of top-down, institutional politics, and the squeezing of political spaces opened by women during the conflict. Is the re-imposition of a conventional gender order a factor in motiving women who reject 'the peace' and remain militarily active within spoiler groups? What role, if any, does gender or feminist activism plays within such dissenting or spoiler groups? Moreover, while women tend to populate the various ranks of non-state, liberation movements, it is perhaps pertinent to examine those military movements which have remained impervious to women's contributions (Henshaw 2016). In addition, recent developments mapping out the complex reasons for women's recruitment to non-state militaries also identifies nascent furrows to plough in the future.

While an exploration such as this text may stand accused of undermining the foundational basis of feminism by accentuating the diversity of women's experiences, however, patriarchy and gender remain primary forces shaping the war and post-war lives of all women, thus providing a vital theoretical link. Just as women's endeavours for bridge-building and peace-making are not taken seriously within formal peace processes, so too combatant women are rarely considered 'real soldiers' by their male comrades (or mainstream IR for that matter). Even in the instances when women do occupy the same roles within military movements, they are treated differently by their gender (Sjoberg 2014: 31). Despite the diversity, breadth and scope of women's experiences, interests and roles, from bridge-builders to bomb-makers, the common denominator shaping their lives is gender and its multiple workings, which invariably privilege men and masculinities always. Regardless of the roles undertaken by women in times of war, unconventional or otherwise, normative models of masculinities and femininities endure, precipitating a gender order of power and relationships that subjugates women and femininity. All feminists have a stake in drawing attention to a diversity of women's roles in conflict transition, including those of former combatants, despite their 'outsiders' outsider' status. All too often, the fissures among women are interpreted by some as undermining the political potential of feminism. Exploring the lives of combatant women and recognising their diverse experiences should not be understood as a point of feminist weakness. Rather than extracting or weakening feminist post-war struggles, exploring the standpoints of combatant women can add significant theoretical understandings to the ways in which differentially positioned women respond to patriarchy in conflict transition. Remaining acutely aware of the differences among women, I argue, ensures that we expose patriarchy is all its various guises.

Concluding thoughts

It would be folly to suggest that the North of Ireland is not in a significantly better position than it was 30 years ago. With armed conflict largely absent, the city centres and rural beauty of the North do not look dissimilar to that of any other region. Peace, however, demands far more than the absence of 'conventional violence' and the North remains deeply polarised, as well as bearing many of the trademark scars of a society emerging from armed conflict. Increasing levels of sectarianism, the extension of inter-communal 'peace walls', issues of parades, commemorations, dealing with the past, contentious (and often violent confrontations) over flags and emblems are indicative that the GFA represents a prudent form of conflict *management* as opposed to conflict *resolution*. Despite the formal declaration of 'peace', the North of Ireland's institutions of government appear to be in perpetual crisis, marred by high levels of mistrust. Despite this, the period of 2007 to December 2016 represented unprecedented levels of relative political stability, and it appeared that the region was beginning to 'normalise' its politics. However, the legacy of the conflict and its bitter residue continued to shape relations between Sinn Féin and the Democratic Unionist Party (DUP). The 'past is always present' in the North of Ireland and the failure to adequately deal with the toxic legacy of that past has led to mistrust and antagonisms. Moreover, major disagreements over 'bread and butter' issues such as austerity, the economy, abortion, and social issues such as marriage equality, LGBT rights, and, of course, Brexit, also highlighted the vast ideological schism between the relatively progressive agenda of Irish republicanism and the more conservative standpoints of unionism. Despite the alleged agreement secured by all political parties in December 2014, the Stormont House Agreement had to be followed up with a further ten weeks of party negotiations the following year culminating in the Fresh Start Agreement in November 2015. While the agreement did address the wrangling over the extent of austerity budgets, it failed, however, to adequately resolve the legacy of the past, combating residual paramilitarism, or confront the vexed issue of flags, emblems and parades. After months of deteriorating relations, events came to a head in January 2017 when Deputy First Minister and former IRA commander Martin McGuinness resigned, and the power-sharing Executive collapsed. At the time of writing (July 2018) there are no significant efforts to restore the Executive. Given the ideological gulf between the two main parties however, and the spectre of Brexit looming, most commentators are convinced that power-sharing governance in the North is heading for cold-storage, and the re-introduction of direct rule from Westminster, London. While the recent 20th anniversary of the GFA in April 2018 should have been an occasion for much reflection and perhaps even celebration, the Irish peace process proved once again, to be a stalled work in progress.

Beyond issues directly related to the armed conflict, many communities, particularly those in disadvantaged areas, continue to endure significant levels of economic deprivation and social exclusion. The latest collapse of global capitalism has taken its toll, with marginalised communities blighted by the double-burden of high unemployment rates and cuts to vital public services. According to the Joseph Rowntree Foundation, which monitors poverty and social exclusion in the North, in the last five years household incomes, poverty rates and unemployment have all worsened in the North of Ireland at levels far greater than in Great Britain.[1] The North of Ireland is a society in which 24 per cent of children live below the poverty line and are twice as likely to be living in consistent poverty than those living in Britain (Shirlow 2012). Between 2007 and 2013, unemployment doubled to 5.8 per cent, average household incomes fell by 10 per cent and poverty rates among young adults rose by 8 per cent. In addition, a 2014 study by Queens University, Belfast, finds that suicide rates have soared, almost doubling in the aftermath of the negotiated settlement.[2] Recent figures indicate an alarming statistic that suicide is now claiming as many lives each year as 'the Troubles' did. While those who propagate the peace model of good governance and neoliberal capitalism may find salutary reassurance in the relative absence of the political violence that marked 'the Troubles', listening to marginalised voices, however, not only disrupts the logic of such approaches but also offers a broader vision of peace and security.

Of great significance is the fact that little has changed for women where they continue to experience high levels of physical and sexual violence, are concentrated in low-level employment, do most of unpaid care and continue to be the most likely to be in poverty (Cockburn 2013; Fearon and Rebouche 2006; O'Keefe 2012: 84). Ostensibly, the GFA peace accord promised so much. Despite those who lauded its political potential to deliver equality for all, contemporary northern Irish society displays little of this much heralded social and political change. The agreement stipulated the equality of opportunity for all and the right of women to politically participate fully. Many feminists and women's groups cited such inclusion as potentially ground-breaking in that it could act as a catalyst for transforming gender relations. Women's lives, particularly working-class women's lives, however, continue to be blighted by poverty, unemployment, unpaid domestic labour, low-paid employment, various forms of physical and sexual violence, marginalisation from institutional politics, and positions of public decision-making (Cockburn 2013; O'Keefe 2013). By any measure the northern Irish peace process has effectively failed to deliver transformative and substantive changes to the lives of women. Even some of the GFA's greatest champions are now lamenting its lack of discernible success (Deiana 2013; Galligan 2013; Side 2009). Of course, none of this should come as a surprise given that the entire process was largely governed by the staples of standard forms of 'conflict resolution'. The story of the Irish peace process is an exclusionary, state-centred, male dominated process, concerned primarily by the management of conflict between two polarised ethno-national/sectarian blocs. While some feminist and women's groups successfully insisted on an equality clause within the agreement, the male architects of peace primarily paid lip service to it, designating it as aspirational as opposed to fundamental. If anything, the Irish peace process thus far demonstrates the limited capabilities of conventional approaches to both peace and women's equality.

Given the levels of structural and cultural violence, coupled with the issues directly related to the legacy of the conflict, the North of Ireland is not a society that bears any semblance to 'a place at peace'. Considering these stark realities, one might expect that the proponents and architects of peace and conflict resolution may wish to reappraise their approaches and perhaps look towards those who have been hitherto excluded from meaningful participation, such as combatant women. Gender equality and women's struggle for emancipation, however, are rarely afforded priority, particularly in conflict transition, and continue to be placed on the back-burner for some other more pressing concern. Feminists who convincingly and consistently demonstrate the centrality of gender to war and conflict resolution are often reminded by the powers that be 'of the need to wait and look at the bigger picture'. Cynthia Enloe retorts with trademark pinpoint precision, asking 'what if patriarchy *is* the big picture?' (2005: 280). This book consistently argued for the need to remain attentive to marginalised voices such as combatant women, as they face that 'big picture'. I am not suggesting, nor have I suggested that former combatants such as republican women hold all the answers but by being attentive to their experiences, we can ensure that patriarchy – in all its many manifestations – remains the big picture.

Notes

1 To view the entire report, see www.jrf.org.uk/publications/monitoring-poverty-and-social-exclusion-northern-ireland-2014
2 For more information on this report, see www.independent.ie/irish-news/suicide-rates-in-northern-ireland-soared-following-the-peace-agreement-26879484.html

Bibliography

Alison, M. 2009. *Women and Political Violence: Female Combatants in Ethno-national conflict.* New York: Routledge.
Anderlini, S. N. 2007. *Women Building Peace: What They Do, Why It Matters*. Boulder and London: Lynne Rienner Publishers.
Basham, V. M. and Catignani, S. 2018. 'War Is Where the Hearth Is: Gendered Labor and the Everyday Reproduction of the Geopolitical in the Army Reserves'. *International Feminist Journal of Politics* 20(2): 153–171.
Buckley, F. 2013. 'Women and Politics in Ireland: The Road to Sex Quotas'. *Irish Political Studies* 28(3): 341–397.
Cockburn, C. 2004. The Continuum of Violence: A Gender Perspective on War and Peace'. Pp. 24–44 in *Sites of Violence: Gender and Conflict Zones*, edited by W. Giles and J. Hyndman. London: University of California Press.
Cockburn, C. 2013. 'A Movement Stalled: Outcomes of Women's Campaign for Equalities and Inclusion in the Northern Ireland Peace Process'. *Interface: A Journal for and about Social Movements* 5(1): 151–182.
Deiana, M-A. 2013. 'Women's Citizenship in Northern Ireland after the 1998 Agreement'. *Irish Political Studies* 28(3): 399–412.
Enloe, C. 2005. 'What if Patriarchy Is "the Big Picture"? An Afterword'. Pp. 280–284 in *Gender, Conflict and Peacekeeping*, edited by D. Mazurana and A. Raven-Roberts. Lanham, MD: Rowman and Littlefield Publishers.

Enloe, C. 2014. *Bananas, Beaches and Bases: Making Feminist Sense of International Politics*, 3rd edn. Berkeley: University of California Press.

Fearon, K. and R. Rebouche. 2006. 'What Happened to the Women?' Gender and Peace in Northern Ireland'. Pp. 280–301 in *Farewell To Arms? Beyond the Good Friday Agreement*, edited by M. Cox, A. Guelke, and F. Stephen. Manchester: Manchester University Press.

Galligan, Y. 2013. 'Gender and Politics in Northern Ireland: The Representation Gap Revisited'. *Irish Political Studies* 28(3): 413–433.

Henshaw, A. 2016. 'Where Women Rebel'. *International Feminist Journal of Politics* 18(1): 39–60, DOI: 10.1080/14616742.2015.1007729

MacKenzie. M. H. 2012. *Female Soldiers in Sierra Leone: Sex, Security, and Post-Conflict Development.* New York: New York University Press.

O'Keefe, T. 2012. 'Sometimes It Would Be Nice to Be a Man: Negotiating Gender Identities after the Good Friday Agreement'. Pp. 83–97 in *Everyday Life After the Irish Conflict*, edited by C. McGratton and E. Meehan. Manchester: Manchester University Press.

O'Keefe, T. 2013. *Feminist Identity Development and Activism in Revolutionary Movements.* London and New York: Palgrave Macmillan.

Racioppi, L. and K. O'Sullivan See. 2001. 'This We Will Maintain: Gender, Ethnonationalism and the Politics of Unionism Northern Ireland'. *Nations and Nationalism* 7(1): 93–112.

Shirlow, P. 2012. *The End of Ulster Loyalism?* Manchester: Manchester University Press.

Side, K. 2009. 'Women's Civil and Political Citizenship in the Post-Good Friday Agreement Period in Northern Ireland'. *Irish Political Studies* 24(1): 67–87.

Sjoberg, L. 2014. *Gender, War, and Conflict.* Cambridge: Polity.

Index

8th amendment, referendum to repeal 95

abortion, issue of 68n1, 95–97, 134–135, 139, 144, 164, 169, 181, 185
Adams, Gerry 23, 33n23, 116, 121, 127, 146n11
African National Congress (ANC) 12–13
Aharoni, Sarai 77, 80
Ahern, Bertie 119
AMNLAE (women's popular organisation) 12, 138
anti-apartheid movement (South Africa) 12, 45
anti-austerity agenda 87
anti-colonial nationalisms 98
Armagh jail 18, 42, 56–59; women's experiences in 58
armed conflicts 4, 7, 16, 49, 57, 63, 65, 75–76, 80–81, 85–88, 90, 92–93, 100–101, 104, 116, 124, 127, 129, 133, 135, 138, 141, 143, 171, 178, 180–182, 185; approaches to resolving 2; dichotomy of 'war and peace' 6; eruption of 1, 46–47, 53, 61; feminist IR theory of 49; gender equality and 52, 151; GFA negotiations 29; male consolidation of power 26; male-dominated realm of 53; military roles in times of 66; in North of Ireland 145; political spaces opened by combatant women during 3; 'post-conflict' moment 3; Provisional IRA (PIRA) 15; Provisional republicanism during 114; 'real' actors in 50; republican movement during 61; republican women's transitioning away from 21, 30; Tupamaros National Liberation Movement (MLN) 44; violence of 5, 27, 41, 73; waging and sustaining of 50; women's lives during 9, 42; women's role as armed activists during 10, 62, 66, 105, 145
arms transportation 54, 59
Association of Women Confronting the National Problem (AMPRONAC) 138
austerity, agenda of 84–85; state-led 87

Ballymurphy 86, 107n6
Bean, Kevin 118, 125
Belfast Agreement 119
biological reproductive role, of women 12, 97
Blair, Tony 119
Bloody Sunday 17, 43
bodily integrity, principle of 92, 95
boom years of capitalism 84
Brewer, John 92
British Army 42, 59; night-time incursions into republican areas 70n13; Special Air Services (SAS) 70n12
British imperialism, in Ireland 76, 79
Brolly, Anne 95–96

Catholicism 135
ceasefire republicans 115, 118
ceasefire soldiers 114–118
Celtic Tiger 107n5
Cherish All Children Equally 95
Chiapas peace process 92
child soldiers, issue of 45
Civil Defence Force (CDF) 45
civil disobedience 61
civil rights protests 16
civil society activism 30, 169–170, 180
civil society organisations 170
Clár na mBan 127–129, 142; growth of 127; informal meetings of women 127; republican movement 127; state power

Clár na mBan continued
   127; 'Women's Agenda for Peace'
   conference (1994) 127
class and gender oppression 84
Clinton, Bill 75, 119
Cockburn, Cynthia 7, 93, 98, 170, 179
Cock, Jacklyn 45
Cohn, Carol 7
collective hero-worship 61
Collective of Female Ex-Combatants 65
combatants: female combatants *see*
   combatant women; masculine definition
   of 49; as militarised masculinity 58
combatant women 2; acquisition of
   political consciousness 99; blurring the
   lines of fighter/supporter 45–50; DDR
   programs 11, 41; definition of 42;
   gender stereotyping of 41; invisibility in
   post-war period 41; male expectations
   of 54; marginalisation in post-war
   narrative 41; marginalisation of 14;
   military roles of 44; outsiders' outsider
   10–15; political activism of 13; 'post-
   conflict' moment 3–6; in post-war
   memorialisation 40; post-war roles of
   21; pregnancy, impact of 54; return to
   pre-war domestic life 3; structural
   barrier, to political participation 14;
   wartime narratives 41; wartime roles
   and sacrifices 11
communal violence 16, 80, 92
community activism 29, 42, 47, 57, 60–61,
   64, 89, 100–102, 122, 124, 125, 128,
   133, 153, 155, 163–166, 168, 183
community politics 125, 162, 164
conflict management 185
conflict resolution 73, 185; model of 74, 186
conflict transition 1–15, 21, 25, 27–28, 30,
   40, 46, 58, 62, 66, 68, 73, 105, 114, 129,
   135, 142, 145, 151, 153, 155, 177, 181,
   183, 184, 187
Connolly, James 81
Conway Mill project 56
Corbett, Jack 168
Coulter, Carol 141
Coulter, Colin 82, 85
courageous female protestor, gender
   identity of 13
cross-community activism 165
cross-community grassroots engagement 9
cultural violence 6, 62, 68, 82, 179, 187
Cumann na mBan: foundation of 66;
   republican movement 66; volunteers of
   59, 65

decision-making, on peace and security 75,
   88, 154, 162, 172, 186
Demilitarisation, Demobilisation, and
   Reintegration (DDR) programs 11, 40–41,
   45, 100, 183; legal discourse of 42;
   reports of women 'being left behind' 11
Democratic Unionist Party (DUP) 40,
   68n1, 87, 122, 185
Department of Social Development 170
division of labour 18, 53, 67, 84, 123,
   158–159
domestic violence 13, 63, 79, 84, 90–91,
   131–134, 165, 183
Dowler, Lorraine 48, 56, 61
Downing Street Declaration (1993) 127
Duck Patrols 70n13
Dukhtaran-e-Millat (DM) 138

eclectic activism 155, 169
economic class 7
electoral democracy 155
Enloe, Cynthia 8, 45, 65, 84, 138, 187
'Entitled Voices - Women in International
   Struggle' conference (2006) 140
ethnic differentiation 7
ethnic identities 77
ethno-national identities 80
ethno-nationalism 178
ethno-national politics 77, 158
ethno-religious tensions 16

Falls Cultural Society 56
Farabundo Martí National Liberation Front
   (FMLN) 12, 45, 132
Farrell, Mairead 31n8, 59, 65
female combatants *see* combatant women
female ex-prisoners, digital database for
   14, 63–64
female IRA prisoners 128
female prisoners, assaults on 18–19,
   32n17, 64
feminine private, notion of 61
femininity, notion of 2, 7–8, 15, 62, 98,
   105, 144, 157, 177, 184
feminist agitation, modes of 29, 114
feminist ethics and politics 166
feminist research, methodologies and
   methods of 19–26
feminist scholarship 2, 4, 10, 12, 67, 74,
   154; in context of war 7
Feminist Security Studies 4
feminist vision of peace and security 75
fighter/supporter, notion of 27, 41, 43,
   45–50, 67–68

fiscal austerity 85
freedom of conscience 95
Fresh Start Agreement (2015) 171, 173n5, 185

Gaelic (Irish language) 106n1, 145n1, 145n2
Galtung, Johan 5, 82
gender-based violence *see* gendered violence
gender differentiation, institutionalisation of 14, 97–98
gender discrimination 3, 11, 27, 74, 92, 146n8, 177
gendered division of labour 18, 53, 67, 84, 123, 158, 159
gendered rituals 158
gendered violence 28, 73, 74, 79, 133; in aftermath of the 1994 ceasefires 90–91; continuum of 97–104, 105; domestic violence 90; eradication of 89, 95; and insecurity 6; intimate partner violence 93; during 'post-conflict' period 90, 92; rape 93; sexual abuse 93; in South Africa 93; in United States 83; 'war on women' campaign 83; against women's bodies 18; women's equality and 88–93; against working-class women 93
gender equality *see* women's equality
gender-equal society 98
gender hierarchy 8
gender identities 13, 19, 90
gender in conflict zones, role of 77
gender inequalities 5, 92
gender job segregation 88
gender occupational segregation 123
gender pay gap 5
gender power relations 8
gender role segregation 5, 10
gender stereotyping, of female combatants 41
Glenholmes, Eibhlín 140–141, 147n14
global capitalism 28, 83, 88, 104–105, 170, 178, 185; collapse of 185
global crisis in capitalism 83
Good Friday Agreement (GFA) 74–75, 118, 137, 152, 178; 'gender equality' provision 89; governance structure for the North of Ireland 120; negotiations for 127; signing of 119; talk's agenda 123; women's experiences of 113
good governance, issues of 73, 151
grassroots activism 13, 99, 125, 132, 139, 162, 166, 180

grassroots anti-imperial movements 98
grassroots democracy, benefits of 125
guerrilla warfare 44

Harding, Sandra 20–21
Hartstock, Nancy 20
Hate Motivation Crime 95
Hen Patrols 59, 70n13
Hoewer, Melanie 92
homophobic attacks 28, 74, 93–95
honey traps 44
housing segregation 79–80
human security, debates regarding 74
hunger strike 56, 69n4, 76; deaths due to 57; women's experiences in 58

imagined community 97
institutional democracy 155
inter-communal violence 16
International Relations (IR) 4, 26
International Women's Day (8 March) 63, 66, 88, 131
In the Footsteps of Anne (2011) 63
Irish nationalism 99, 107n10
Irish peace process: Belfast Agreement 119; ceasefire soldiers 114–118; *versus* Chiapas peace process 92; *Clár na mBan* 127–129; d'Hondt formula for 120; *fait accompli* 126; gendered casualty of 129–144; Good Friday Agreement *see* Good Friday Agreement (GFA); international mediation in 119; 'leadership-led' culture during 126; North–South Ministerial Council 120; post-war republican politics and 114–118; reconfiguring gender roles during 118–129; Sinn Féin vertical lines of control during 126; Sinn Féin women's department and 129–144
Irish Republican Army (IRA) 2, 15; ban on women as volunteers of 54; bombing campaign 59; ceasefire of 1994 63, 113; cessation of military operations 119; *Green Book, The* 41–42, 47; male-dominated leadership and membership 51; Operation Harvest (1962) 69n5; operations against the British Army 42; participation of women 18, 50; republican women's struggle for full inclusion within 54; struggle for recognition in commemoration 57; unarmed struggle 113; volunteers in 41–42
Irish Republican History Museum 63, 65

192 Index

Irish Republicanism 15, 17, 31n10, 66, 107n10, 141, 146n4, 185

Lederach, John-Paul 5
left-wing military movement 44
Lesbian Gay Bisexual Transgender (LGBT) 131; anti-discrimination legislation 94; effect of marginalising 94; rights of 19; violence against 90
loose talk, notion of 60
Luisa Amanda Espinoza Association of Nicaraguan Women (AMNLAE) 12, 138

McAliskey, Bernadette 93
McDowell, Sara 14, 60–61
McEvoy, Sandra 14
McIntyre, Anthony 147n19
MacKenzie, Megan 11, 26, 40, 48
male expectations, of combatant women 54
male heroics and acts of valour, concept of 60
male public, notion of 61
male/violence and female/peace, dichotomies of 10
masculinity 2, 7, 67, 106, 177, 179; adversarial 123, 158; concepts of 98; formal politics of 158; hegemonic 61; militarised 58, 62; normative 50; notion of 8, 49, 157; oppressive 105; performance and evaluation of 50; privileging of 8
mass mobilisation 114, 121, 125–127; of republican community 155
Members for the Legislative Assembly (MLA) 120
'militant' politics 143
militarism 42–43, 50, 62, 67; masculine definition of 59
military reconnaissance 54
military war of liberation 42
mirror searches 19
Mitchell, George 119
Moser, Caroline 5
Muilleoir, Máirtín Ó 86
multi-national corporations 86

national identities 77, 80
nationalist movements 2, 11–12, 14, 29, 54, 98, 103, 126, 177, 179, 181–182
neo-liberal austerity, effects of 28, 74, 86, 183
neo-liberal capitalism 74, 81–88, 105, 123

non-cooperation, campaign of 18
non-state liberation movements, participation of women within 19, 54
non-state military movements 6, 10, 50, 62
Northern Ireland Act (1998) 152
Northern Ireland Women's Coalition (NIWC) 119, 124, 152
Northern Ireland Women's European Platform (NIWEP) 170
North of Ireland 58–59, 69n5, 75, 79, 138; barriers to women's participation in 159; British jurisdiction over 77; dismantling of 129; EU peace funding to 170; gender division of labour within 123, 159; GFA governance structure for 120; housing segregation in 79; institutional politics in 165; institutions of government 185; Irish Republic claim over 120; new post-conflict politics 154; 'post-conflict' life in 88; as post-conflict prosperous and progressive society 82; post-war experiences of republican women in 73; public sector employment in 84; reality of women's political organising in 171; removing the British from 83; as society at peace 85; Women's Centres in 164–165, 169; working class communities in 85
North–South Ministerial Council 120
No-Wash protest 18–19, 32n17

O'Keefe, Theresa 61, 103
Operation Harvest (1962) 69n5
Oslo Accord (1993) 13

Paisley, Ian 68n1
Palestinian Authority (PA) 13
parliamentary politics, culture of 29, 151, 154, 158, 162, 169
partition of Ireland 28, 69n8, 74, 76, 104, 106n3, 178
Pathak, Bishnu 44
patriarchal power, reconstruction of 1
patriarchy 187; concept of 3, 8, 19–20, 27, 41, 49–51, 104; in conflict transition 68, 184; congenital formations of 52; eradication of 93, 98, 136; feminists struggle against 62, 183–184; institutionalised 98; intersecting forces of 74; masculinity and 106; sexism and 105
peace activist, women's role as 10
peace-building 10, 75, 85, 88, 104, 165
peace dividend 85–86, 88, 165

peace processes, in Africa 92
peace walls 79–80, 185
Peeler 79, 82, 106n4
People's Liberation Front (EPLF), Eritrea 54
person with a weapon 27, 41, 45, 50
Police Service of Northern Ireland (PSNI) 23, 33n22, 78, 106n2
political activism 3, 13–14, 27–29, 73, 99–101, 113, 143, 153, 158–159, 165, 169, 180; shoe-horning of 113
political demobilisation 126
political rights and citizenship, re-establishment of 155
political struggle 6, 12–13, 28, 62, 76, 81, 100–102, 104, 113, 129, 132, 137, 169, 171, 180, 182; institutionalisation of 113
Porter, Elizabeth 95, 164, 169
'post-conflict' moment, theory of 3–6
post-conflict social reconstruction 75
post-conflict society 6, 80
'post-violence' society 92
post-war activism 3, 151, 153
post-war peace processes 5; role of women in 1
post-war politics 118, 152, 172
post-war reconstruction 73
post-war republican politics 114–118
power and power differentials 7
Power, Maria 139
pregnancy, impact on combatant women 54
prisoner rights, issues of 19
prison protests, of late 1970s and early 1980s 56; commemoration relating to 63; deaths of the Hunger Strikers 57; women's contribution to 57–58
prison regime, for women 18–19
prison struggle of 1976–1981 19
professionalisation, process of 118
Progressive Unionist Party 119
protection racket 154
Provisional IRA (PIRA) 15, 23; bomb attack on British military targets 59; bombs in England of 'the Troubles' 59; Hen Patrols 59
Provisional republicanism 28, 76, 89, 113–114, 129, 141, 167, 180
Provisional republican movement 17, 68, 96, 114, 126–127, 129, 160, 162, 182, 184

racial identities 77
racist crimes 95

rape 18, 91, 93, 96–97, 130, 172n4
religious war 16
reproductive health care 89, 95
reproductive rights, issues of 19, 28, 74, 89–90, 92, 95–97, 105, 134, 143, 183
Republican commemoration: acts of 56; architects of memorialisation 55; awareness regarding 'invisibility' in 58; on collective resistance 55; commemoration relating to the prison protests 63; dominant narrative within 58; formal processes of 60; and 'invisibility' of women 54–62; IRA struggle for recognition in 57; male-led 61; re-writing themselves back into history 63–67; role in shaping of collective memories 54; as type of symbolic warfare 61; wall murals 58; on war fought by male combatants 58; on women's wartime contributions 58
republican feminist consciousness, development of 19
republican memorialisation 40, 46, 55, 59; acts of 58; regarding the prison protests 56
Republican Movement 14–15, 17, 19, 22, 26, 28–30, 46–52, 54, 57, 59–63, 66, 68, 95–96, 99–100, 102, 113, 114, 118, 122–123, 125–130, 136–137, 139, 141, 143, 145, 155, 166, 172n4, 179–180, 182–184
republicans at peace 74–81
republican women: approaches towards armed conflict 124; commemoration relating to the prison protests 63; dichotomy of 'fighter/supporter' 49; ex-prisoners, digital database for 64; insecurity experienced by 75; and meaning of combatant 41–45; military roles of 44–45; no link to England 74–81; participation in non-state liberation movements 54; post-war politics of 153; re-writing themselves back into history 63–67; roles and contributions within armed struggle 40; similarities with Kashmir all-women groups 138; struggle for a British withdrawal from Ireland 77; struggle for full inclusion within the IRA 54; writing and publishing own stories in magazines 63
'reserve army' thesis 141
residential segregation *see* housing segregation

Index

Revolutionary United Front (RUF) 45
Richter-Devroe, Sophie 13
right to life, of the unborn 95
Robinson, Peter 68n1
Roddy McCorley Society 63
Royal Ulster Constabulary (RUC) 16, 31n7, 53, 69n8, 78–79, 106n3

Sandinista National Liberation Front (FSLN) 138
Sandinista organisations 12
Sands, Bobby 45–46, 59, 61, 69n4, 69n9
Saward, Michael 151
second-wave feminism 151
self-determination, principle of 19, 95–97, 102, 127, 181
sexual violence 4, 91, 93, 97, 164, 186
Sheela na Gig 128–129; disbandment of 129
Shekhawat, Seema 9, 44, 121, 138
Sinn Féin 15, 22, 40, 61, 66, 76, 89, 167; anti-austerity agenda 87; *Ard Comhairle* 130; *Ard Fheis* 25, 95, 115, 130; Bernie works for 57; Border Campaign 47; conflict transition period 118; development of 115; electoral success 114; 'Entitled Voices - Women in International Struggle' conference (2006) 140; Equality Department 135, 140, 142–143; female elected representatives 159, 161; freedom of conscience 95; as gender-balanced party 133; gendered casualty of peace 129–144; independent women's voice within 127; involvement in government 119; leadership 115; lines of control during the peace process 126; participatory rights for women 134; party politics 56; political representative of 128; on repeal the 8th amendment 95; 'reserve army' thesis 141; socialist ideology of 86; Women's Department 19, 29, 63, 129–144, 180, 182; Women's Manifesto 139
Sjoberg, Laura 7–8, 74, 90
Smith, Dorothy 20
social capital 120
social justice 5–6, 77, 81–82, 85, 99, 104, 123, 124, 128, 161, 166
social movement, theory of 98, 114–115, 134, 151, 162
society at peace, discourse of 76, 78, 80, 85
South of Ireland 68n1, 83, 86, 89, 95, 134
Spark, Ceridwen 168

Special Category Prisoners 32n16
Squires, Judith 151, 172
state-centric political institutions 158
state security, issues of 3, 27, 73, 88
street activism 125, 155
street rioting 61
strip searching, of women prisoners 19, 32n18
structural violence 5, 28, 82, 106, 168
struggle, continuum of 97–104

Tar Anall (ex-prisoners' group) 66, 164
Third Force 68n1
transnational capitalism 83
the Troubles 60, 79, 107n6, 115–116, 119, 121, 164, 173n5, 182; mass mobilisation of 125
Tupamaros National Liberation Movement (MLN) 44

Ulster Defence Association (UDA) 31n9, 119, 146n5
Ulster Democratic Party 119
Ulster Freedom Fighters (UFF) 17, 31n9, 119, 146n5
Ulster Resistance (1986) 68n1
Ulster Unionist Party 69n1, 131
Ulster Volunteer Force (UVF) 31n10, 119, 146n4
Umkhonto weSizwe (MK) 45
unemployment rates 86, 186
United Nations SCR 1325 10, 30, 144, 154, 172n1
UN Security Council 35, 88

violence against women *see* gendered violence
vote management 115

war and peace, diplomatic dichotomy of 73
Ward, Margaret 141
'war on women' campaign 83
wartime violence 4
wealth and justice, redistribution of 77
What Did You Do in the War Mammy? (video documentary) 63
women and armed struggle, notion of 50–54
'women and peace' hypothesis 9, 77, 104
'women as backbone' discourse 122
women as victims, notion of 9
women, gender, and conflict transition, study of 7–10
Women In An Ireland Of Equals 139

Women In Struggle (exhibition) 65
'Women's Agenda for Peace' conference (1994) 127
Women's Aid Federation Northern Ireland 91
women's 'behind the scenes' work, depiction of 122
women's empowerment 11, 154
women's equality 74, 137, 151, 187; conceptualising of 88–97; gender-based violence 88–93; homophobia and 93–95; national self-determination and 127; reproductive rights 95–97
Women's Garden of Remembrance 63
women's grassroots activism 13, 99, 166
women's insecurity, depiction of 74
women's participation: in armed conflict 42; in non-state military movements 6
women's peace activism 77
women's political activism 14, 27, 73, 143
women's post-war activism 151–154; grassroots and community organising 162–171; institutional politics and conflict transition 154–162; and work–life balance 159
women's propensity for peace, myth of 41
women's relationship to war and peace, feminist theorising of 8
women's reproductive rights 28, 74, 90, 95–97
Women's Resource and Development Agency (WRDA) 84
women's stories, from the republican struggle 56
women's struggle, after armed struggle 178–184
women's wartime roles, scope of 1, 11, 41
work–life balance 159